GIRL GENIUS

AGATHA HETERODYNE
&
THE BEETLEBURG CLANK

A Gaslamp Fantasy with
ADVENTURE, ROMANCE & MAD SCIENCE

Story by Kaja & Phil Foglio
Pencils by Phil Foglio • Inks by Brian Snoddy
Colors by Cheyenne Wright

AIRSHIP ENTERTAINMENT

OTHER BOOKS FROM AIRSHIP ENTERTAINMENT AND STUDIO FOGLIO

Girl Genius® Graphic Novels

Girl Genius Volume One:
Agatha Heterodyne and the Beetleburg Clank

Girl Genius Volume Two:
Agatha Heterodyne and the Airship City

Girl Genius Volume Three:
Agatha Heterodyne and the Monster Engine

Girl Genius Volume Four:
Agatha Heterodyne and the Circus of Dreams

Girl Genius Volume Five:
Agatha Heterodyne and the Clockwork Princess

Girl Genius Volume Six:
Agatha Heterodyne and the Golden Trilobite

Girl Genius Volume Seven:
Agatha Heterodyne and the Voice of the Castle

Girl Genius Volume Eight:
Agatha Heterodyne and the Chapel of Bones

Girl Genius Volume Nine:
Agatha Heterodyne and the Heirs of the Storm

Other Graphic Novels

What's New with Phil & Dixie Collection

Robert Asprin's MythAdventures®

Buck Godot, zap gun for hire:
• *Three Short Stories*
• *PSmIth*
• *The Gallimaufry*

Girl Genius® is published by:
Airship Entertainment™, a happy part of Studio Foglio, LLC
2400 NW 80th St #129 Seattle WA 98117-4449, USA

Please visit our Web sites at www.airshipbooks.com and www.girlgenius.net

Story by Phil & Kaja Foglio. Pencils by Phil Foglio. Inks by Brian Snoddy. Colors by Cheyenne Wright (main story) and Laurie E. Smith (Electric Coffin). Airship City illustration colored by Mark McNabb. Cover colored by Kaja Foglio. Logos, Lettering, Artist Bullying & Book Design by Kaja. Fonts mostly by Comicraft– www.comicbookfonts.com. Invaluable art assistance by Cheyenne Wright, Savannah Goodwin and Alice Bentley.

Most of the material in this collection was originally published in black-and-white in the Girl Genius comic book issues 1-3, and later in black-and-white as the *Girl Genius Collection Volume One.* This is the first color edition of the *Girl Genius Collection Volume One.*

Published simultaneously in Hardcover (ISBN# 978-1-890856-49-6)
and Softcover (ISBN# 978-1-890856-50-2) Editions.

Color Edition, First Printing: June 2009 • PRINTED IN THE USA

This book is dedicated to the Girl Genius discussion group on *Yahoo,* who makes us feel loved, forgives us when a book is late, and never lets a mistake pass unnoticed. Argh.

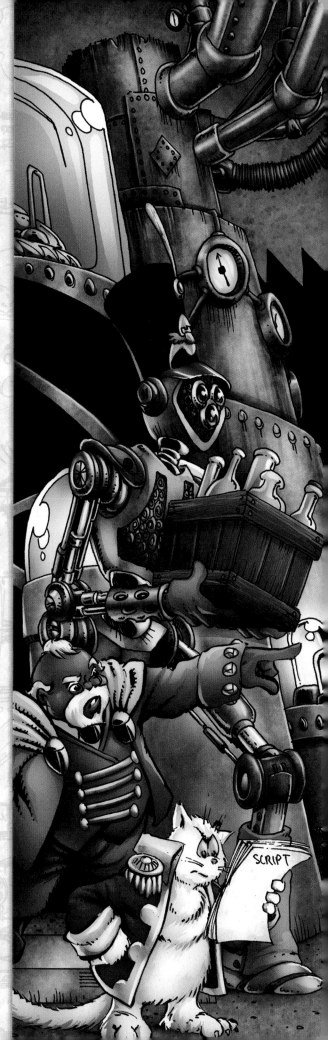

Kaja Foglio

Professor Foglio first became aware of the power of Creative History while listening to the excuses of fellow students who had failed to produce their homework. Her doctoral work brought scientific recognition to the long hidden canis operisphagus, or "homework-eating dog" which, as we now know, infests most of our major schools and universities. She first became interested in the history of the Heterodyne family during the infamous "Nymphenburg Pudding Incident" when she was mistaken for Agatha by an angry mob of dessert chefs from whom she barely escaped. Her subsequent research has earned her the grudging acclaim and jealous rivalry of many of her academic colleagues. She enjoys exotic travel (as long as nobody is trying to kill her), harpsichord music and airship racing.

Phil Foglio

Professor Foglio spends most of his time in the field collecting legends, folksongs, anecdotes and gossip relating to the gifted and their effects on village society and "folk science." This is a bit odd, as he was originally hired by Transylvania Polygnostic to teach modern dance. He first became interested in Heterodyne stories while doing research on simple automatons and was actually present when Agatha unleashed her "Battle Circus" upon Baron Wulfenbach. Through subsequent research, bribery and wild speculation, the professor has managed to fill in a great many of the narrative gaps in the life of Agatha Heterodyne. He enjoys entomology, botany, kite flying, and, in moderation, modern dance.

Brian Snoddy

Professor Snoddy is TPU's resident Zombie Master. His introductory class Revenant Control and Ethics (If Any) is well-attended and has a long waiting list. He was brought on board the Girl Genius project when Professors Foglio and Foglio realized that their proposed research might actually involve a certain amount of danger in the field, and that an army of zombie servants couldn't hurt. Hurt them, at any rate.

Professor Snoddy is responsible for the gorgeous linework throughout the main story, for which we thank him most gratefully.

Laurie E. Smith

Professor Smith was one of the last travellers to return from the Americas before all contact with the continent was cut off. She has devoted her years at Transylvania Polygnostic to the study of an unusual type of snail thought to be found only within a fifty yard radius of the faculty lounge (the one with the really GOOD coffee) but was persuaded to abandon her primary work long enough to join the Girl Genius research team. Her beautiful color work on the short story at the end of this book is greatly appreciated, as is her willingness to finish it even in the face of a hideous mystery flu later determined to be caused by snails in her coffee. Her dedication is an ornament to the profession.

Cheyenne Wright

Professor Wright spent his last sabbatical captaining the light airship: *Queen Bang's Revenge.* Although he claims it was "merely a pleasure cruise," the University board is investigating the fact that the Dept. of Very Nearly True History is able to publish Vol. 1 of Girl Genius in full color, despite having had no budget for the last six years. Also, they claim: "He never even sent us a postcard."

SCRIPT

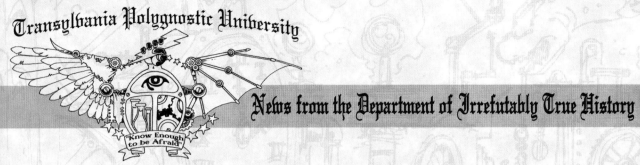

Transylvania Polygnostic University

"Know Enough to be Afraid"

News from the Department of Irrefutably True History

Transylvania Polygnostic University students[1] who read sensationalistic novels when they should be studying or conducting important research will all be familiar with the exploits of the legendary Agatha Heterodyne.

We, in the Department of Irrefutably True History, have long felt that the life of this exceptional person is worthy of attention of a more scholarly nature. Thus, as an aid to students taking our new series of courses, we are pleased to offer the following textbook in an easy-to-follow pictorial format.

Unscrupulous foreign publishers, concerned only with profit, have distorted the historical facts concerning Agatha Heterodyne, her family, and her associates to the point that the narrative contained within this account will no doubt be entirely new to the majority of readers. We trust you will consider these differences in story with the gravity that befits intelligent students who know what is good for them and agree that we, as experts, are the final authority on these matters.[2] You'll know it's true because we, your instructors, say so.

These courses and their associated textbooks are based upon our meticulous research of the last ten years, in which we gratefully acknowledge the aid of the Department of Alternate Realities and Temporal Uncertainty. Here you will find the actual, factual account of what happened in the early years of Agatha Heterodyne's career, starting from the lowest point in her life–her final day as a student here at Transylvania Polygnostic.

Thanks to the support we receive from the current administration at TPU, our students are hereby authorized to peruse these texts during other, less interesting classes (such as Prof. Strout's Theoretical Potential of Pickled Herring as a Low-Cost Power Source lectures). In exchange you are expected to maintain good grades, curb your monsters and not blow up school property if you can possibly avoid it.

And finally, students, remember—your future arch-nemeses are out there somewhere, studying hard. Don't make it easy for them.

–Professors Foglio & Foglio
Department of Irrefutably True History
Transylvania Polygnostic University

1 and faculty–you know who you are.

2 Occasional guesswork and narrative license have been applied in cases where facts were uncertain or where documented occurrences would have been more amusing if only they had happened in some other way. Other than that, it's all true. We swear.

This is a story about Science. Or Magic. Or possibly both.

There have always been those with the Spark-people who seem to be able to tinker with the laws of physics as we know them. This sort of person can be the worst of evil mad scientists or a tremendous force for Good.

The last members of the great house Heterodyne stood as the models against which all other heroes of their time were measured. With a collection of like-minded companions, they travelled the globe negotiating peace, stopping monsters and shutting down doomsday devices. Their exploits were the stuff of legends.

And then they disappeared. Our story begins some years later.

Prologue

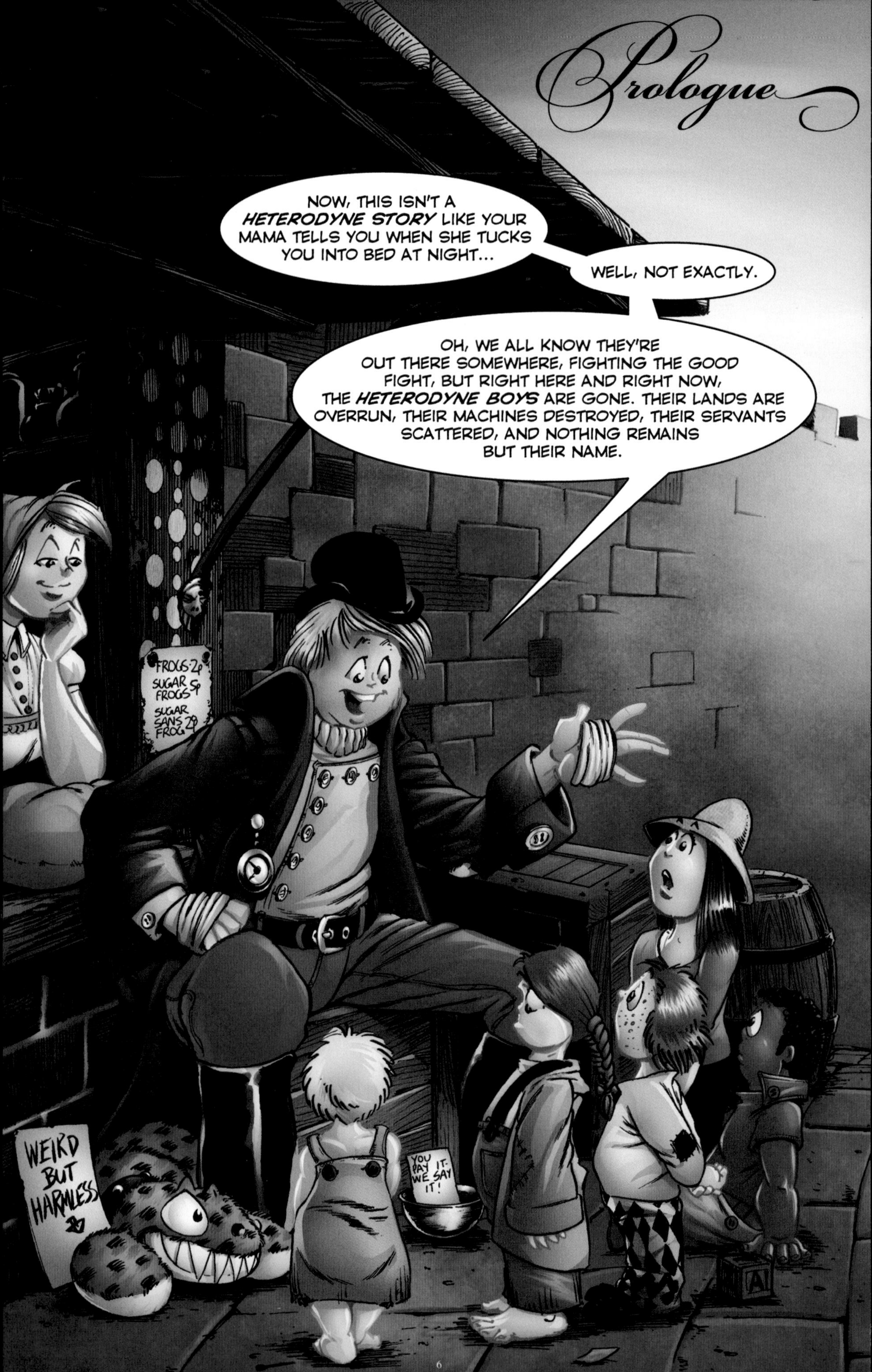
NOW, THIS ISN'T A *HETERODYNE STORY* LIKE YOUR MAMA TELLS YOU WHEN SHE TUCKS YOU INTO BED AT NIGHT...
WELL, NOT EXACTLY.
OH, WE ALL KNOW THEY'RE OUT THERE SOMEWHERE, FIGHTING THE GOOD FIGHT, BUT RIGHT HERE AND RIGHT NOW, THE *HETERODYNE BOYS* ARE GONE. THEIR LANDS ARE OVERRUN, THEIR MACHINES DESTROYED, THEIR SERVANTS SCATTERED, AND NOTHING REMAINS BUT THEIR NAME.
FROGS-2p
SUGAR FROGS 5p
SUGAR SANS FROG 2p
WEIRD BUT HARMLESS
YOU PAY IT- WE SAY IT!

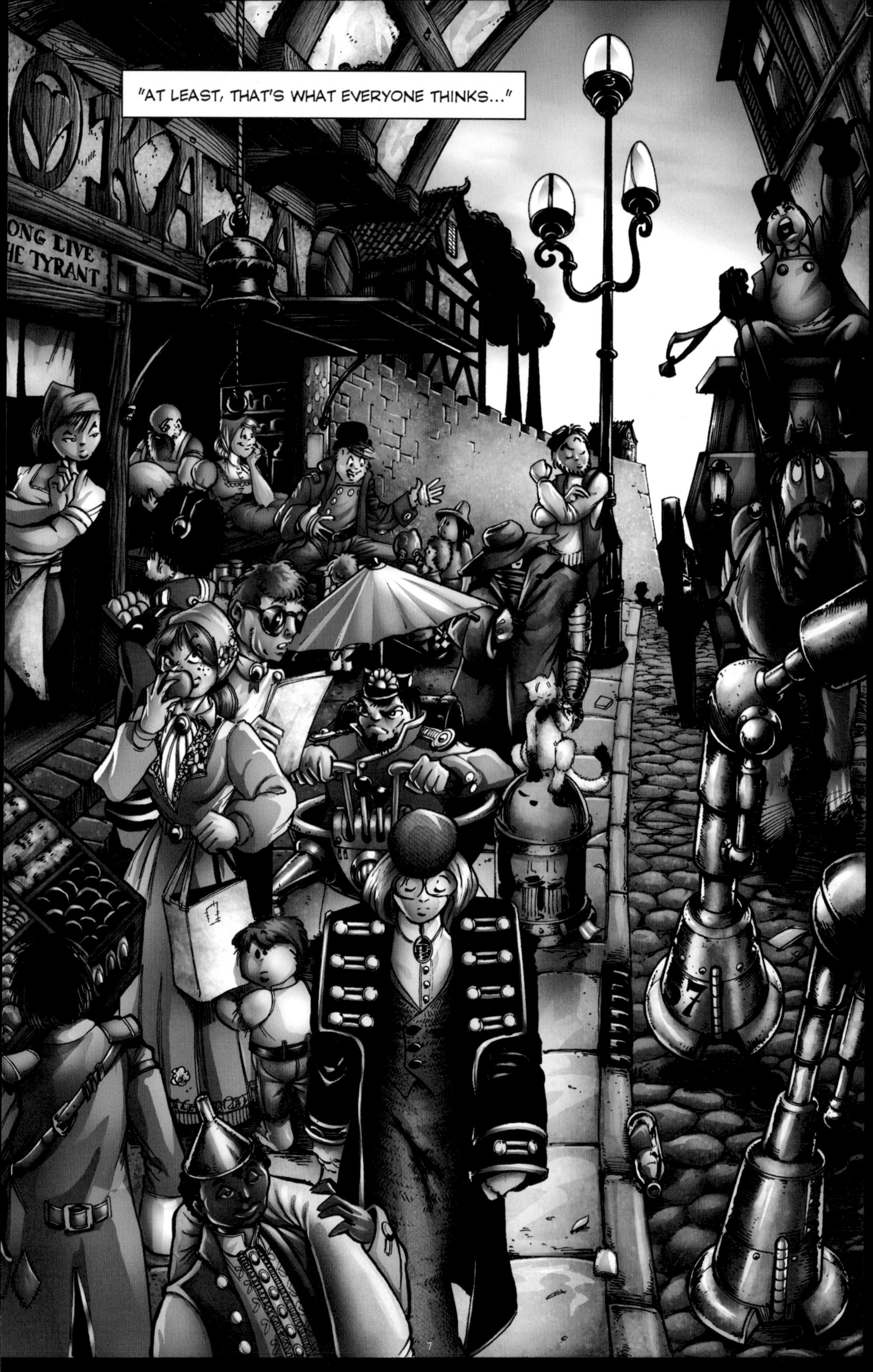
"AT LEAST, THAT'S WHAT EVERYONE THINKS..."
LONG LIVE THE TYRANT
7

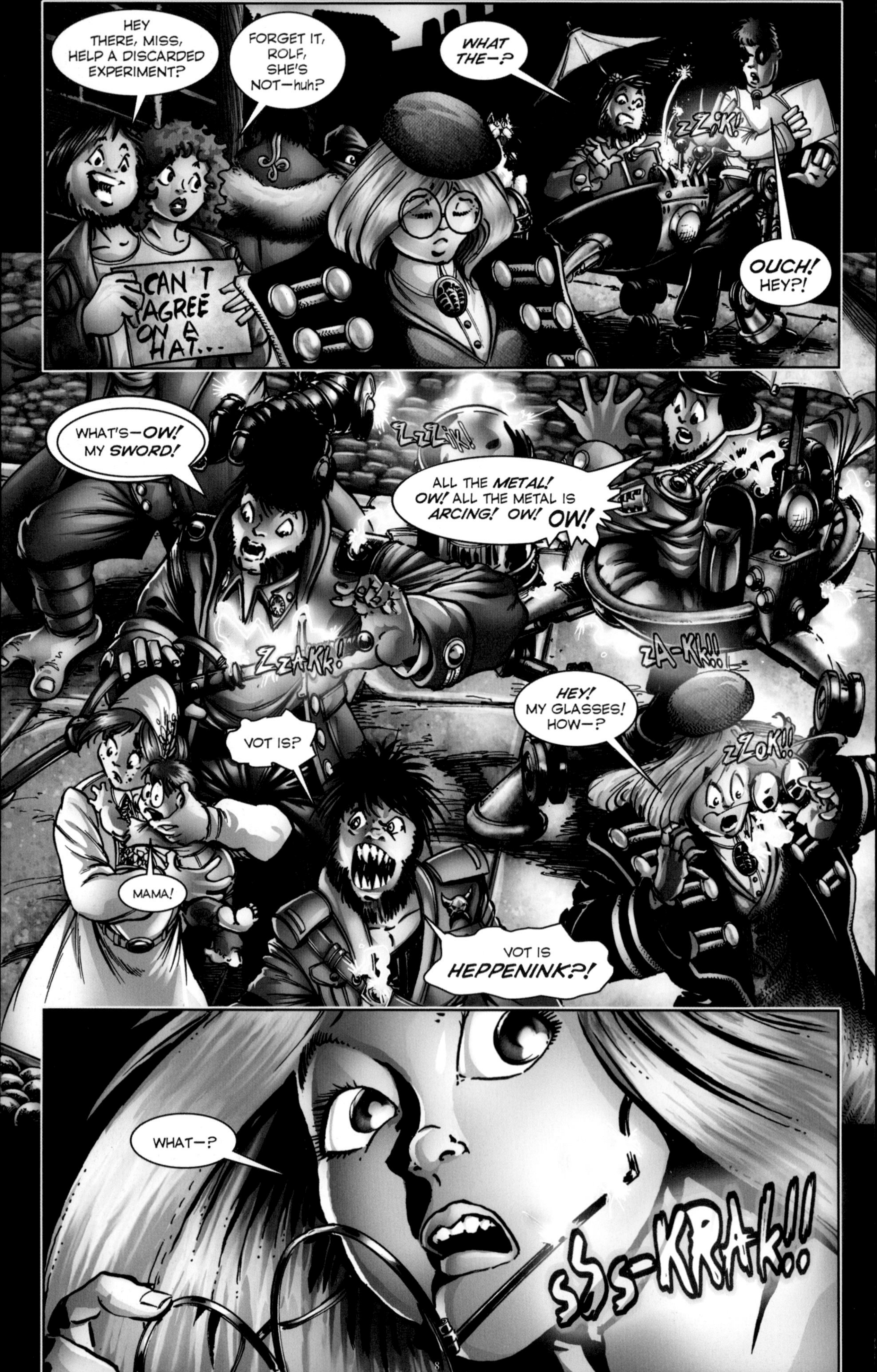

HEY THERE, MISS, HELP A DISCARDED EXPERIMENT?
CAN'T AGREE ON A HAT...
FORGET IT, ROLF, SHE'S NOT—huh?
WHAT THE—?
zZzK!
OUCH! HEY?!
WHAT'S—OW! MY SWORD!
ZzLik!
ALL THE METAL! OW! ALL THE METAL IS ARCING! OW! OW!
ZzAKk!
zA-Kk!!
HEY! MY GLASSES! HOW—?
zZOK!!
VOT IS?
MAMA!
VOT IS HEPPENINK?!
WHAT—?
sSs-KRAK!!

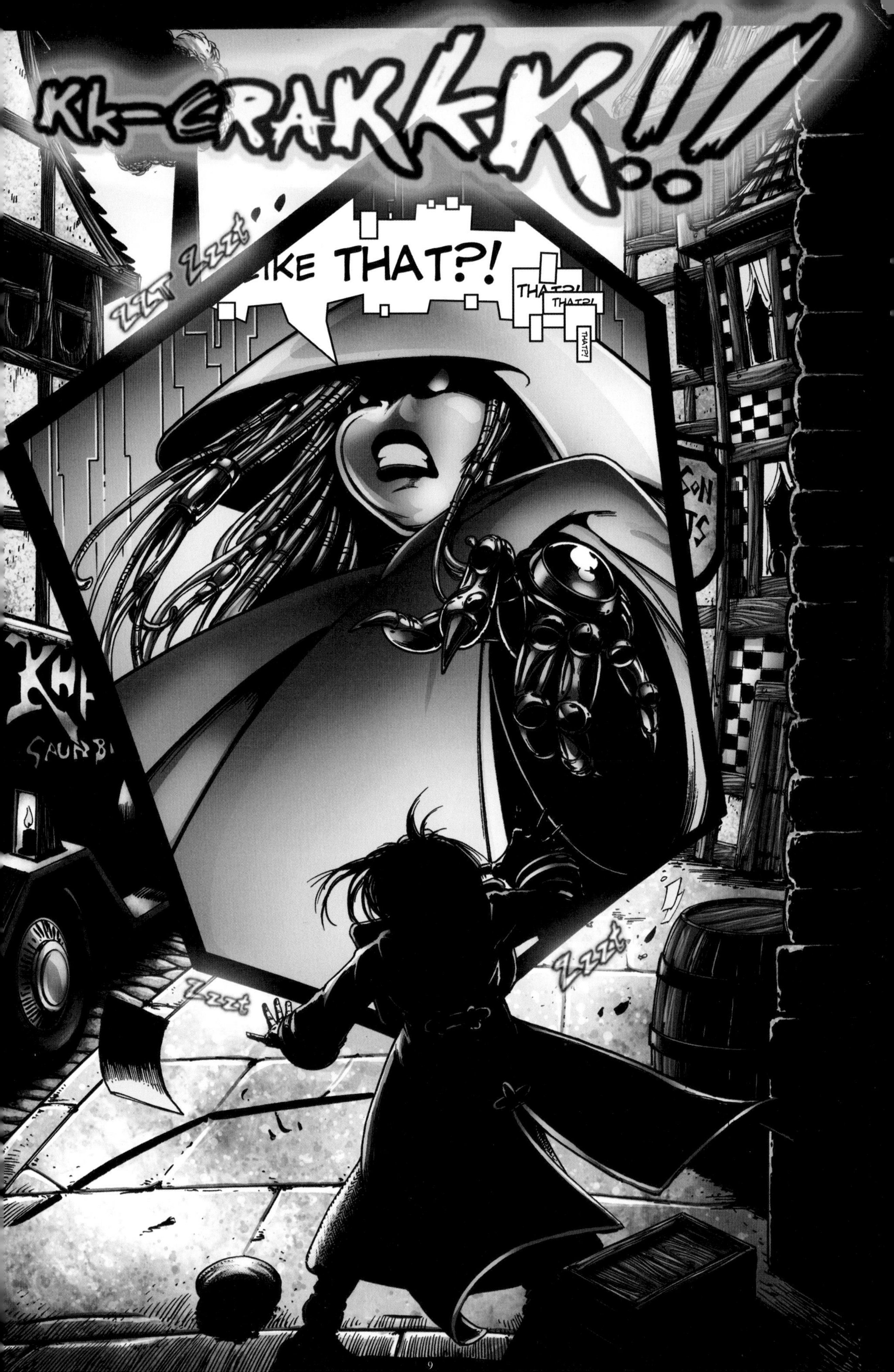
KK-CRAKKK!!
ZZZT ZZZT..
LIKE THAT?!
THAT?!
THAT?!
THAT?!
ZZZT
ZZZT

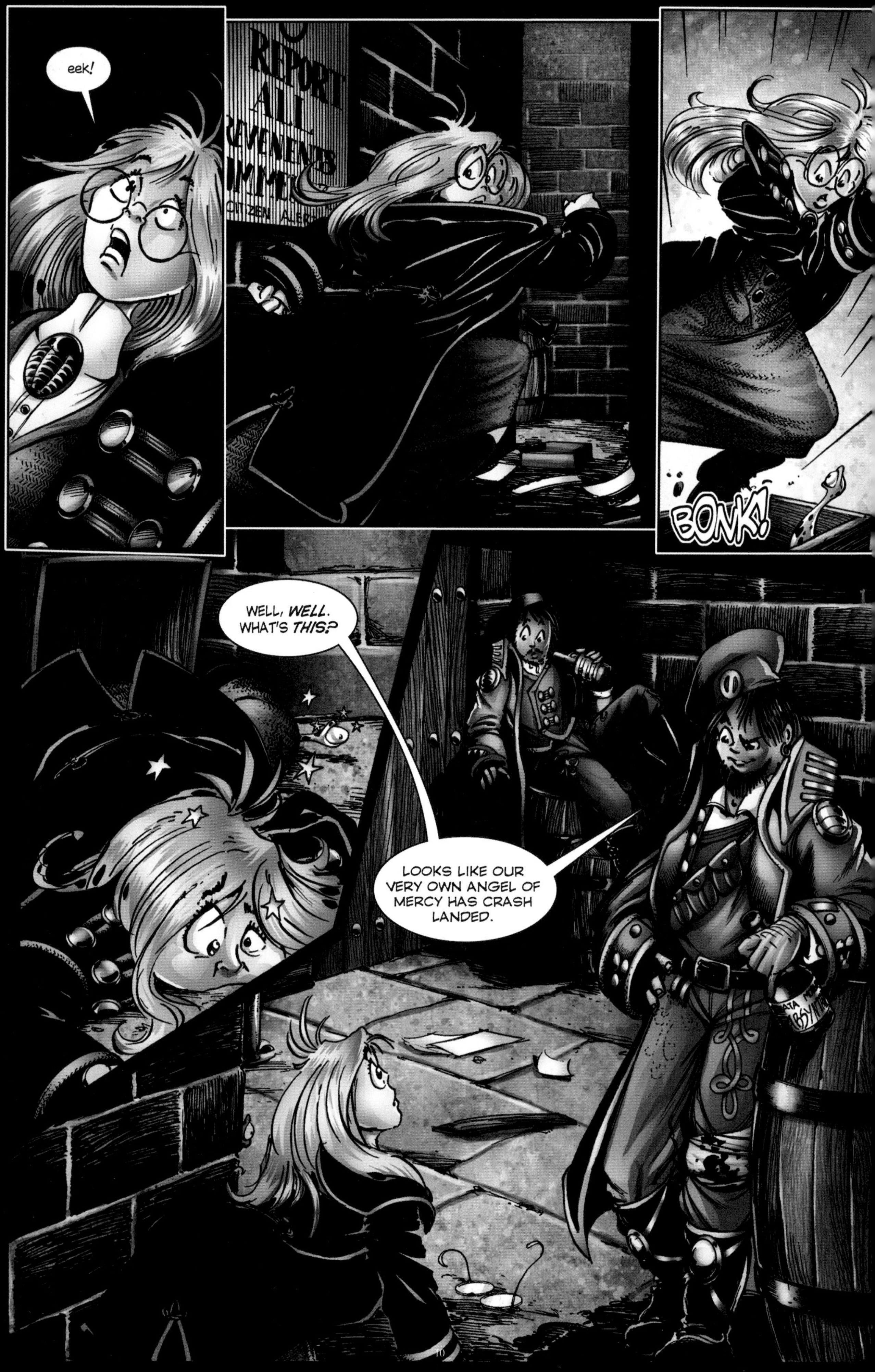
eek!
REPORT ALL
BONK!
WELL, WELL. WHAT'S THIS?
LOOKS LIKE OUR VERY OWN ANGEL OF MERCY HAS CRASH LANDED.

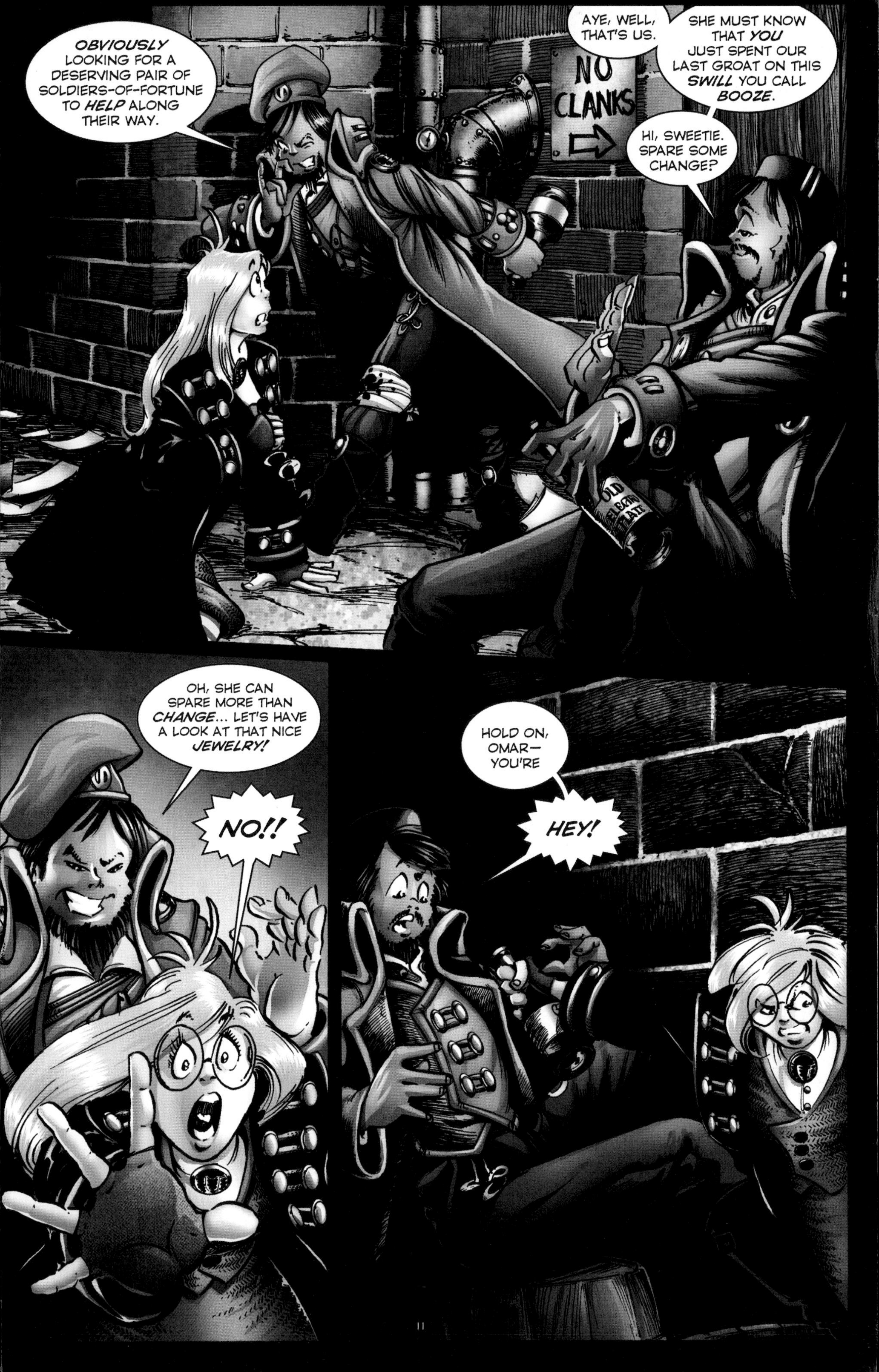
OBVIOUSLY LOOKING FOR A DESERVING PAIR OF SOLDIERS-OF-FORTUNE TO HELP ALONG THEIR WAY.
AYE, WELL, THAT'S US.
SHE MUST KNOW THAT YOU JUST SPENT OUR LAST GROAT ON THIS SWILL YOU CALL BOOZE.
NO CLANKS
HI, SWEETIE. SPARE SOME CHANGE?
OH, SHE CAN SPARE MORE THAN CHANGE... LET'S HAVE A LOOK AT THAT NICE JEWELRY!
NO!!
HOLD ON, OMAR— YOU'RE
HEY!

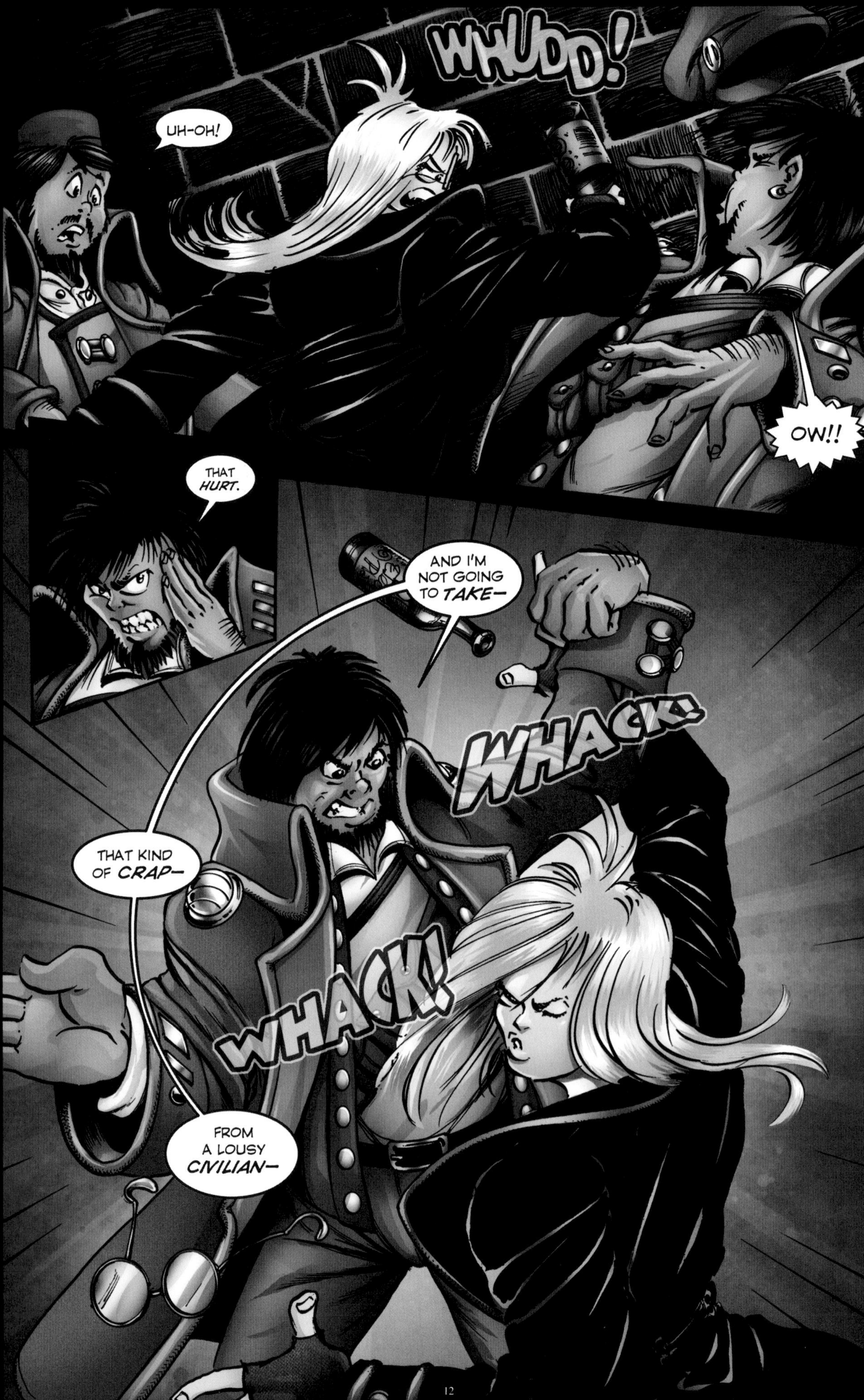
WHUDD!
UH-OH!
OW!!
THAT HURT.
AND I'M NOT GOING TO TAKE—
WHACK!
THAT KIND OF CRAP—
WHACK!
FROM A LOUSY CIVILIAN—

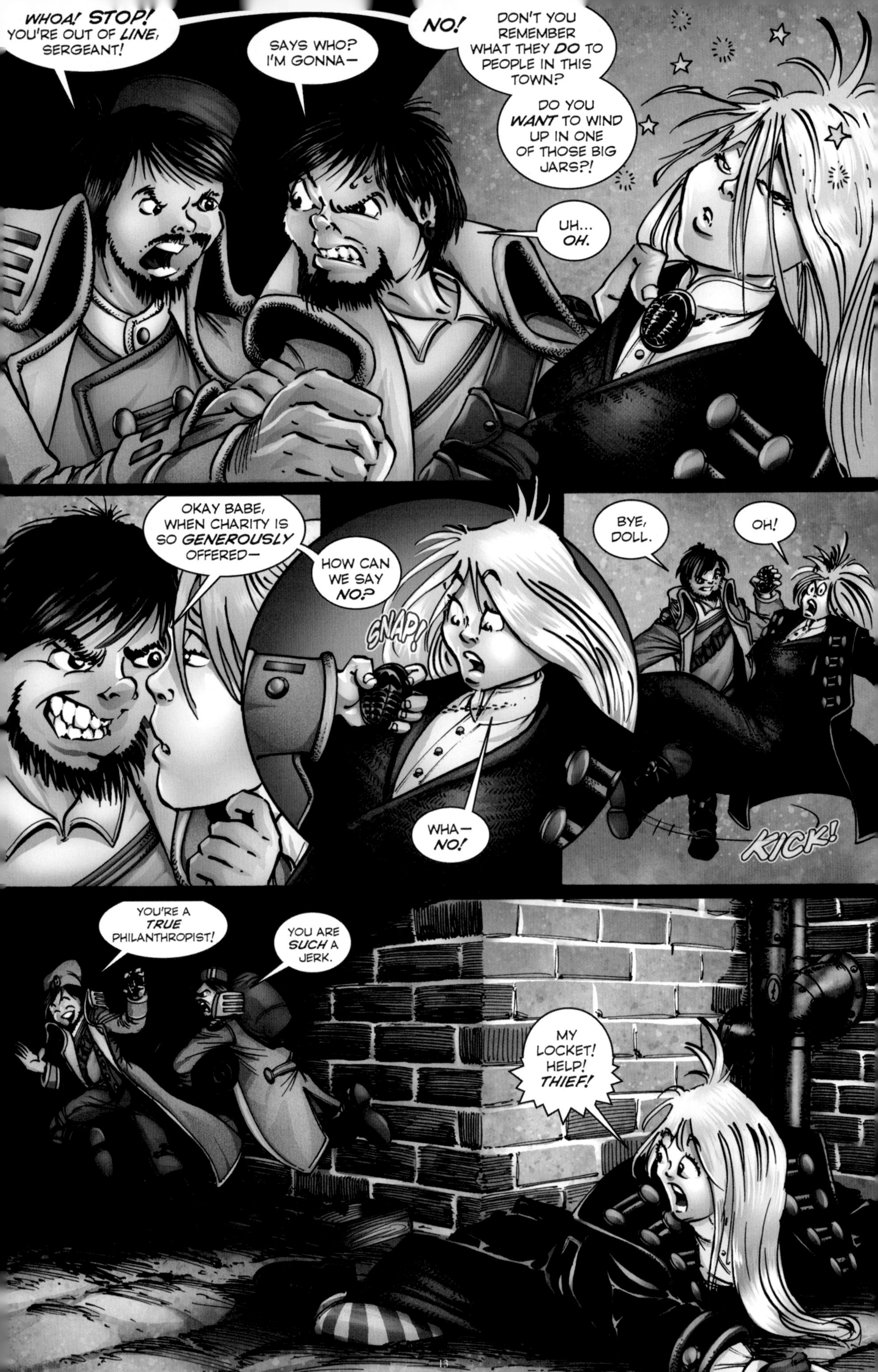
WHOA! STOP! YOU'RE OUT OF LINE, SERGEANT!
SAYS WHO? I'M GONNA—
NO!
DON'T YOU REMEMBER WHAT THEY DO TO PEOPLE IN THIS TOWN?
DO YOU WANT TO WIND UP IN ONE OF THOSE BIG JARS?!
UH... OH.
OKAY BABE, WHEN CHARITY IS SO GENEROUSLY OFFERED—
HOW CAN WE SAY NO?
SNAP!
WHA— NO!
BYE, DOLL.
OH!
KICK!
YOU'RE A TRUE PHILANTHROPIST!
YOU ARE SUCH A JERK.
MY LOCKET! HELP! THIEF!

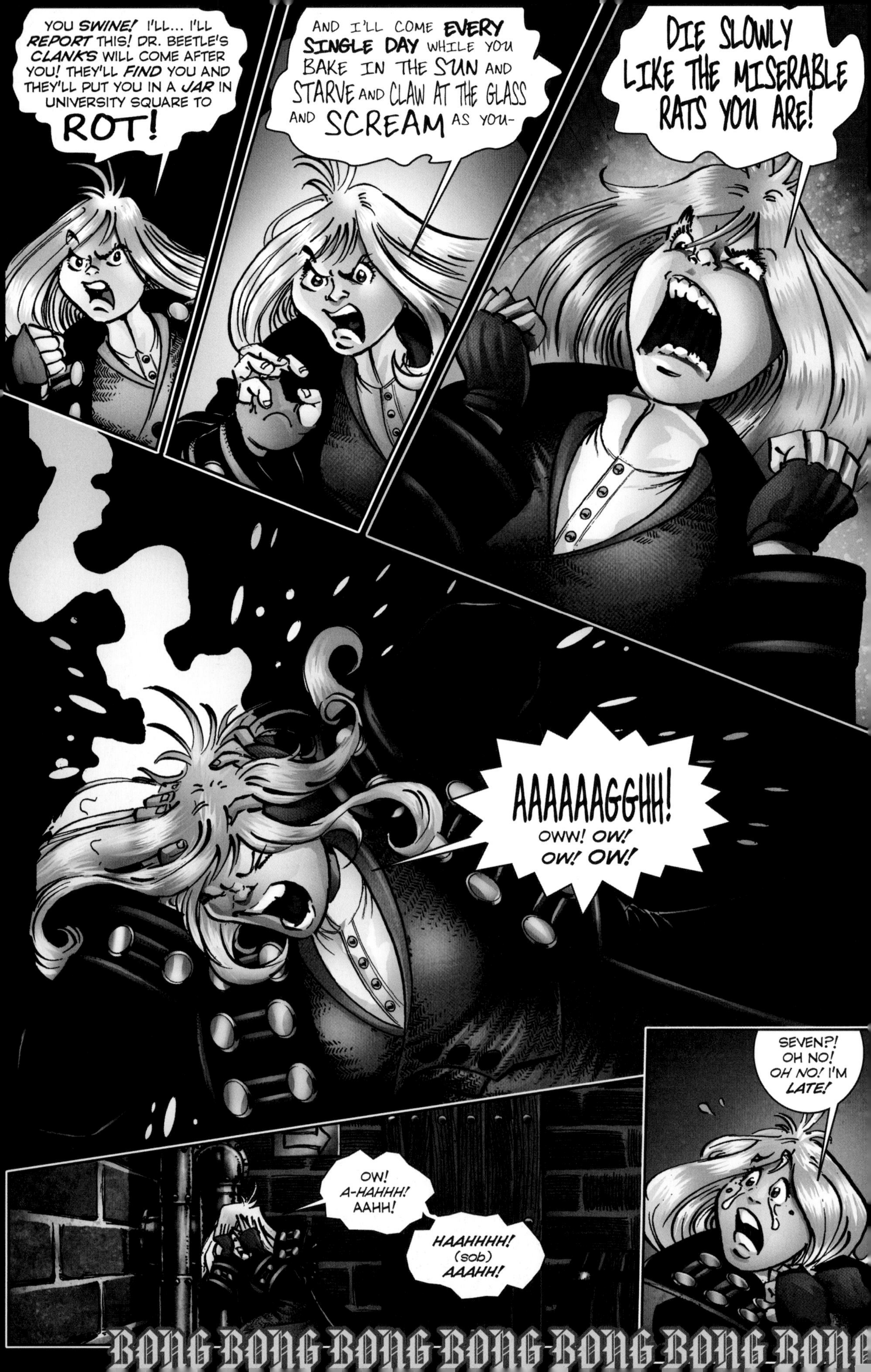
YOU SWINE! I'LL... I'LL REPORT THIS! DR. BEETLE'S CLANKS WILL COME AFTER YOU! THEY'LL FIND YOU AND THEY'LL PUT YOU IN A JAR IN UNIVERSITY SQUARE TO ROT!
AND I'LL COME EVERY SINGLE DAY WHILE YOU BAKE IN THE SUN AND STARVE AND CLAW AT THE GLASS AND SCREAM AS YOU-
DIE SLOWLY LIKE THE MISERABLE RATS YOU ARE!
AAAAAAGGHH! OWW! OW! OW! OW!
SEVEN?! OH NO! OH NO! I'M LATE!
OW! A-HAHHH! AAHH!
HAAHHHH! (sob) AAAHH!
BONG-BONG-BONG-BONG-BONG-BONG-BONG

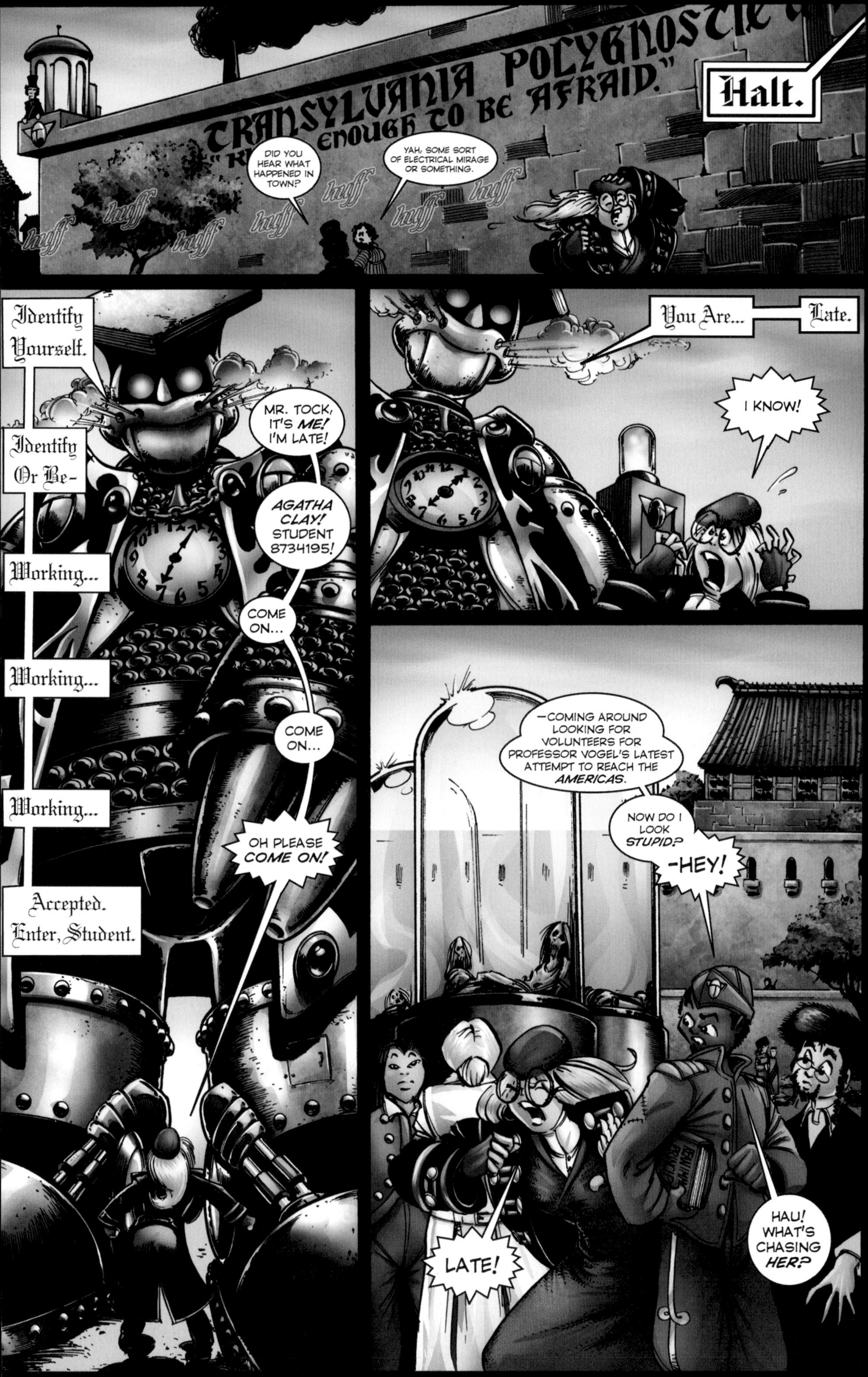
TRANSYLVANIA POLYGNOSTIC
"KN... ENOUGH TO BE AFRAID."
Halt.
DID YOU HEAR WHAT HAPPENED IN TOWN?
YAH, SOME SORT OF ELECTRICAL MIRAGE OR SOMETHING.
huff huff huff huff huff huff huff huff
Identify Yourself.
MR. TOCK, IT'S ME! I'M LATE!
Identify Or Be-
AGATHA CLAY! STUDENT 8734195!
Working...
COME ON...
Working...
COME ON...
Working...
OH PLEASE COME ON!
Accepted. Enter, Student.
You Are... Late.
I KNOW!
—COMING AROUND LOOKING FOR VOLUNTEERS FOR PROFESSOR VOGEL'S LATEST ATTEMPT TO REACH THE AMERICAS.
NOW DO I LOOK STUPID?
-HEY!
LATE!
HAU! WHAT'S CHASING HER?

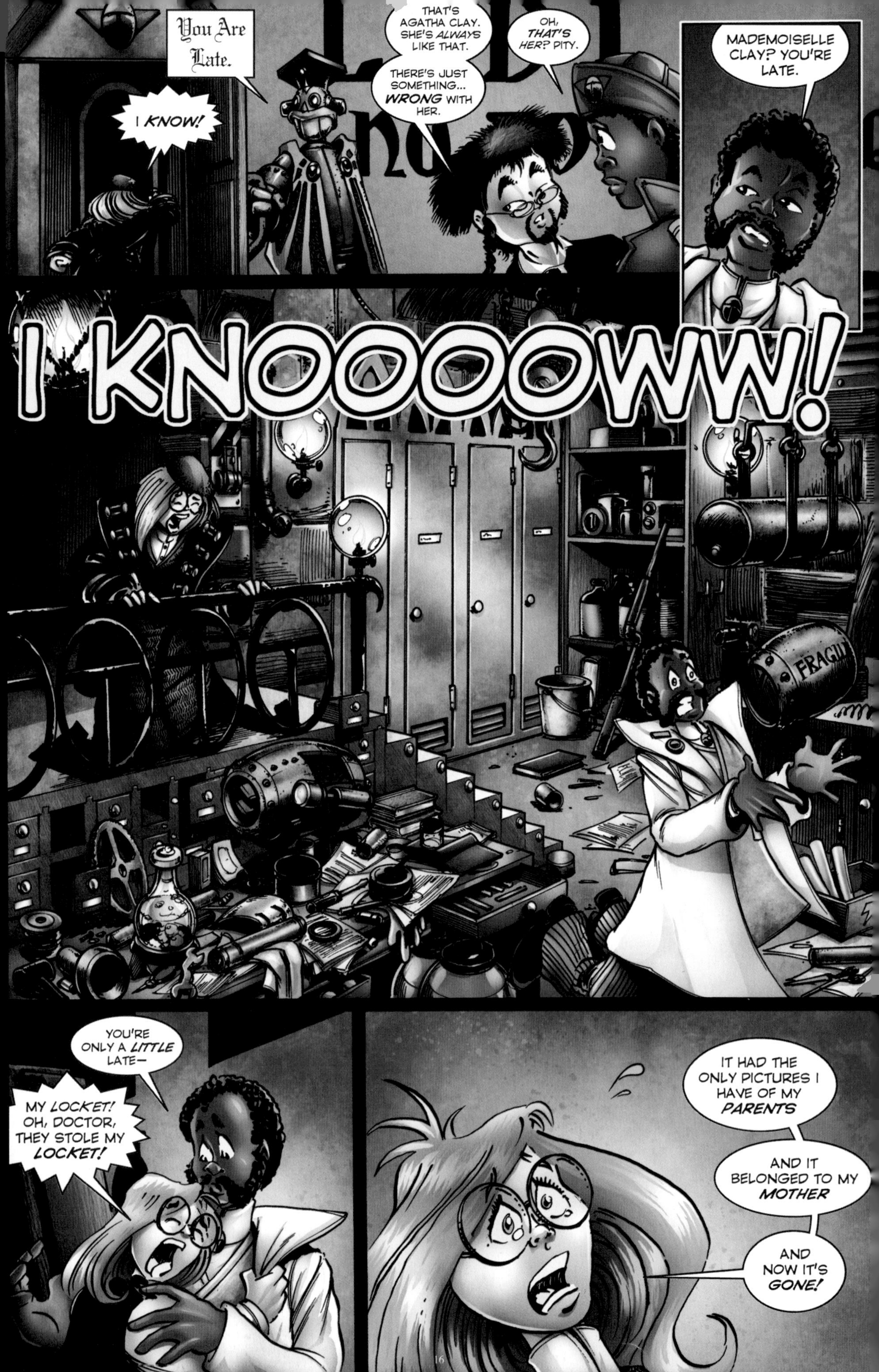
You Are Late.
I KNOW!
THAT'S AGATHA CLAY. SHE'S ALWAYS LIKE THAT.
THERE'S JUST SOMETHING... WRONG WITH HER.
OH, THAT'S HER? PITY.
MADEMOISELLE CLAY? YOU'RE LATE.
I KNOOOOWW!
FRAGIL
YOU'RE ONLY A LITTLE LATE—
MY LOCKET! OH, DOCTOR, THEY STOLE MY LOCKET!
IT HAD THE ONLY PICTURES I HAVE OF MY PARENTS
AND IT BELONGED TO MY MOTHER
AND NOW IT'S GONE!

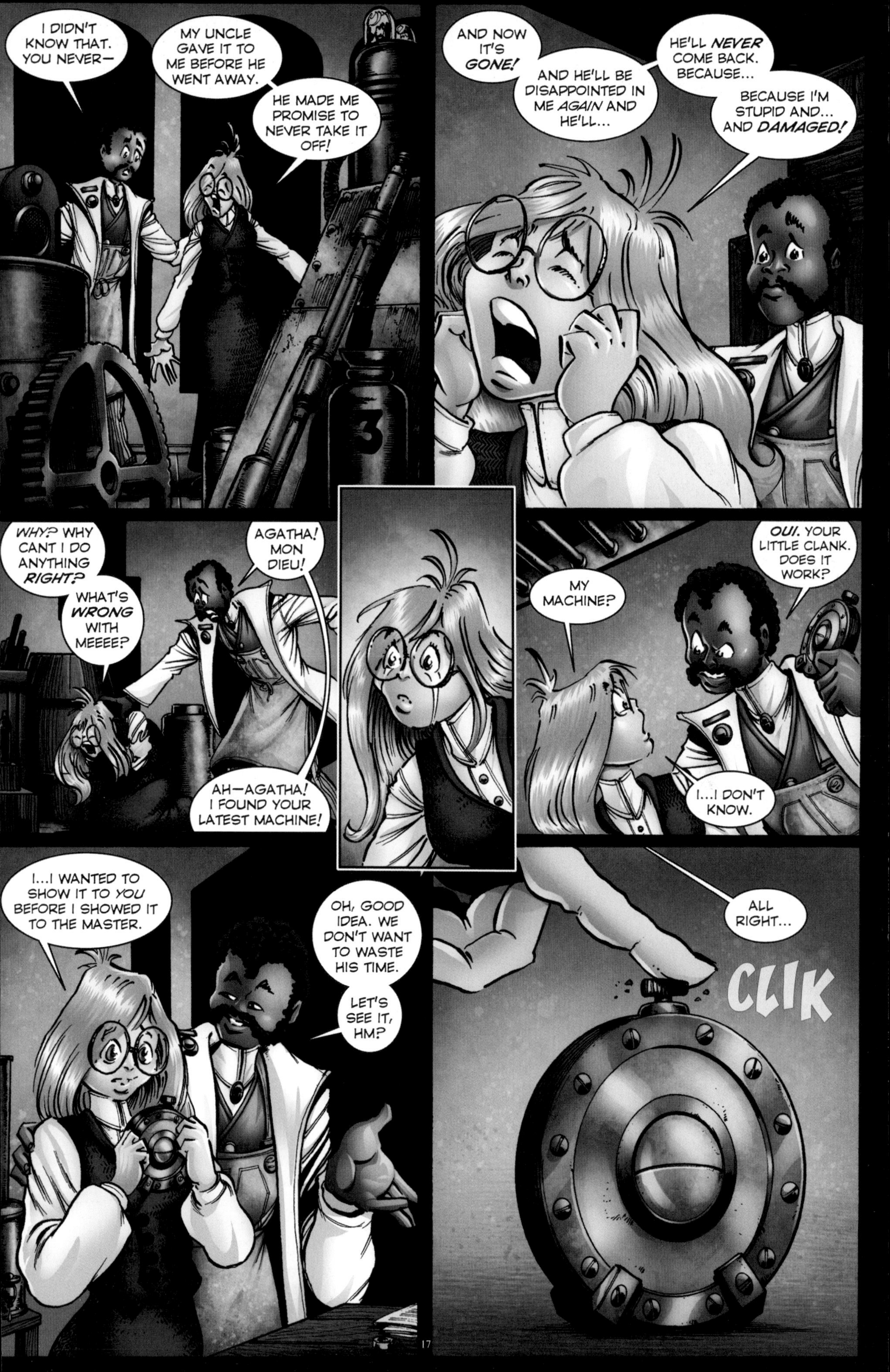
I DIDN'T KNOW THAT. YOU NEVER—
MY UNCLE GAVE IT TO ME BEFORE HE WENT AWAY.
HE MADE ME PROMISE TO NEVER TAKE IT OFF!
AND NOW IT'S GONE!
AND HE'LL BE DISAPPOINTED IN ME AGAIN AND HE'LL...
HE'LL NEVER COME BACK. BECAUSE...
BECAUSE I'M STUPID AND... AND DAMAGED!
WHY? WHY CANT I DO ANYTHING RIGHT?
WHAT'S WRONG WITH MEEEE?
AGATHA! MON DIEU!
AH—AGATHA! I FOUND YOUR LATEST MACHINE!
MY MACHINE?
OUI. YOUR LITTLE CLANK. DOES IT WORK?
I...I DON'T KNOW.
I...I WANTED TO SHOW IT TO YOU BEFORE I SHOWED IT TO THE MASTER.
OH, GOOD IDEA. WE DON'T WANT TO WASTE HIS TIME.
LET'S SEE IT, HM?
ALL RIGHT...
CLIK

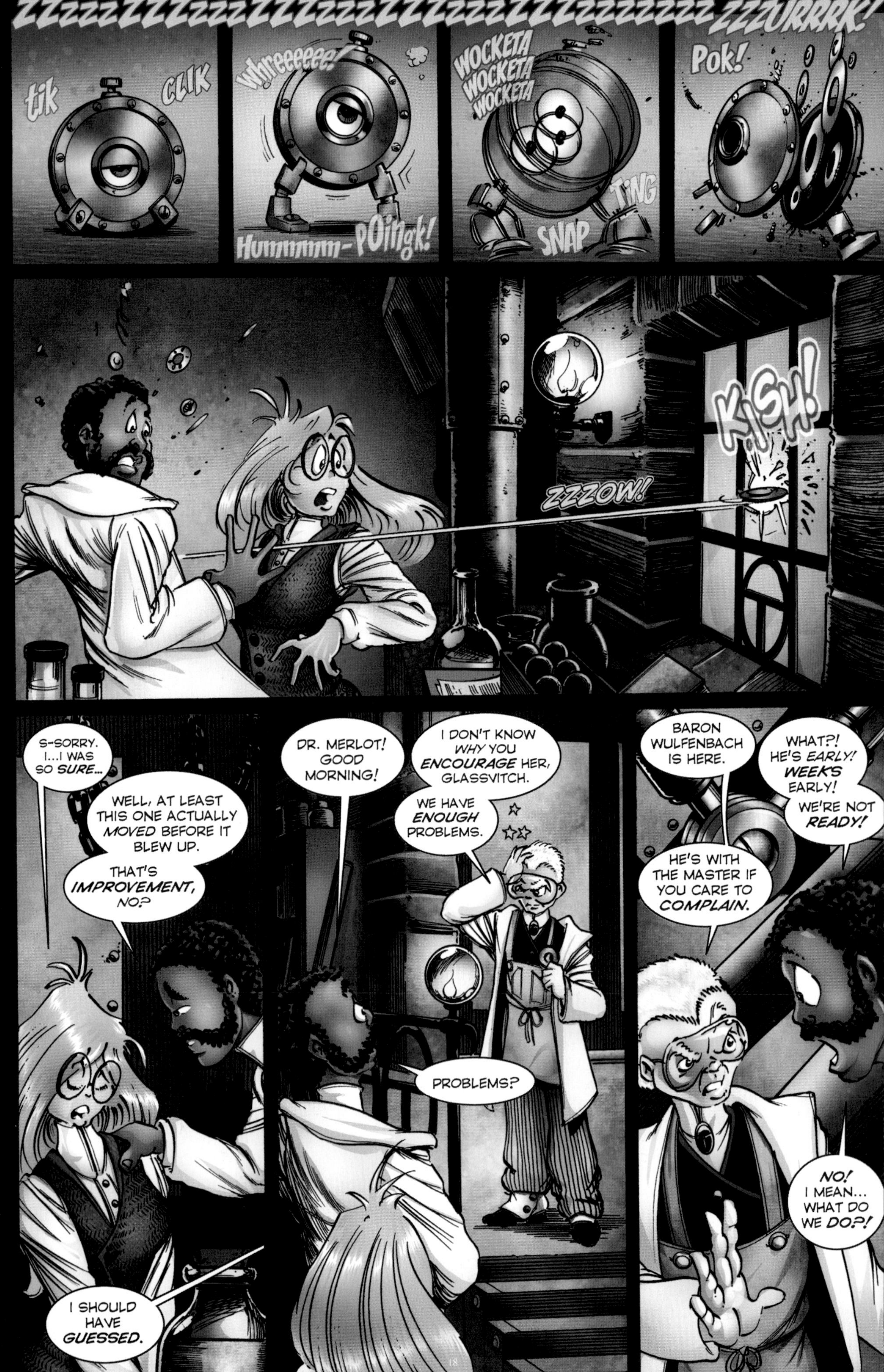
ZZzzzZZZzzzZZZzzzZZZzzzZZZzzzZZZzzzzzzzz ZZZURRRK!
tik
CLIK
Whreeeeee!
Hummmm-POingk!
WOCKETA WOCKETA WOCKETA
SNAP
TING
Pok!
KiSH!
ZZZOW!
S-SORRY. I...I WAS SO *SURE...*
WELL, AT LEAST THIS ONE ACTUALLY *MOVED* BEFORE IT BLEW UP.
THAT'S *IMPROVEMENT*, NO?
I SHOULD HAVE *GUESSED.*
DR. MERLOT! GOOD MORNING!
I DON'T KNOW *WHY* YOU *ENCOURAGE* HER, GLASSVITCH.
WE HAVE *ENOUGH* PROBLEMS.
PROBLEMS?
BARON WULFENBACH IS HERE.
WHAT?! HE'S *EARLY! WEEKS* EARLY!
WE'RE NOT *READY!*
HE'S WITH THE MASTER IF YOU CARE TO *COMPLAIN.*
NO! I MEAN... WHAT DO WE *DO?!*

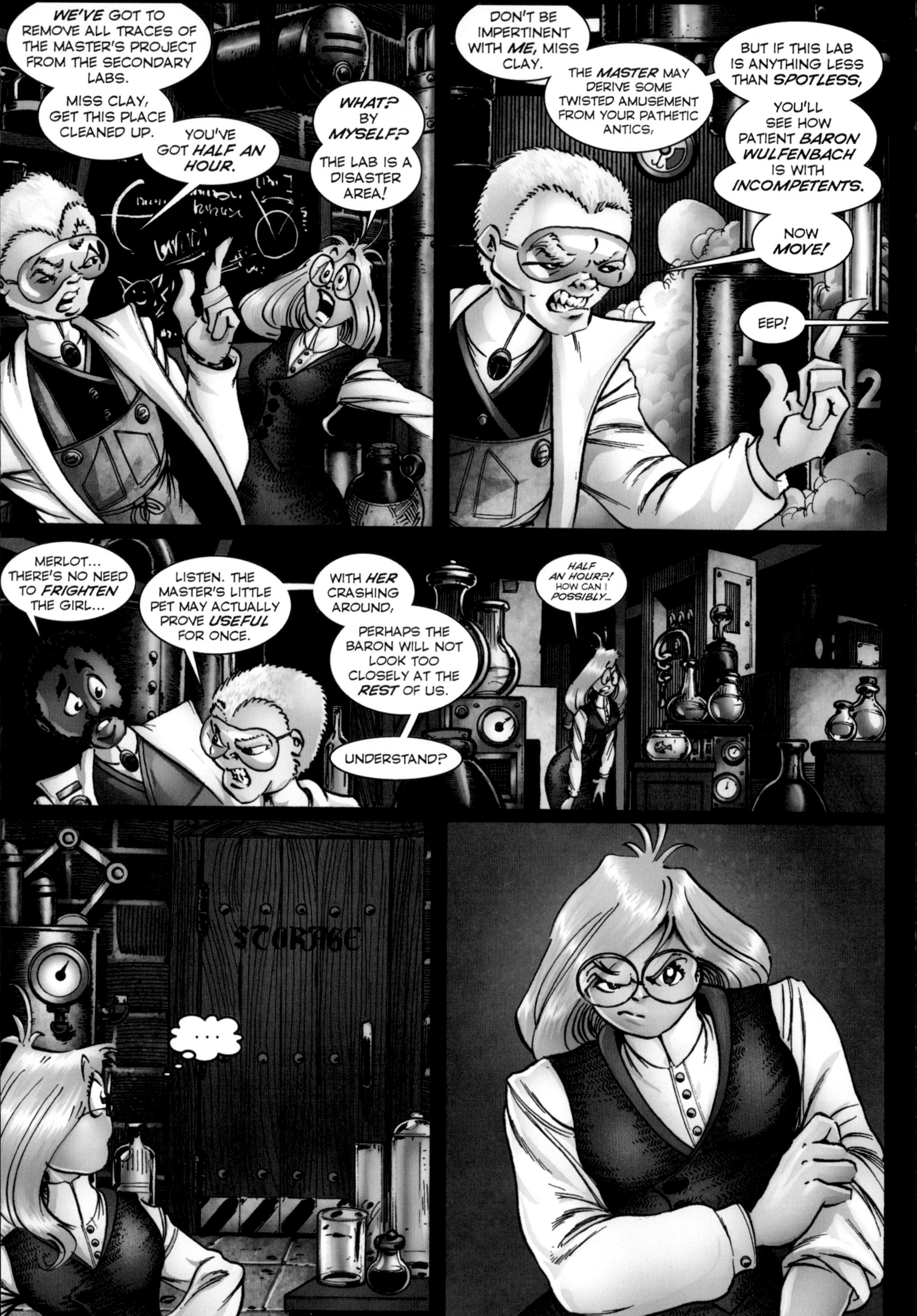
WE'VE GOT TO REMOVE ALL TRACES OF THE MASTER'S PROJECT FROM THE SECONDARY LABS.
MISS CLAY, GET THIS PLACE CLEANED UP.
YOU'VE GOT HALF AN HOUR.
WHAT? BY MYSELF?
THE LAB IS A DISASTER AREA!
DON'T BE IMPERTINENT WITH ME, MISS CLAY.
THE MASTER MAY DERIVE SOME TWISTED AMUSEMENT FROM YOUR PATHETIC ANTICS,
BUT IF THIS LAB IS ANYTHING LESS THAN SPOTLESS,
YOU'LL SEE HOW PATIENT BARON WULFENBACH IS WITH INCOMPETENTS.
NOW MOVE!
EEP!
MERLOT... THERE'S NO NEED TO FRIGHTEN THE GIRL...
LISTEN. THE MASTER'S LITTLE PET MAY ACTUALLY PROVE USEFUL FOR ONCE.
WITH HER CRASHING AROUND,
PERHAPS THE BARON WILL NOT LOOK TOO CLOSELY AT THE REST OF US.
UNDERSTAND?
HALF AN HOUR?! HOW CAN I POSSIBLY...
STORAGE
...

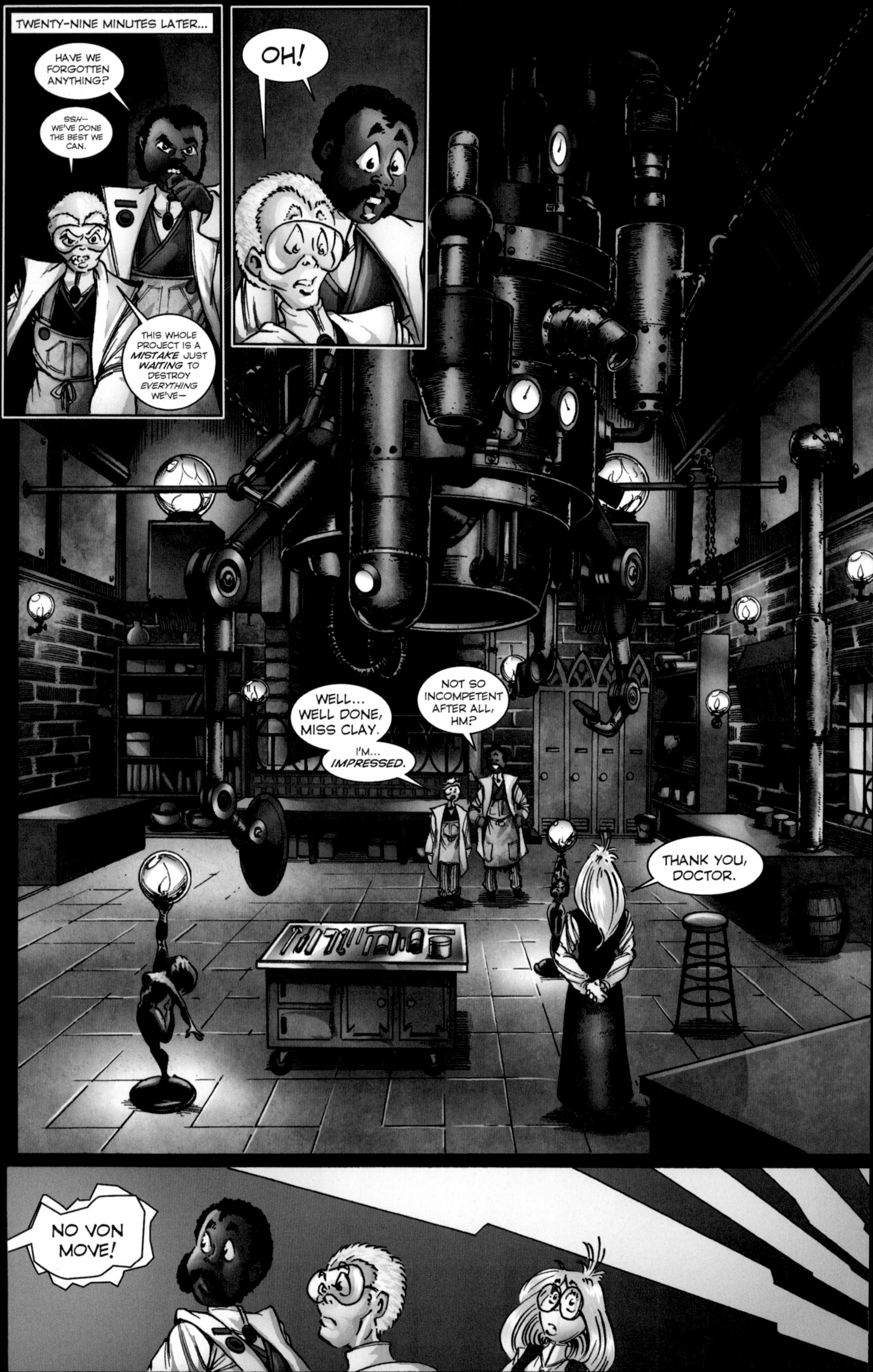
TWENTY-NINE MINUTES LATER...
HAVE WE FORGOTTEN ANYTHING?
SSH— WE'VE DONE THE BEST WE CAN.
THIS WHOLE PROJECT IS A MISTAKE JUST WAITING TO DESTROY EVERYTHING WE'VE—
OH!
WELL... WELL DONE, MISS CLAY.
I'M... IMPRESSED.
NOT SO INCOMPETENT AFTER ALL, HM?
THANK YOU, DOCTOR.
NO VON MOVE!

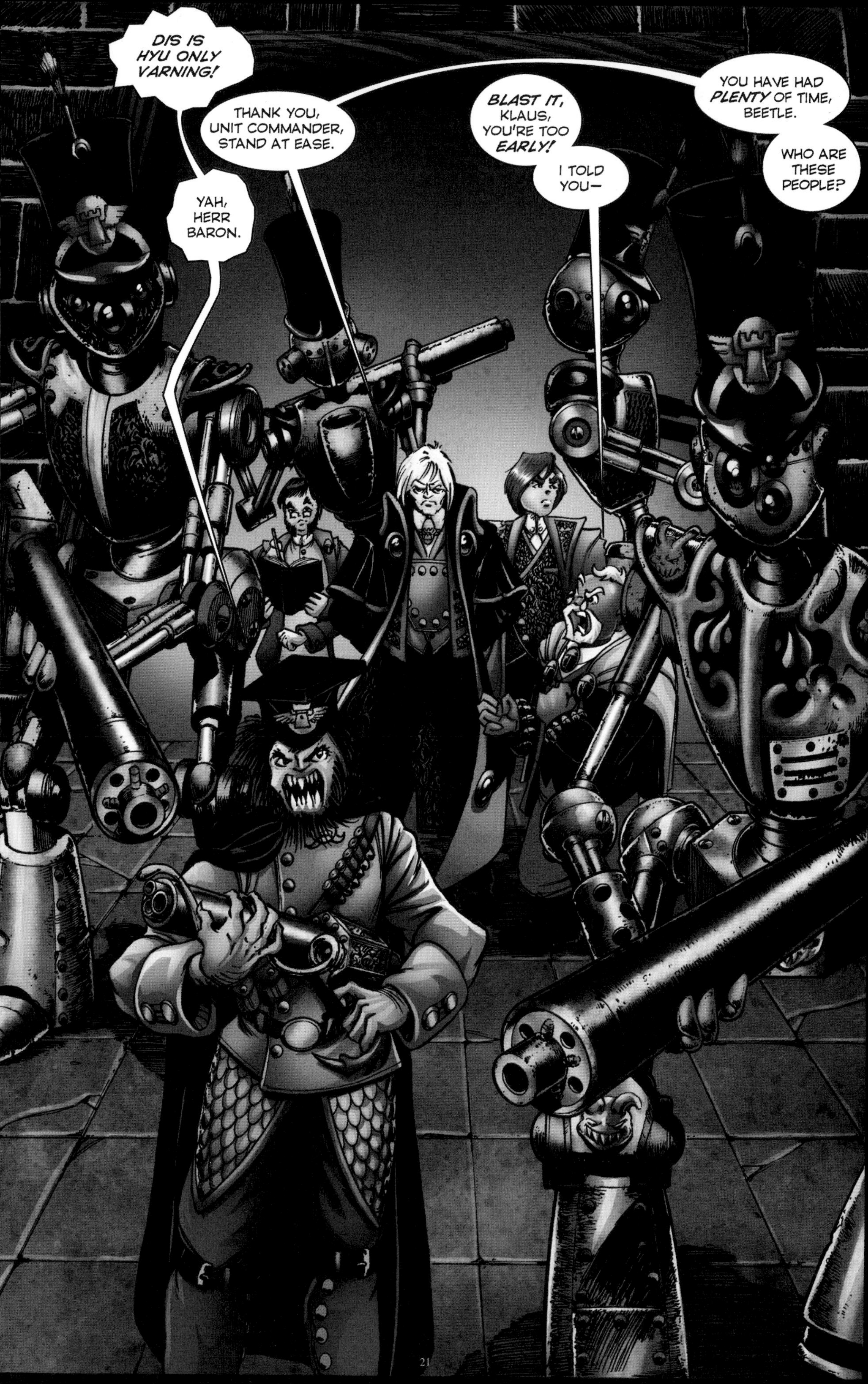

DIS IS HYU ONLY VARNING!
THANK YOU, UNIT COMMANDER, STAND AT EASE.
YAH, HERR BARON.
BLAST IT, KLAUS, YOU'RE TOO *EARLY!*
I TOLD YOU—
YOU HAVE HAD *PLENTY* OF TIME, BEETLE.
WHO ARE THESE PEOPLE?

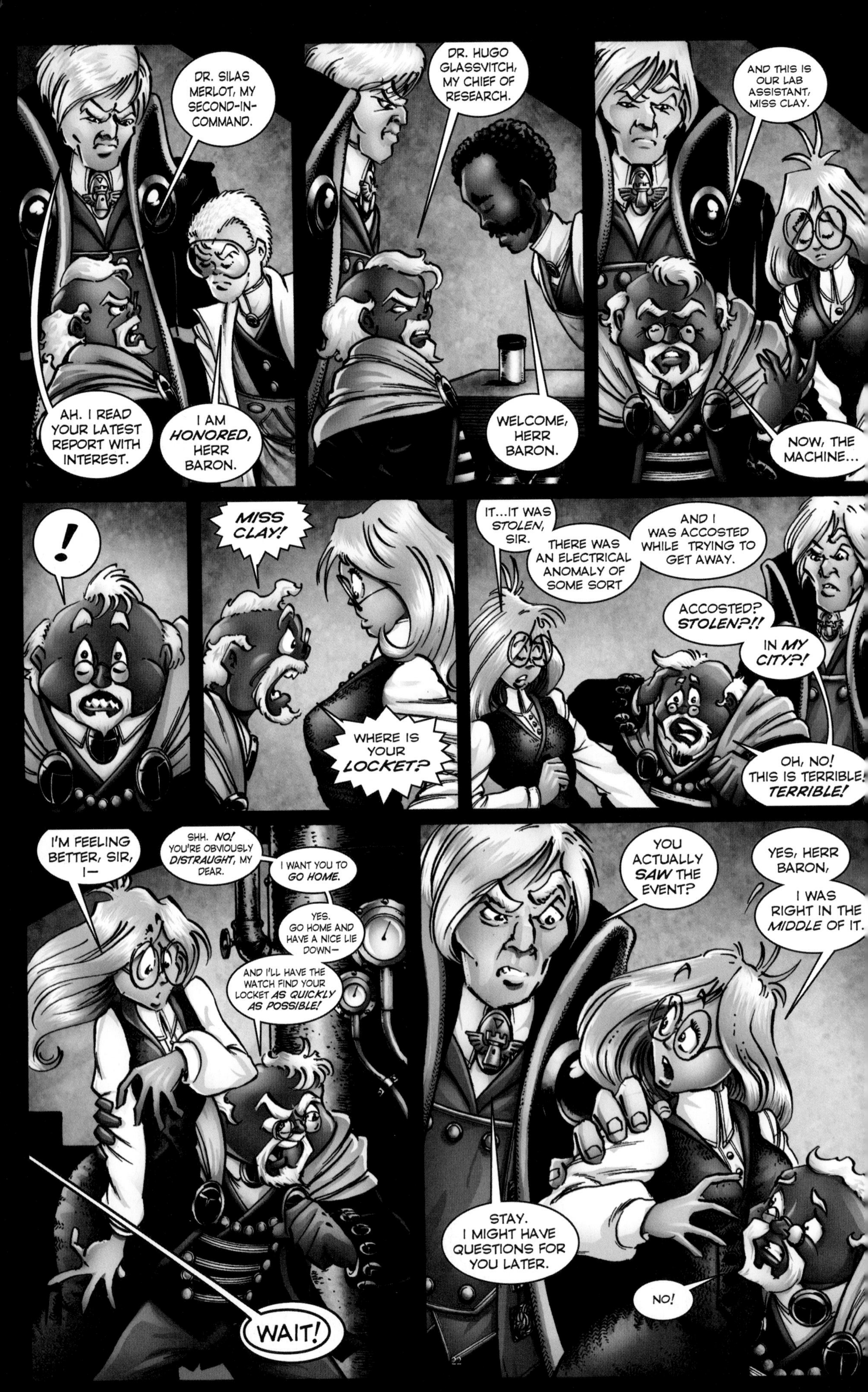
DR. SILAS MERLOT, MY SECOND-IN-COMMAND.
AH. I READ YOUR LATEST REPORT WITH INTEREST.
I AM *HONORED,* HERR BARON.
DR. HUGO GLASSVITCH, MY CHIEF OF RESEARCH.
WELCOME, HERR BARON.
AND THIS IS OUR LAB ASSISTANT, MISS CLAY.
NOW, THE MACHINE...
!
MISS CLAY!
WHERE IS YOUR *LOCKET?*
IT...IT WAS *STOLEN,* SIR.
THERE WAS AN ELECTRICAL ANOMALY OF SOME SORT
AND I WAS ACCOSTED WHILE TRYING TO GET AWAY.
ACCOSTED? *STOLEN?!!*
IN *MY CITY?!*
OH, NO! THIS IS TERRIBLE! *TERRIBLE!*
I'M FEELING BETTER, SIR, I—
SHH. *NO!* YOU'RE OBVIOUSLY *DISTRAUGHT,* MY DEAR.
I WANT YOU TO *GO HOME.*
YES. GO HOME AND HAVE A NICE LIE DOWN—
AND I'LL HAVE THE WATCH FIND YOUR LOCKET *AS QUICKLY AS POSSIBLE!*
WAIT!
YOU ACTUALLY *SAW* THE EVENT?
YES, HERR BARON,
I WAS RIGHT IN THE *MIDDLE* OF IT.
STAY. I MIGHT HAVE QUESTIONS FOR YOU LATER.
NO!

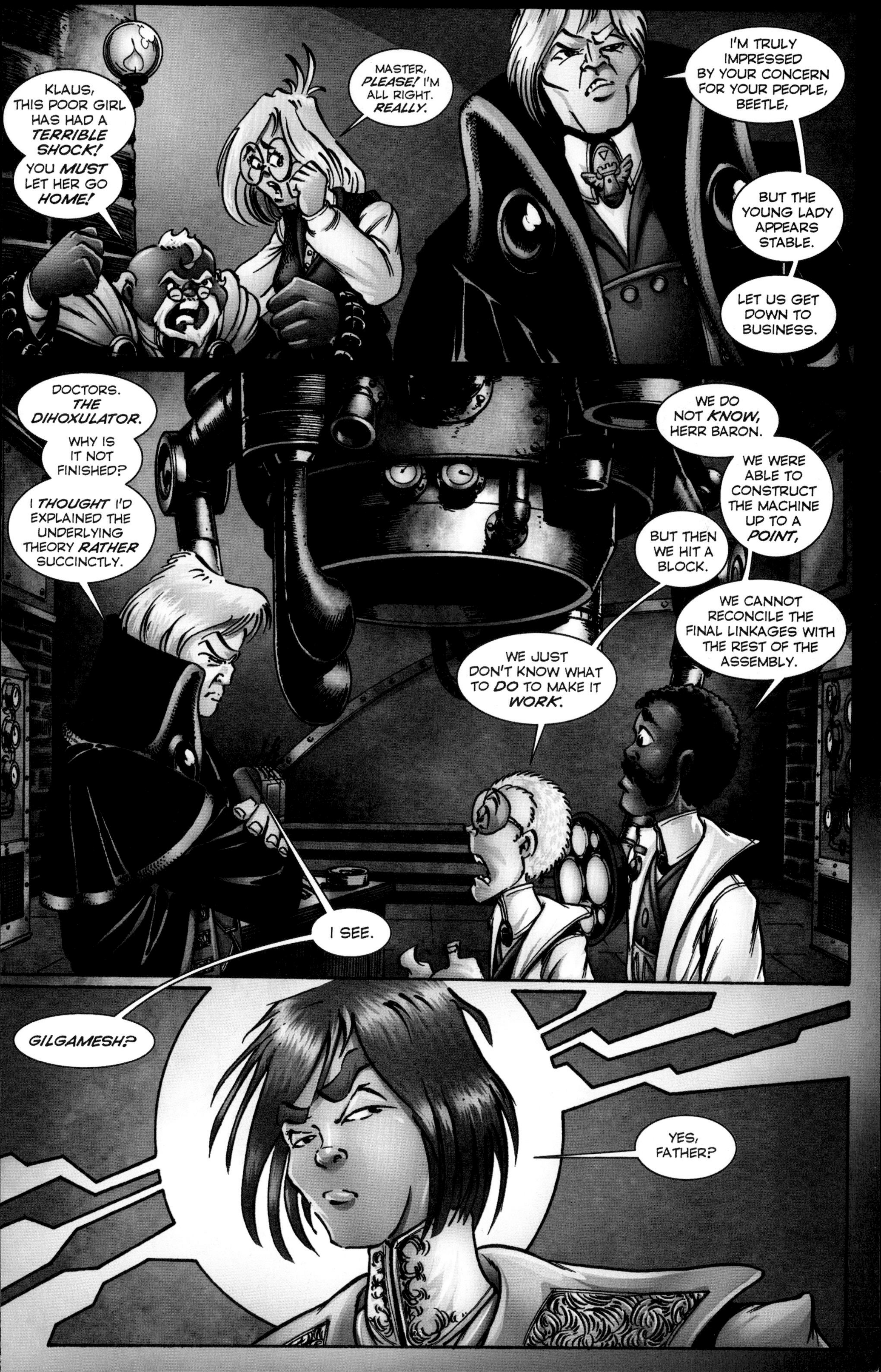

KLAUS, THIS POOR GIRL HAS HAD A *TERRIBLE SHOCK!*
YOU *MUST* LET HER GO *HOME!*
MASTER, *PLEASE!* I'M ALL RIGHT. *REALLY.*
I'M TRULY IMPRESSED BY YOUR CONCERN FOR YOUR PEOPLE, BEETLE,
BUT THE YOUNG LADY APPEARS STABLE.
LET US GET DOWN TO BUSINESS.
DOCTORS. *THE DIHOXULATOR.*
WHY IS IT NOT FINISHED?
I *THOUGHT* I'D EXPLAINED THE UNDERLYING THEORY *RATHER* SUCCINCTLY.
WE DO NOT *KNOW,* HERR BARON.
WE WERE ABLE TO CONSTRUCT THE MACHINE UP TO A *POINT,*
BUT THEN WE HIT A BLOCK.
WE CANNOT RECONCILE THE FINAL LINKAGES WITH THE REST OF THE ASSEMBLY.
WE JUST DON'T KNOW WHAT TO *DO* TO MAKE IT *WORK.*
I SEE.
GILGAMESH?
YES, FATHER?

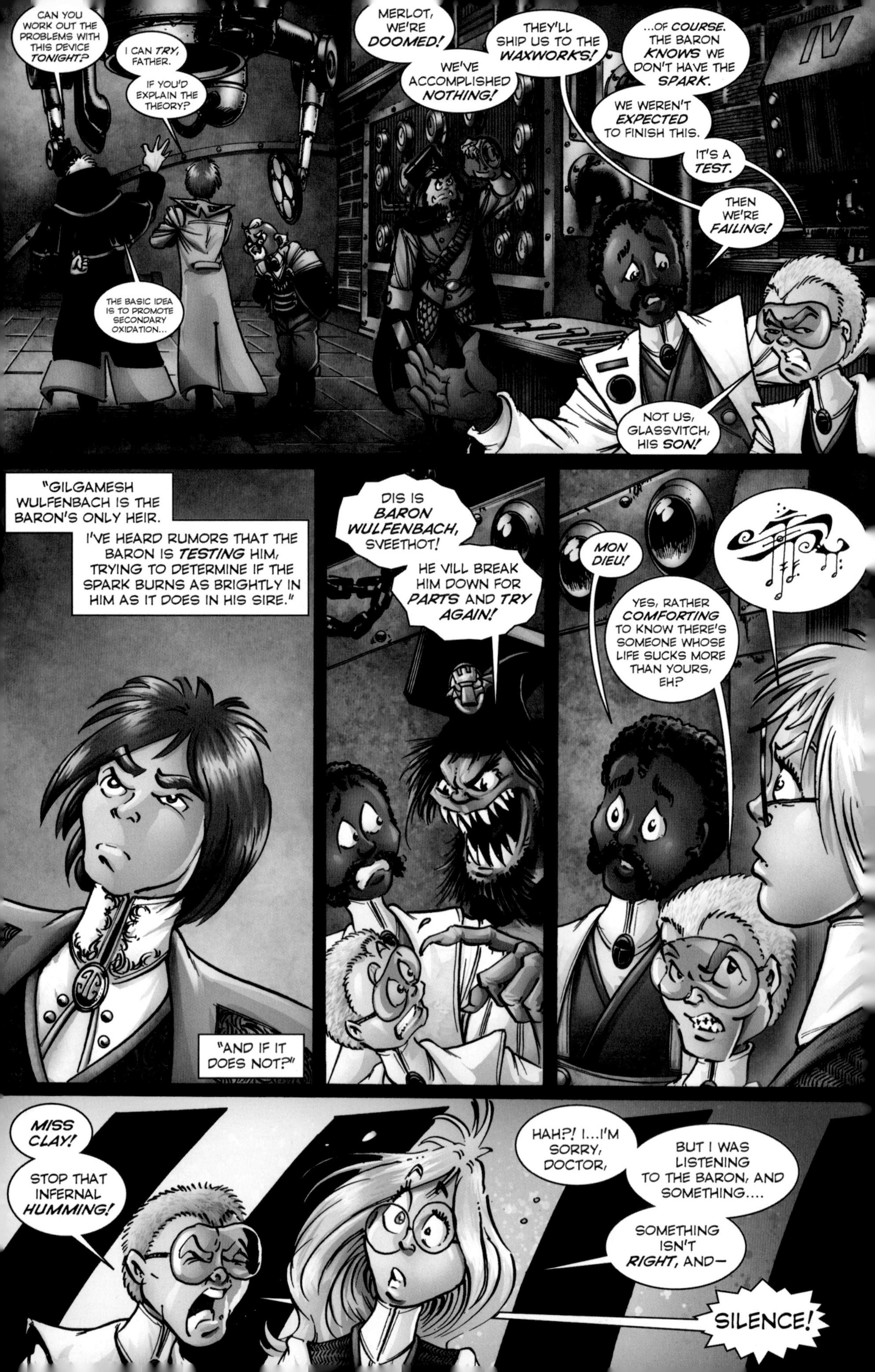
CAN YOU WORK OUT THE PROBLEMS WITH THIS DEVICE TONIGHT?
I CAN TRY, FATHER.
IF YOU'D EXPLAIN THE THEORY?
THE BASIC IDEA IS TO PROMOTE SECONDARY OXIDATION...
MERLOT, WE'RE DOOMED!
WE'VE ACCOMPLISHED NOTHING!
THEY'LL SHIP US TO THE WAXWORKS!
...OF COURSE. THE BARON KNOWS WE DON'T HAVE THE SPARK.
WE WEREN'T EXPECTED TO FINISH THIS.
IT'S A TEST.
THEN WE'RE FAILING!
NOT US, GLASSVITCH, HIS SON!
"GILGAMESH WULFENBACH IS THE BARON'S ONLY HEIR.
I'VE HEARD RUMORS THAT THE BARON IS TESTING HIM, TRYING TO DETERMINE IF THE SPARK BURNS AS BRIGHTLY IN HIM AS IT DOES IN HIS SIRE."
"AND IF IT DOES NOT?"
DIS IS BARON WULFENBACH, SVEETHOT!
HE VILL BREAK HIM DOWN FOR PARTS AND TRY AGAIN!
MON DIEU!
YES, RATHER COMFORTING TO KNOW THERE'S SOMEONE WHOSE LIFE SUCKS MORE THAN YOURS, EH?
MISS CLAY!
STOP THAT INFERNAL HUMMING!
HAH?! I...I'M SORRY, DOCTOR,
BUT I WAS LISTENING TO THE BARON, AND SOMETHING....
SOMETHING ISN'T RIGHT, AND—
SILENCE!

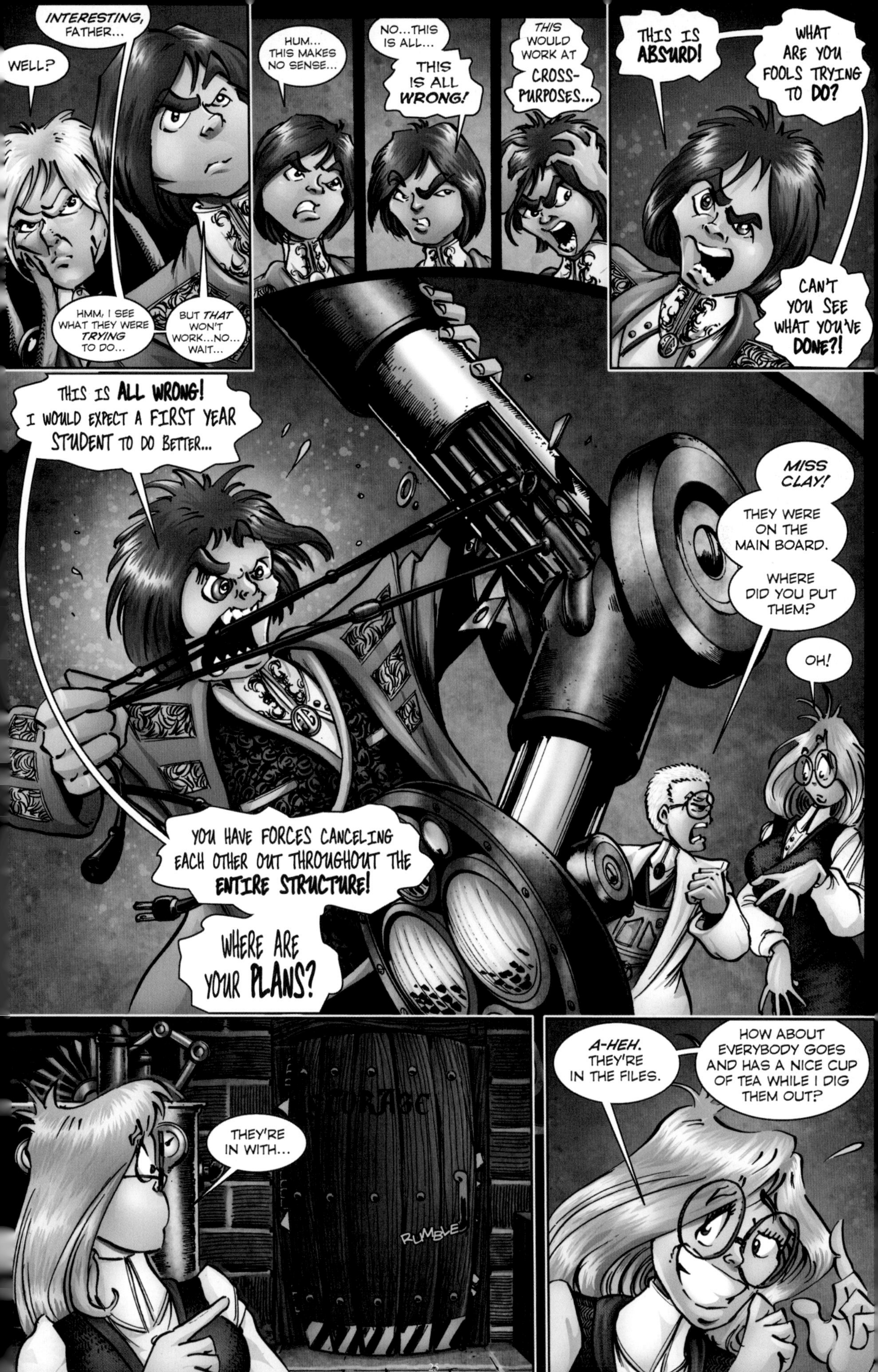

WELL?
INTERESTING, FATHER...
HMM, I SEE WHAT THEY WERE *TRYING* TO DO...
BUT *THAT* WON'T WORK...NO... WAIT...
HUM... THIS MAKES NO SENSE...
NO...THIS IS ALL...
THIS IS ALL *WRONG!*
THIS WOULD WORK AT CROSS-PURPOSES...
THIS IS **ABSURD!**
WHAT ARE YOU FOOLS TRYING TO **DO?**
CAN'T YOU SEE WHAT YOU'VE **DONE?!**
THIS IS **ALL WRONG!** I WOULD EXPECT A FIRST YEAR STUDENT TO DO BETTER...
MISS CLAY!
THEY WERE ON THE MAIN BOARD.
WHERE DID YOU PUT THEM?
OH!
YOU HAVE FORCES CANCELING EACH OTHER OUT THROUGHOUT THE **ENTIRE STRUCTURE!**
WHERE ARE YOUR **PLANS?**
THEY'RE IN WITH...
RUMBLE
A-HEH. THEY'RE IN THE FILES.
HOW ABOUT EVERYBODY GOES AND HAS A NICE CUP OF TEA WHILE I DIG THEM OUT?

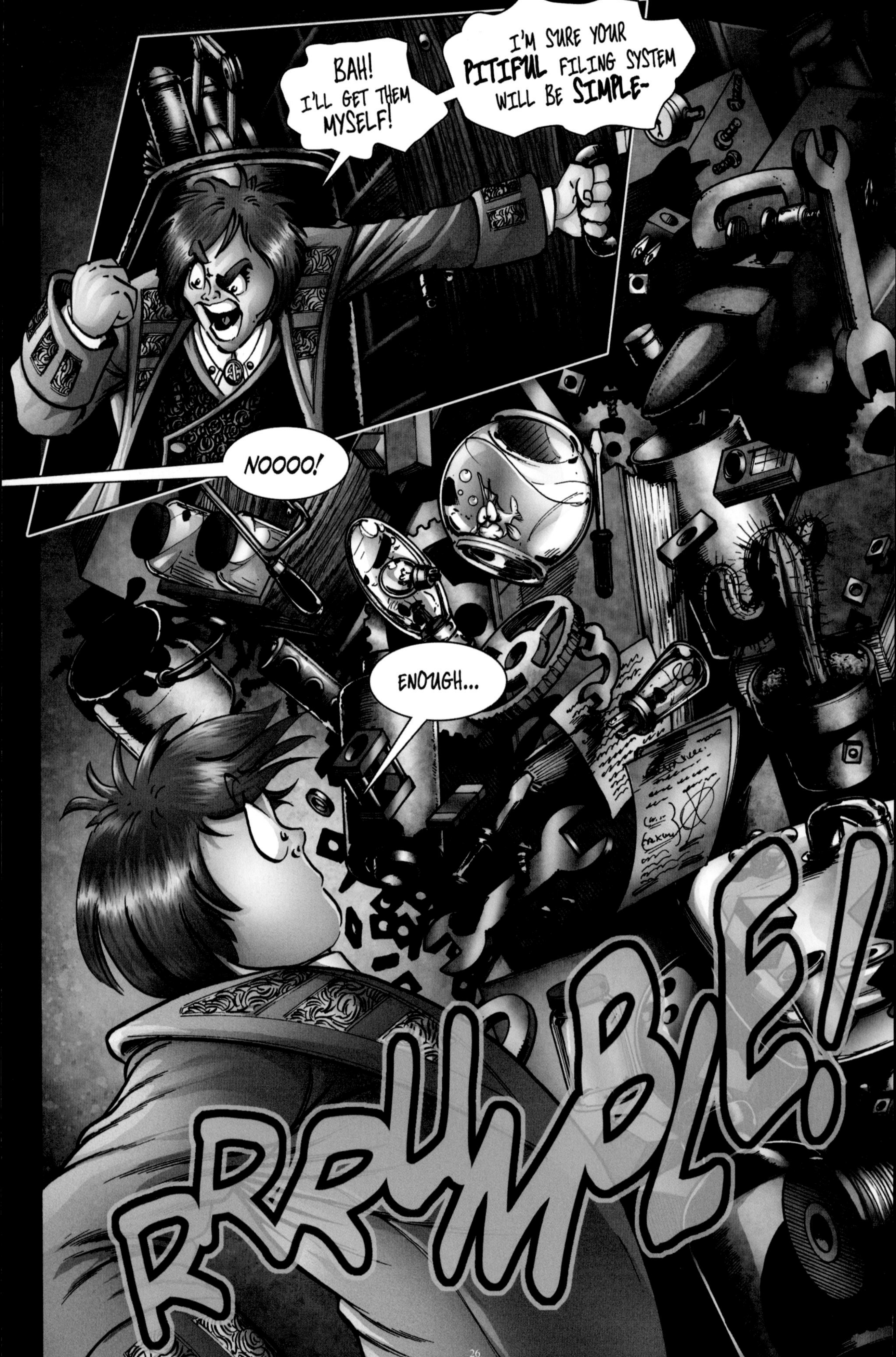
BAH! I'LL GET THEM MYSELF!
I'M SURE YOUR PITIFUL FILING SYSTEM WILL BE SIMPLE-
NOOOO!
ENOUGH...
RRUMBLE!

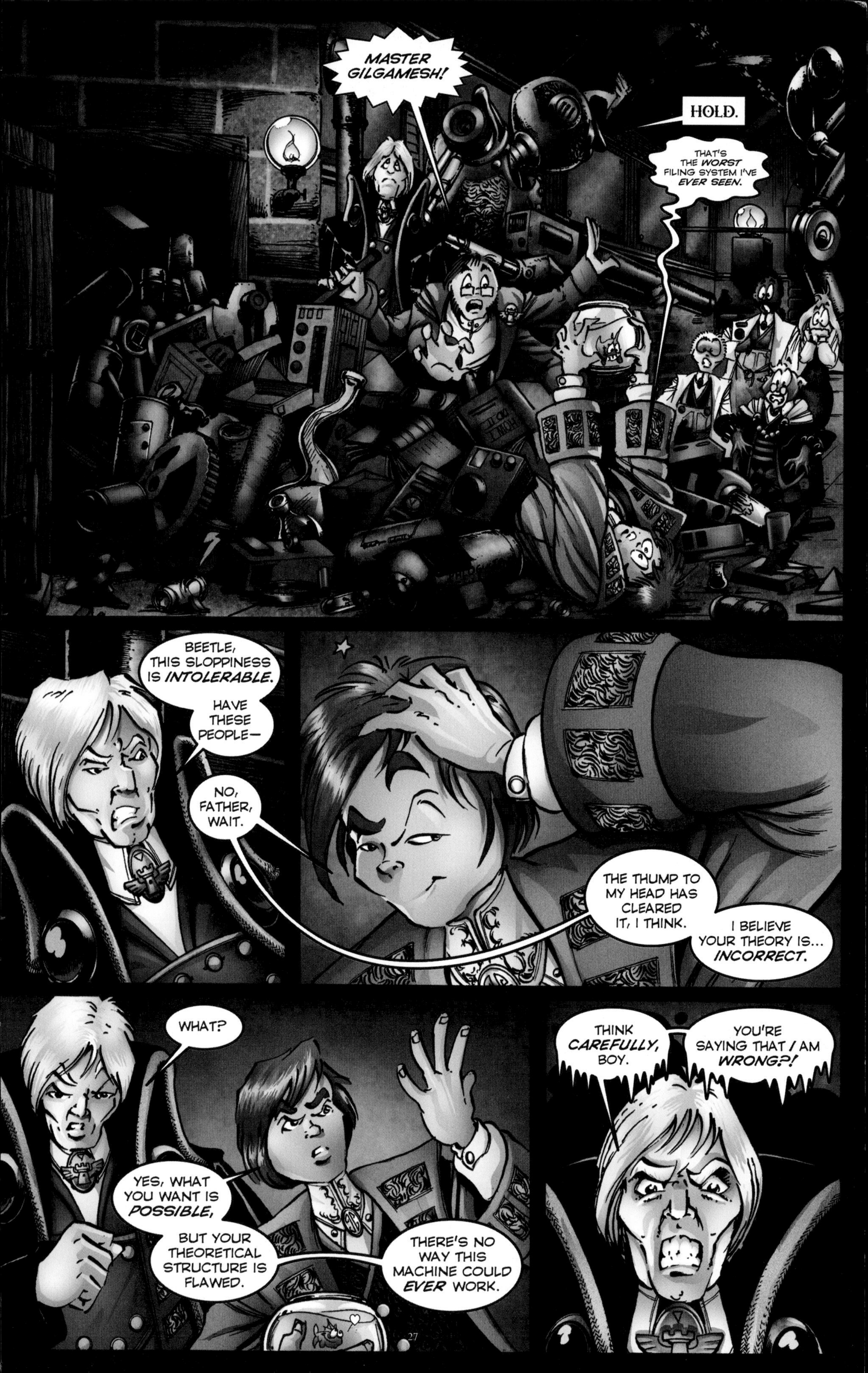
MASTER GILGAMESH!
HOLD.
THAT'S THE *WORST* FILING SYSTEM I'VE *EVER SEEN.*
BEETLE, THIS SLOPPINESS IS *INTOLERABLE.*
HAVE THESE PEOPLE—
NO, FATHER, WAIT.
THE THUMP TO MY HEAD HAS CLEARED IT, I THINK.
I BELIEVE YOUR THEORY IS... *INCORRECT.*
WHAT?
YES, WHAT YOU WANT IS *POSSIBLE,*
BUT YOUR THEORETICAL STRUCTURE IS FLAWED.
THERE'S NO WAY THIS MACHINE COULD *EVER* WORK.
THINK *CAREFULLY,* BOY.
YOU'RE SAYING THAT *I* AM *WRONG?!*

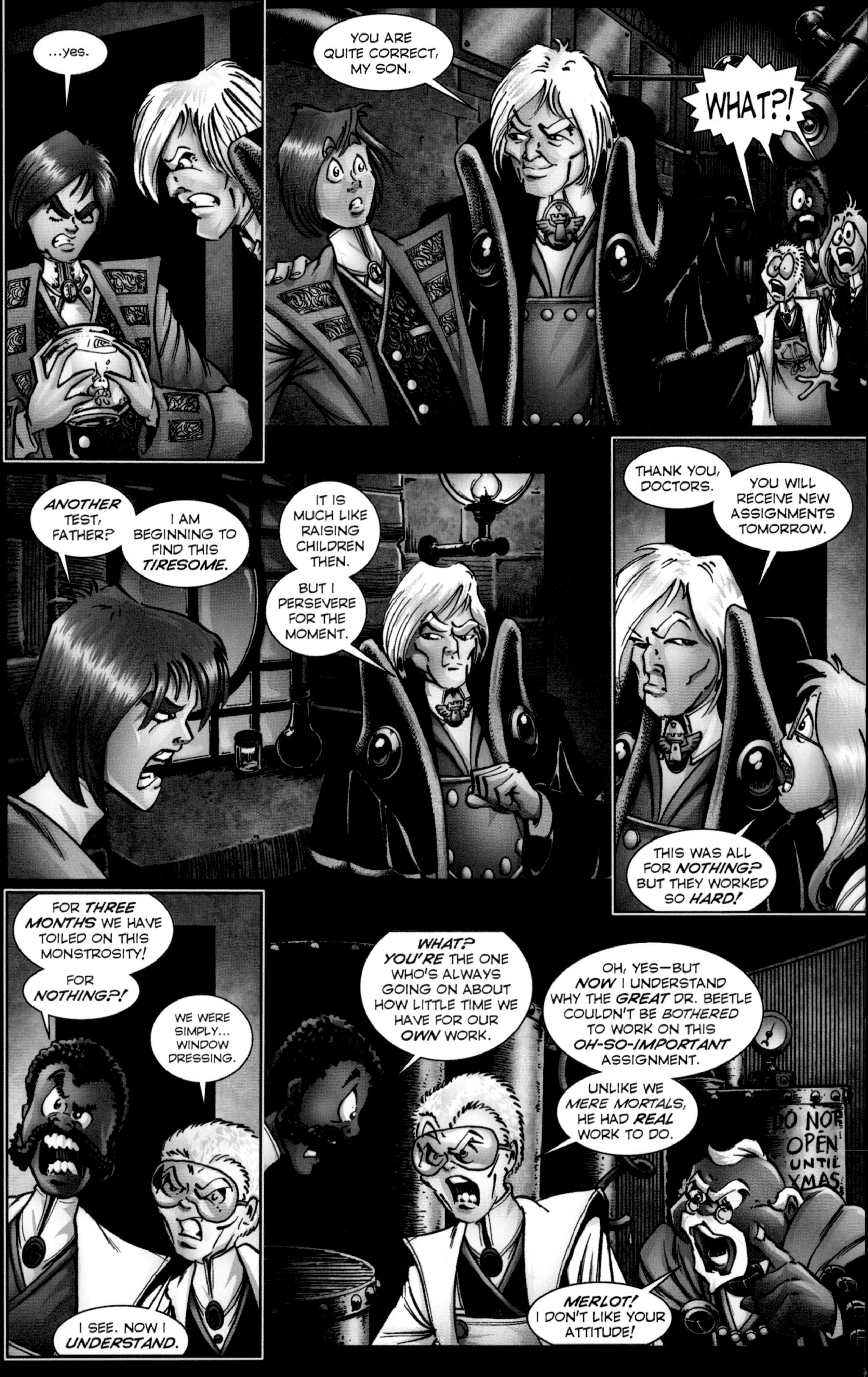
...yes.
YOU ARE QUITE CORRECT, MY SON.
WHAT?!
ANOTHER TEST, FATHER?
I AM BEGINNING TO FIND THIS TIRESOME.
IT IS MUCH LIKE RAISING CHILDREN THEN.
BUT I PERSEVERE FOR THE MOMENT.
THANK YOU, DOCTORS.
YOU WILL RECEIVE NEW ASSIGNMENTS TOMORROW.
THIS WAS ALL FOR NOTHING? BUT THEY WORKED SO HARD!
FOR THREE MONTHS WE HAVE TOILED ON THIS MONSTROSITY!
FOR NOTHING?!
WE WERE SIMPLY... WINDOW DRESSING.
I SEE. NOW I UNDERSTAND.
WHAT? YOU'RE THE ONE WHO'S ALWAYS GOING ON ABOUT HOW LITTLE TIME WE HAVE FOR OUR OWN WORK.
OH, YES—BUT NOW I UNDERSTAND WHY THE GREAT DR. BEETLE COULDN'T BE BOTHERED TO WORK ON THIS OH-SO-IMPORTANT ASSIGNMENT.
UNLIKE WE MERE MORTALS, HE HAD REAL WORK TO DO.
DO NOT OPEN UNTIL XMAS
MERLOT! I DON'T LIKE YOUR ATTITUDE!

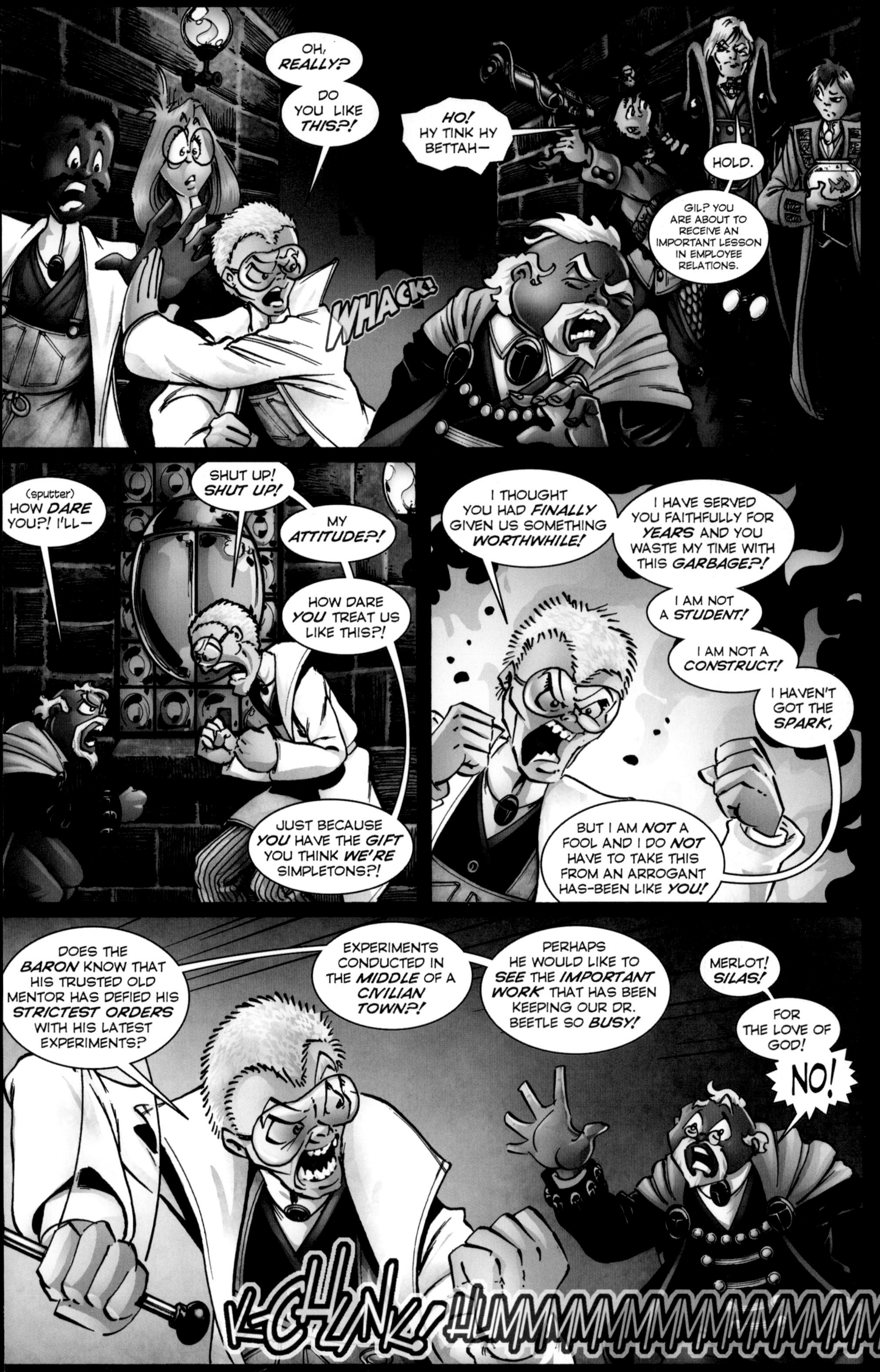
OH, REALLY?
DO YOU LIKE THIS?!
HO! HY TINK HY BETTAH—
HOLD.
GIL? YOU ARE ABOUT TO RECEIVE AN IMPORTANT LESSON IN EMPLOYEE RELATIONS.
WHACK!
(sputter) HOW DARE YOU?! I'LL—
SHUT UP! SHUT UP!
MY ATTITUDE?!
HOW DARE YOU TREAT US LIKE THIS?!
JUST BECAUSE YOU HAVE THE GIFT YOU THINK WE'RE SIMPLETONS?!
I THOUGHT YOU HAD FINALLY GIVEN US SOMETHING WORTHWHILE!
I HAVE SERVED YOU FAITHFULLY FOR YEARS AND YOU WASTE MY TIME WITH THIS GARBAGE?!
I AM NOT A STUDENT!
I AM NOT A CONSTRUCT!
I HAVEN'T GOT THE SPARK,
BUT I AM NOT A FOOL AND I DO NOT HAVE TO TAKE THIS FROM AN ARROGANT HAS-BEEN LIKE YOU!
DOES THE BARON KNOW THAT HIS TRUSTED OLD MENTOR HAS DEFIED HIS STRICTEST ORDERS WITH HIS LATEST EXPERIMENTS?
EXPERIMENTS CONDUCTED IN THE MIDDLE OF A CIVILIAN TOWN?!
PERHAPS HE WOULD LIKE TO SEE THE IMPORTANT WORK THAT HAS BEEN KEEPING OUR DR. BEETLE SO BUSY!
MERLOT! SILAS!
FOR THE LOVE OF GOD!
NO!
K-CHUNK! HUMMMMMMMMMMMMMMM

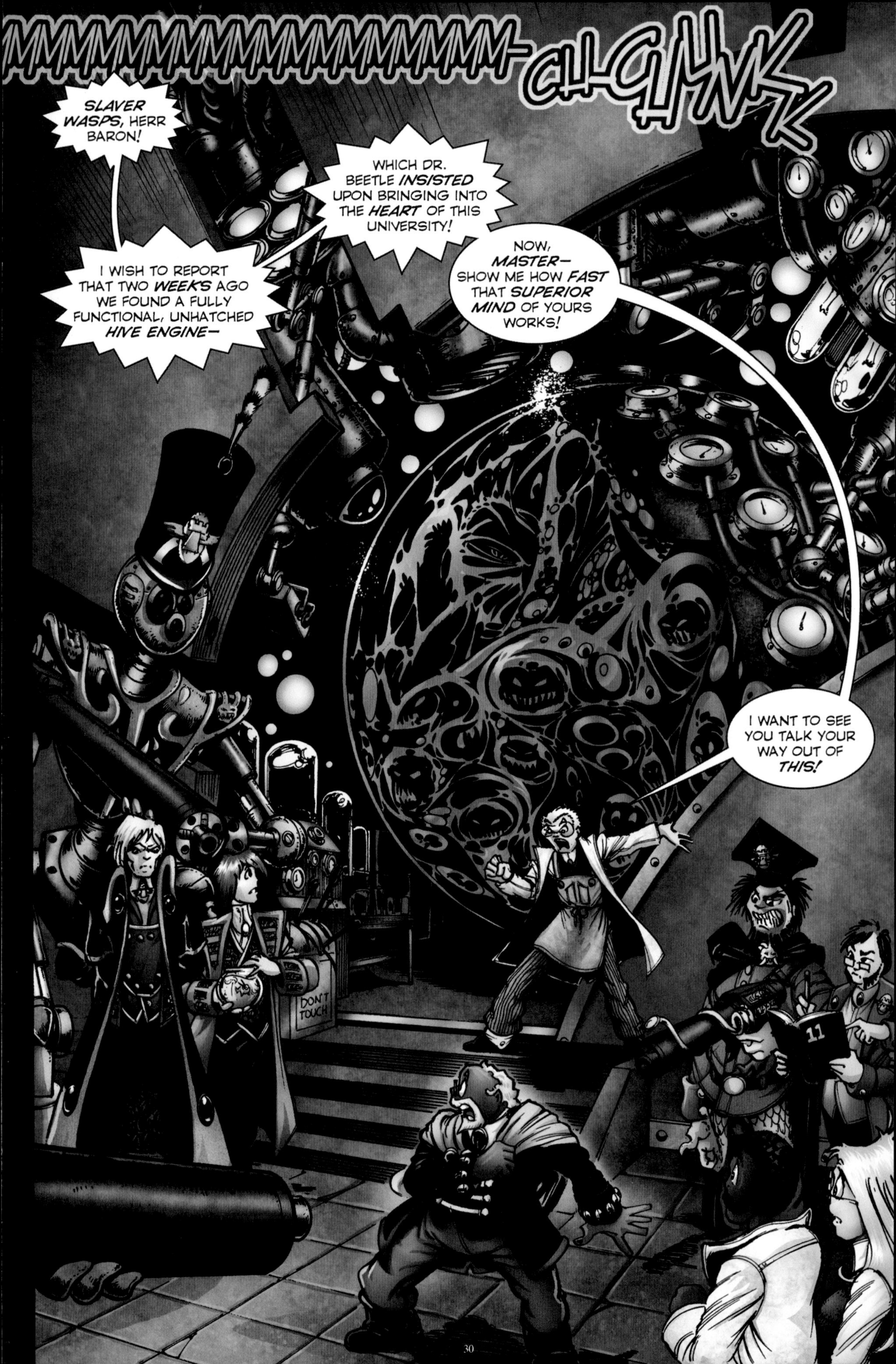
MMMMMMMMMMMMMMMMMMMM—CHUGUNK
SLAVER WASPS, HERR BARON!
I WISH TO REPORT THAT TWO WEEKS AGO WE FOUND A FULLY FUNCTIONAL, UNHATCHED HIVE ENGINE—
WHICH DR. BEETLE INSISTED UPON BRINGING INTO THE HEART OF THIS UNIVERSITY!
NOW, MASTER— SHOW ME HOW FAST THAT SUPERIOR MIND OF YOURS WORKS!
I WANT TO SEE YOU TALK YOUR WAY OUT OF THIS!
DON'T TOUCH

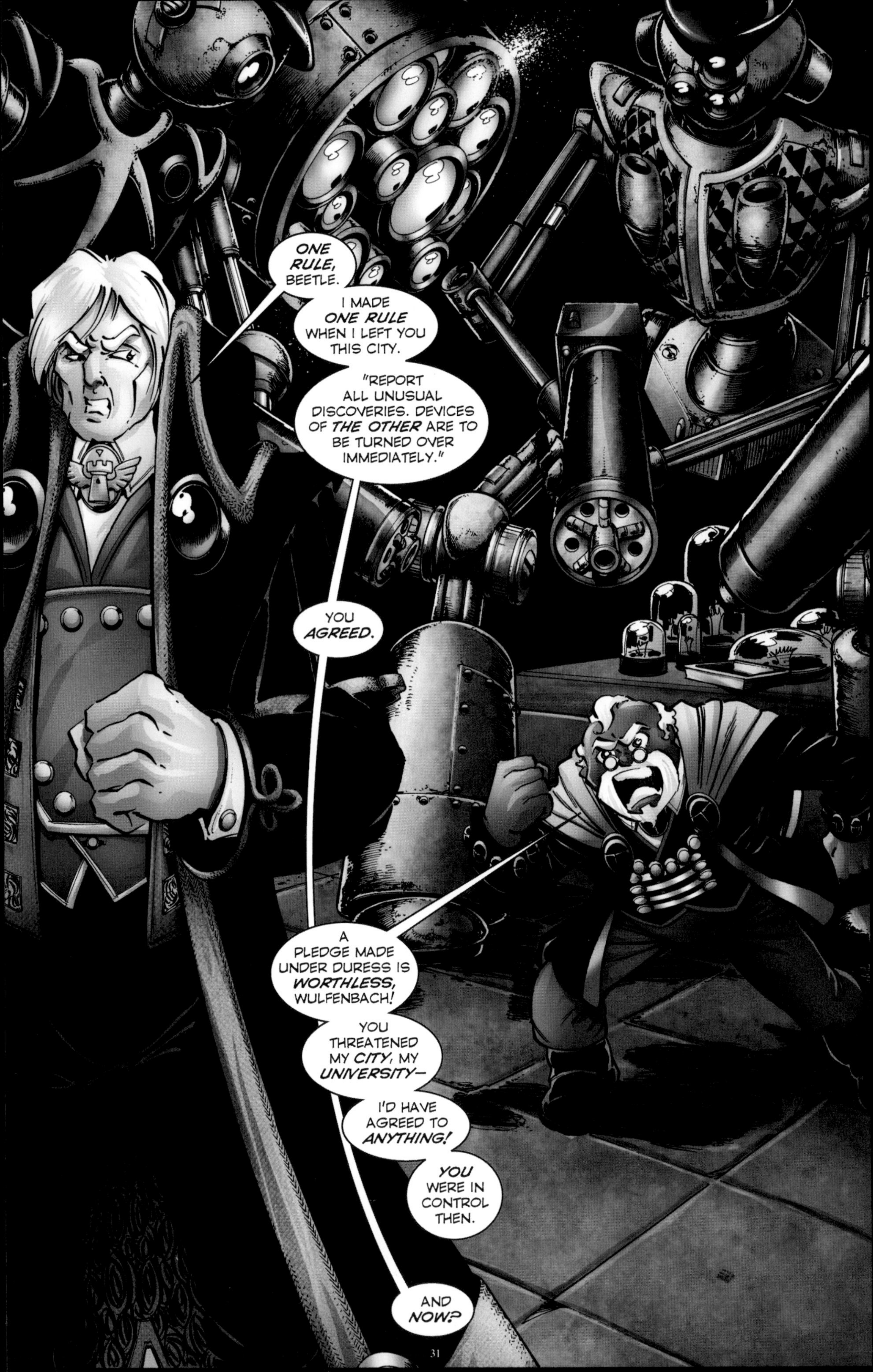
ONE RULE, BEETLE.
I MADE ONE RULE WHEN I LEFT YOU THIS CITY.
"REPORT ALL UNUSUAL DISCOVERIES. DEVICES OF THE OTHER ARE TO BE TURNED OVER IMMEDIATELY."
YOU AGREED.
A PLEDGE MADE UNDER DURESS IS WORTHLESS, WULFENBACH!
YOU THREATENED MY CITY, MY UNIVERSITY—
I'D HAVE AGREED TO ANYTHING!
YOU WERE IN CONTROL THEN.
AND NOW?

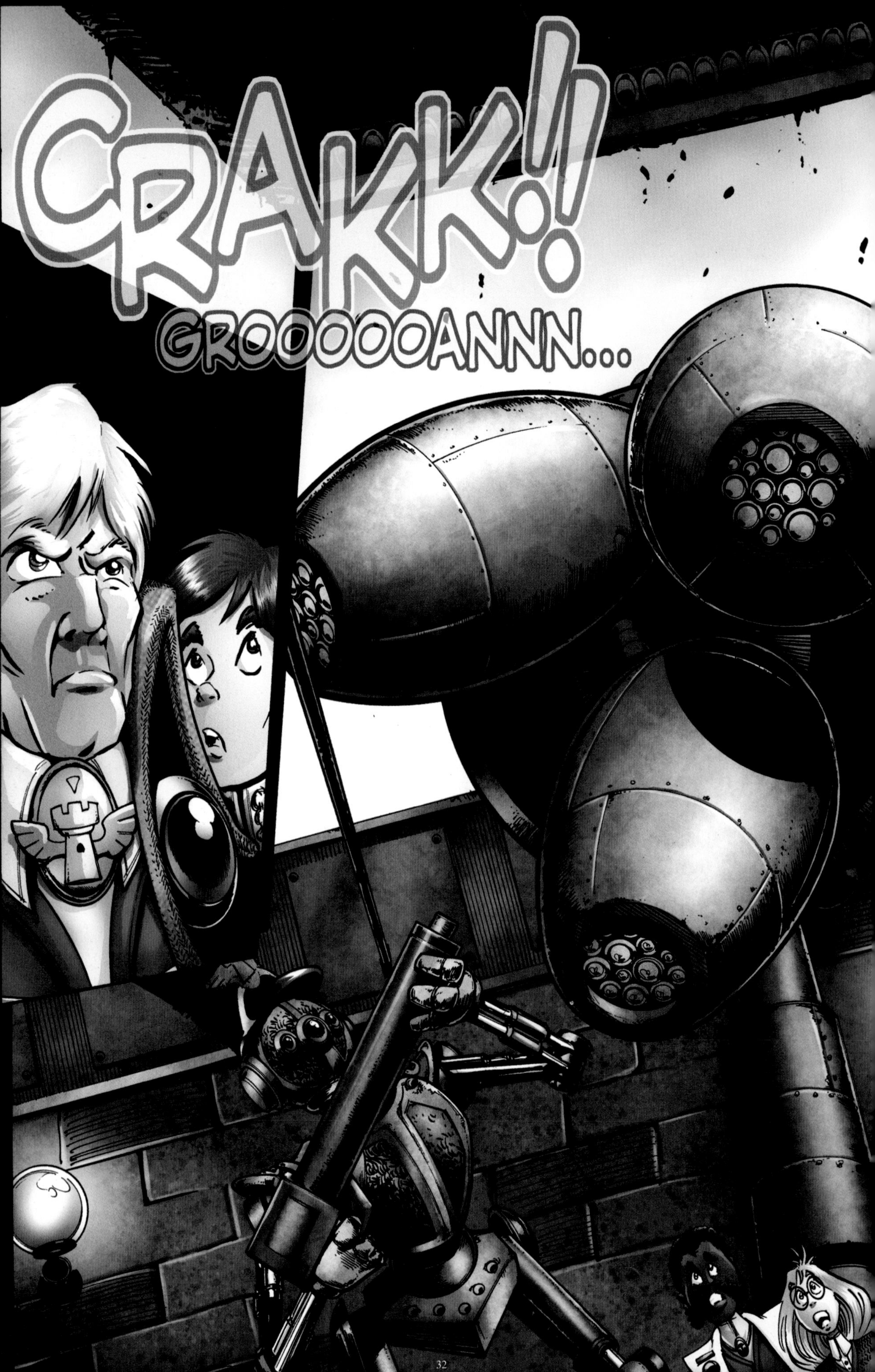
CRAKK!!
GROOOOOOANNN...

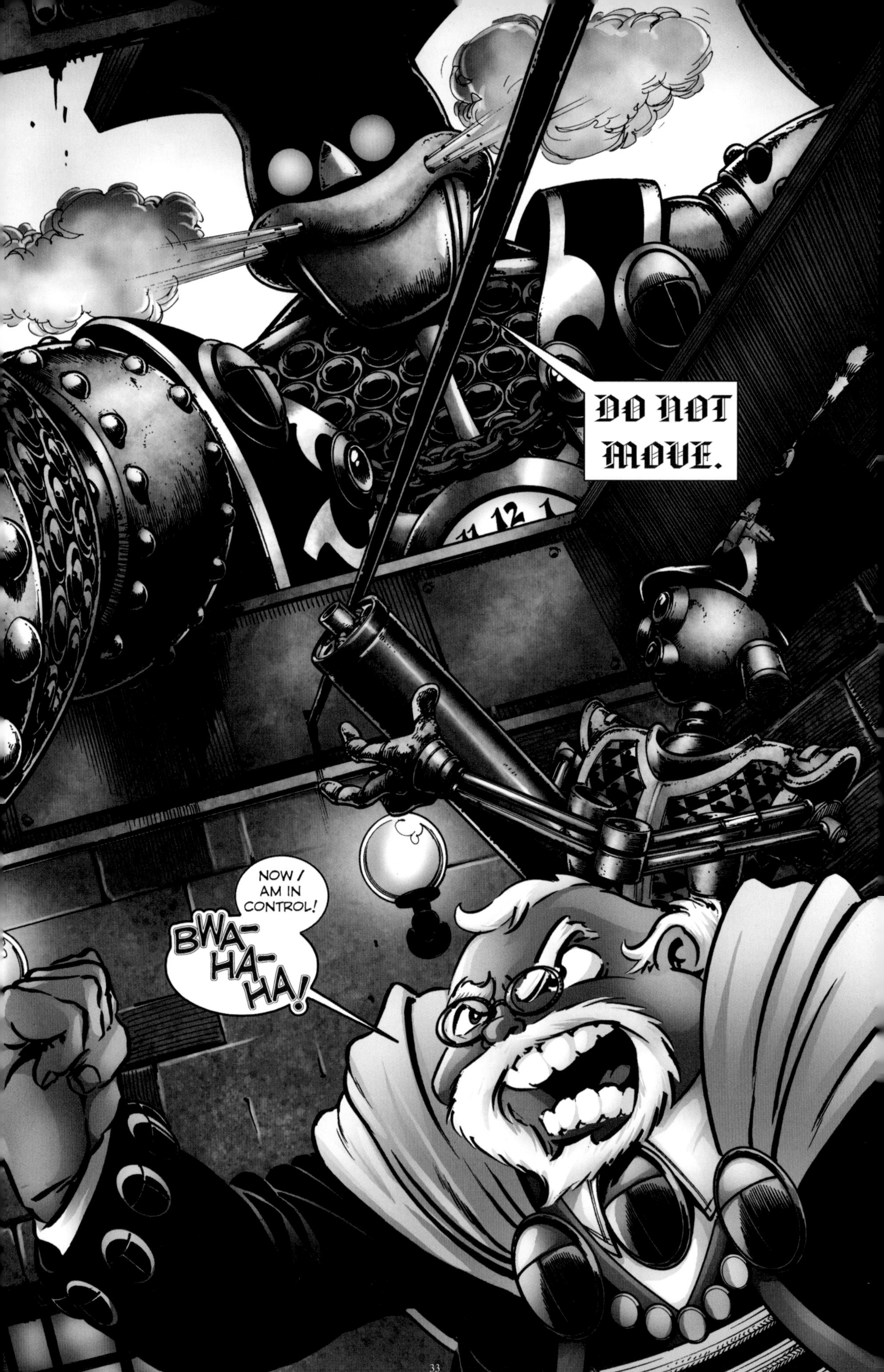
DO NOT MOVE.
NOW I AM IN CONTROL!
BWA-HA-HA!

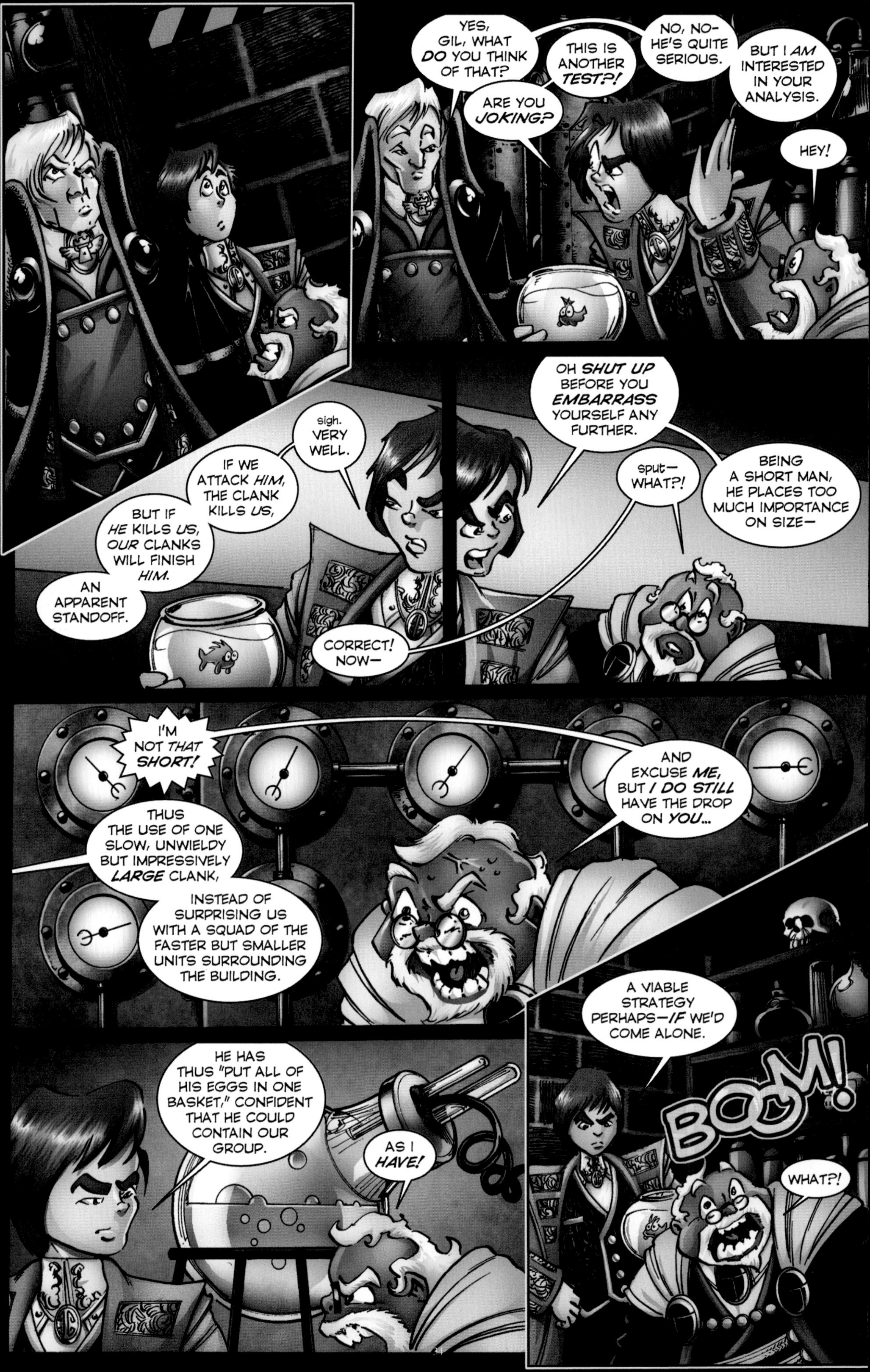
YES, GIL, WHAT DO YOU THINK OF THAT?
THIS IS ANOTHER TEST?!
ARE YOU JOKING?
NO, NO— HE'S QUITE SERIOUS.
BUT I AM INTERESTED IN YOUR ANALYSIS.
HEY!
sigh. VERY WELL.
IF WE ATTACK HIM, THE CLANK KILLS US,
BUT IF HE KILLS US, OUR CLANKS WILL FINISH HIM.
AN APPARENT STANDOFF.
CORRECT! NOW—
OH SHUT UP BEFORE YOU EMBARRASS YOURSELF ANY FURTHER.
sput— WHAT?!
BEING A SHORT MAN, HE PLACES TOO MUCH IMPORTANCE ON SIZE—
I'M NOT THAT SHORT!
THUS THE USE OF ONE SLOW, UNWIELDY BUT IMPRESSIVELY LARGE CLANK,
INSTEAD OF SURPRISING US WITH A SQUAD OF THE FASTER BUT SMALLER UNITS SURROUNDING THE BUILDING.
AND EXCUSE ME, BUT I DO STILL HAVE THE DROP ON YOU...
HE HAS THUS "PUT ALL OF HIS EGGS IN ONE BASKET," CONFIDENT THAT HE COULD CONTAIN OUR GROUP.
AS I HAVE!
A VIABLE STRATEGY PERHAPS—IF WE'D COME ALONE.
BOOM!
WHAT?!

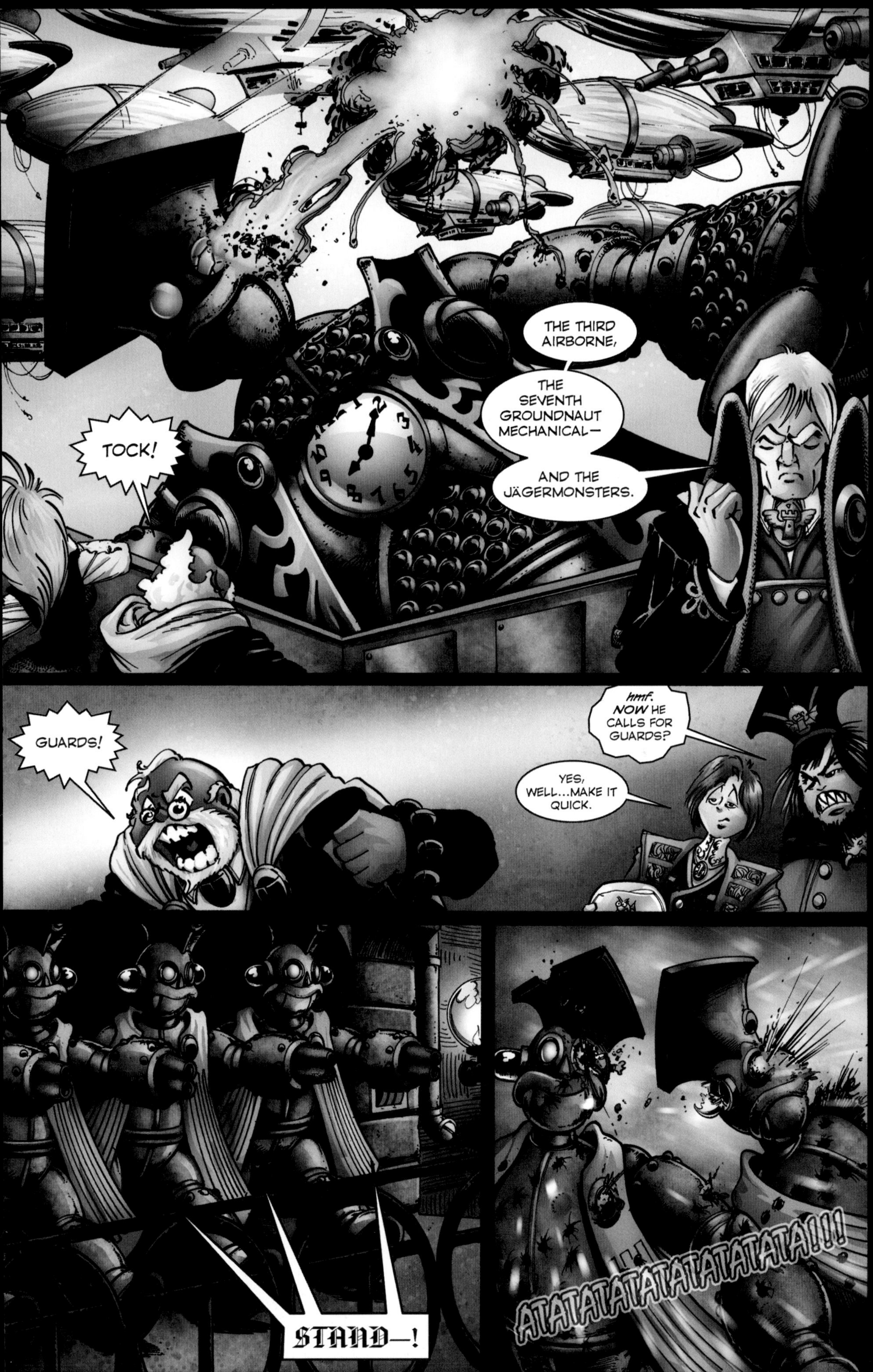
THE THIRD AIRBORNE,
THE SEVENTH GROUNDNAUT MECHANICAL—
AND THE JÄGERMONSTERS.
TOCK!
GUARDS!
hmf. NOW HE CALLS FOR GUARDS?
YES, WELL...MAKE IT QUICK.
STAND—!
ATATATATATATATATATATA!!!

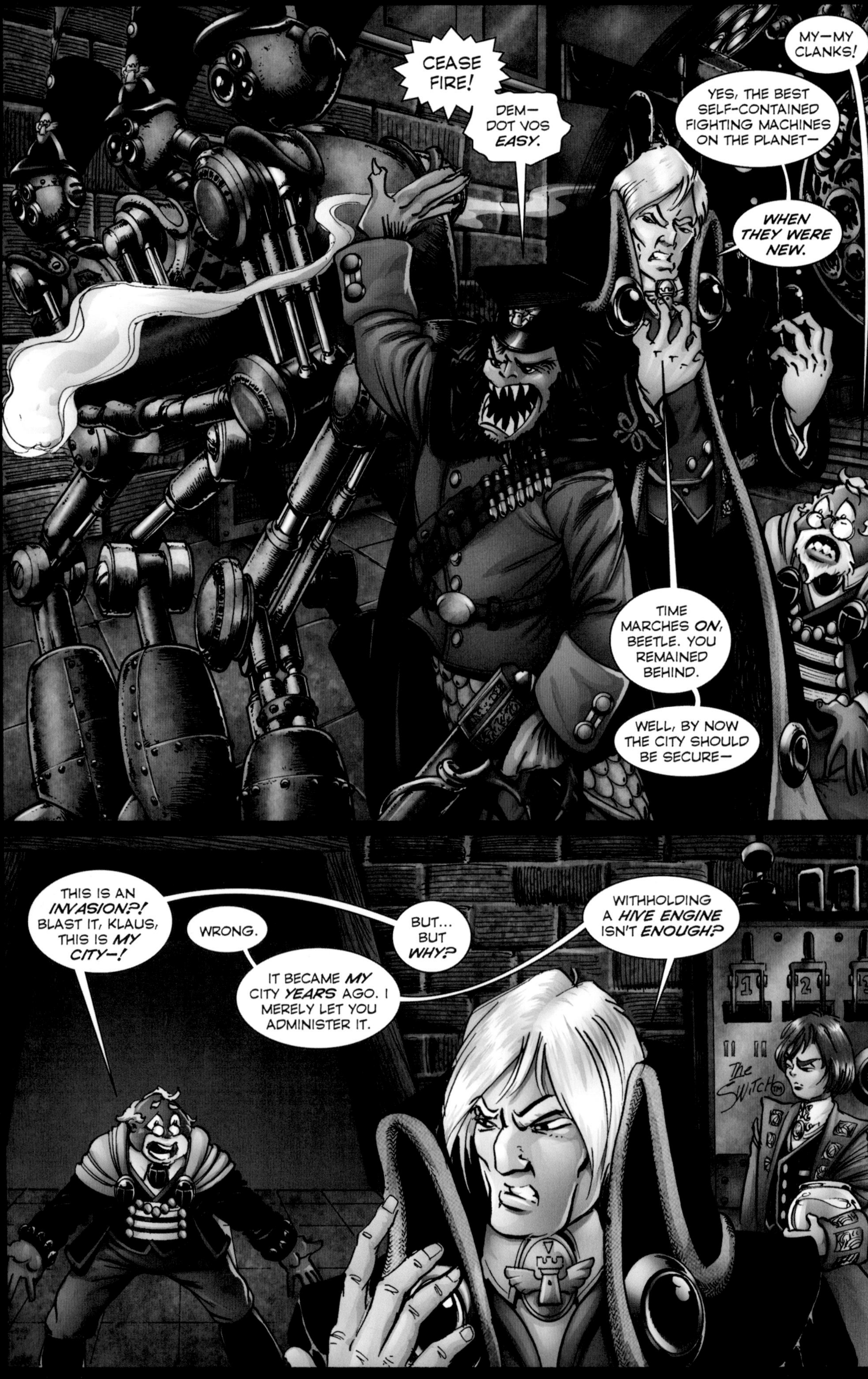
CEASE FIRE!
DEM—DOT VOS *EASY*.
MY—MY CLANKS!
YES, THE BEST SELF-CONTAINED FIGHTING MACHINES ON THE PLANET—
WHEN THEY WERE NEW.
TIME MARCHES *ON*, BEETLE. YOU REMAINED BEHIND.
WELL, BY NOW THE CITY SHOULD BE SECURE—
THIS IS AN *INVASION?!* BLAST IT, KLAUS, THIS IS *MY CITY—!*
WRONG.
IT BECAME *MY* CITY *YEARS* AGO. I MERELY LET YOU ADMINISTER IT.
BUT... BUT *WHY?*
WITHHOLDING A *HIVE ENGINE* ISN'T *ENOUGH?*
The SWITCH™
1
2

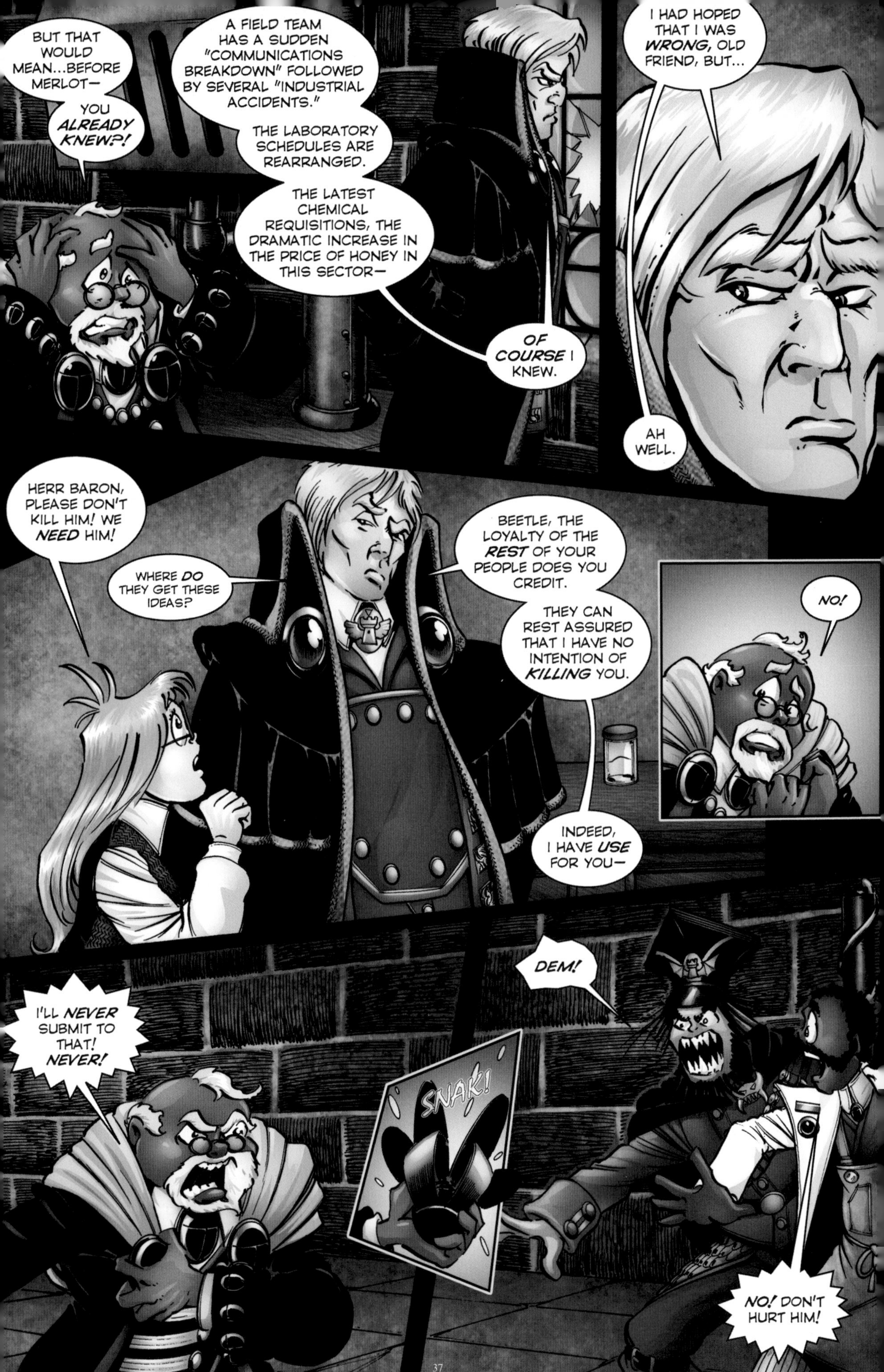
BUT THAT WOULD MEAN...BEFORE MERLOT—
YOU ALREADY KNEW?!
A FIELD TEAM HAS A SUDDEN "COMMUNICATIONS BREAKDOWN" FOLLOWED BY SEVERAL "INDUSTRIAL ACCIDENTS."
THE LABORATORY SCHEDULES ARE REARRANGED.
THE LATEST CHEMICAL REQUISITIONS, THE DRAMATIC INCREASE IN THE PRICE OF HONEY IN THIS SECTOR—
OF COURSE I KNEW.
I HAD HOPED THAT I WAS WRONG, OLD FRIEND, BUT...
AH WELL.
HERR BARON, PLEASE DON'T KILL HIM! WE NEED HIM!
WHERE DO THEY GET THESE IDEAS?
BEETLE, THE LOYALTY OF THE REST OF YOUR PEOPLE DOES YOU CREDIT.
THEY CAN REST ASSURED THAT I HAVE NO INTENTION OF KILLING YOU.
INDEED, I HAVE USE FOR YOU—
NO!
I'LL NEVER SUBMIT TO THAT! NEVER!
SNAK!
DEM!
NO! DON'T HURT HIM!

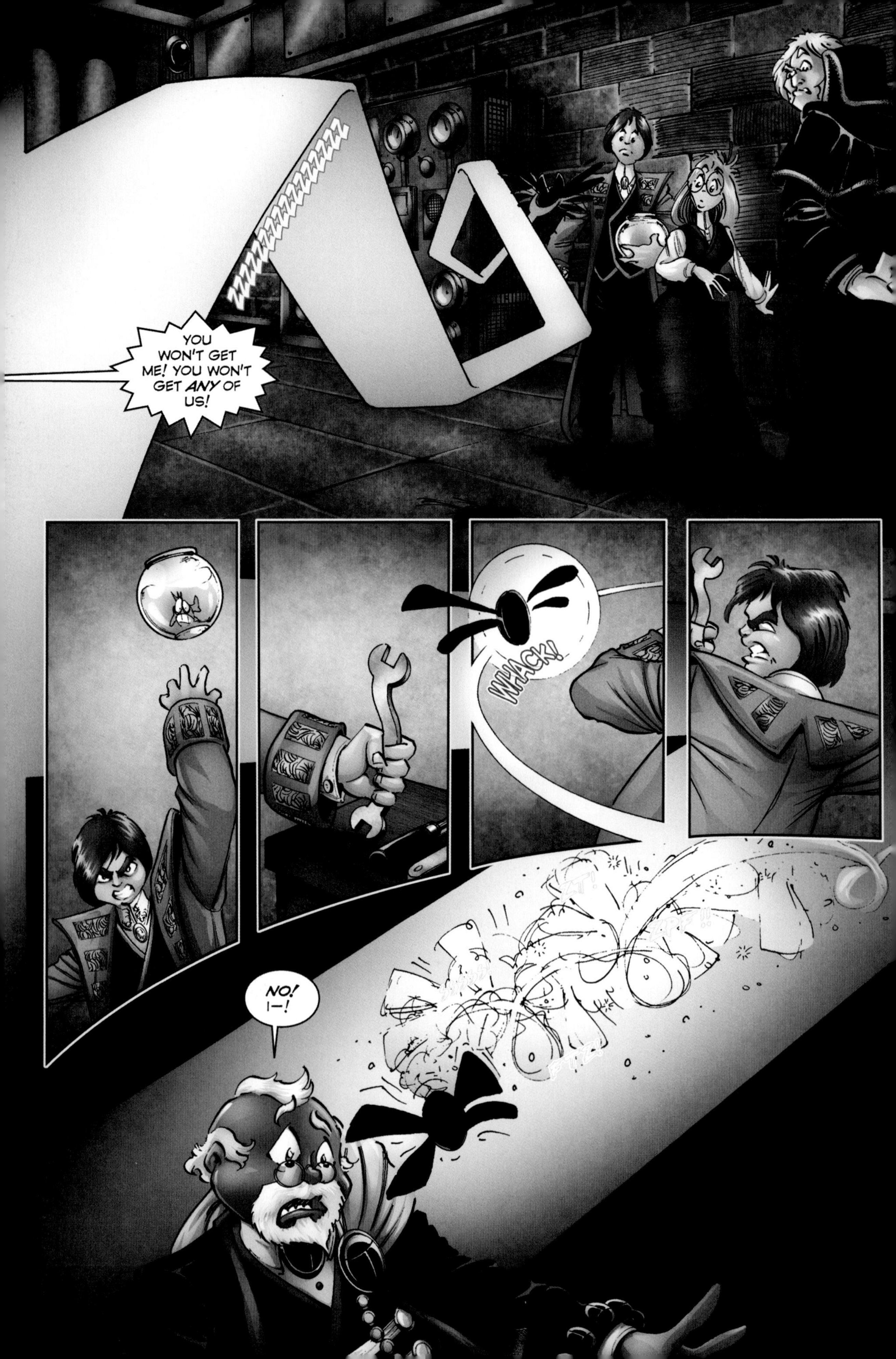
ZZZZZZZZZZZZZZZZZZZ
YOU WON'T GET ME! YOU WON'T GET ANY OF US!
WHACK!
ZT!
ZAP!!
FTZ!
NO! I--!

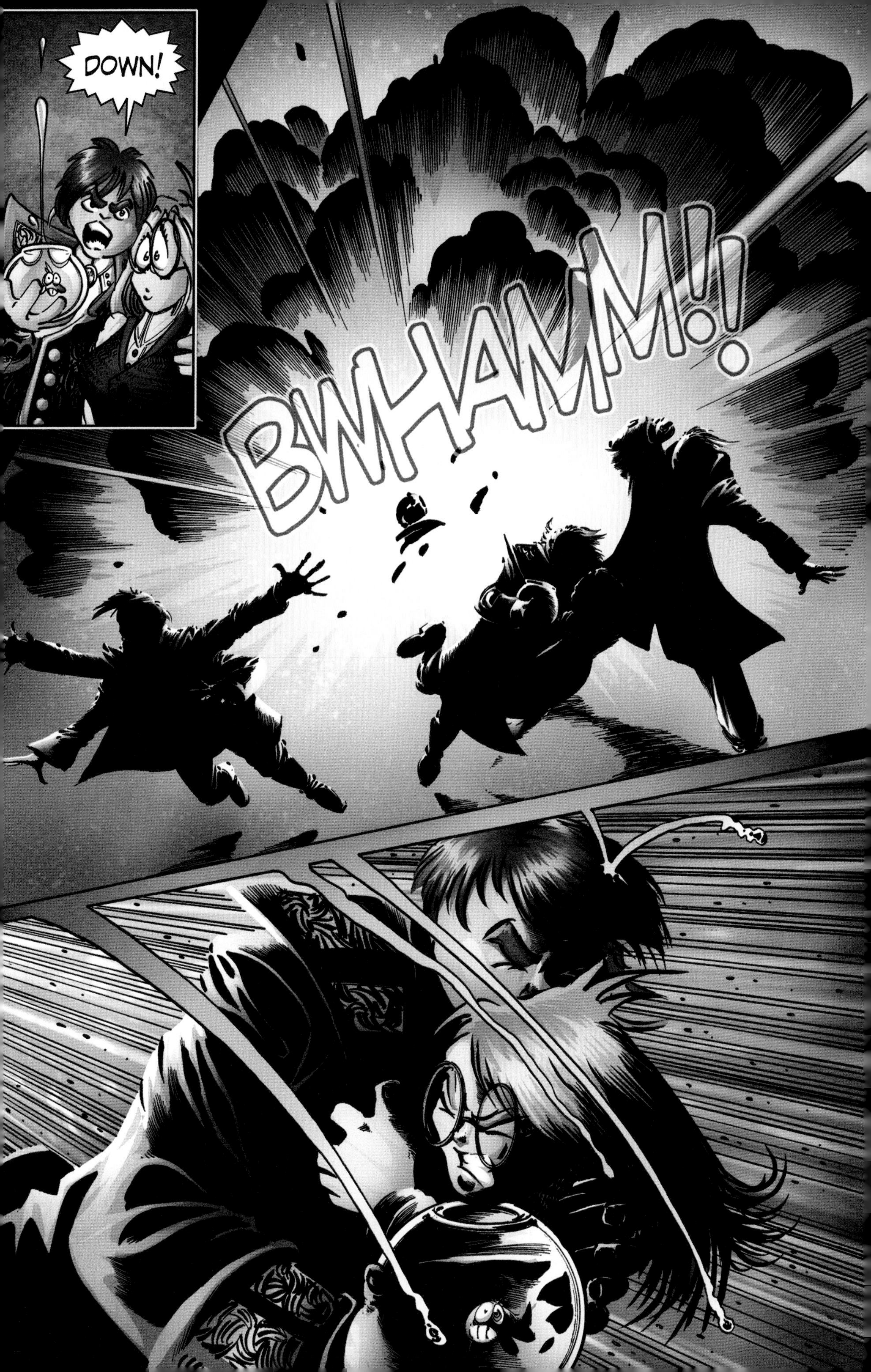
DOWN!
BWHAMM!!

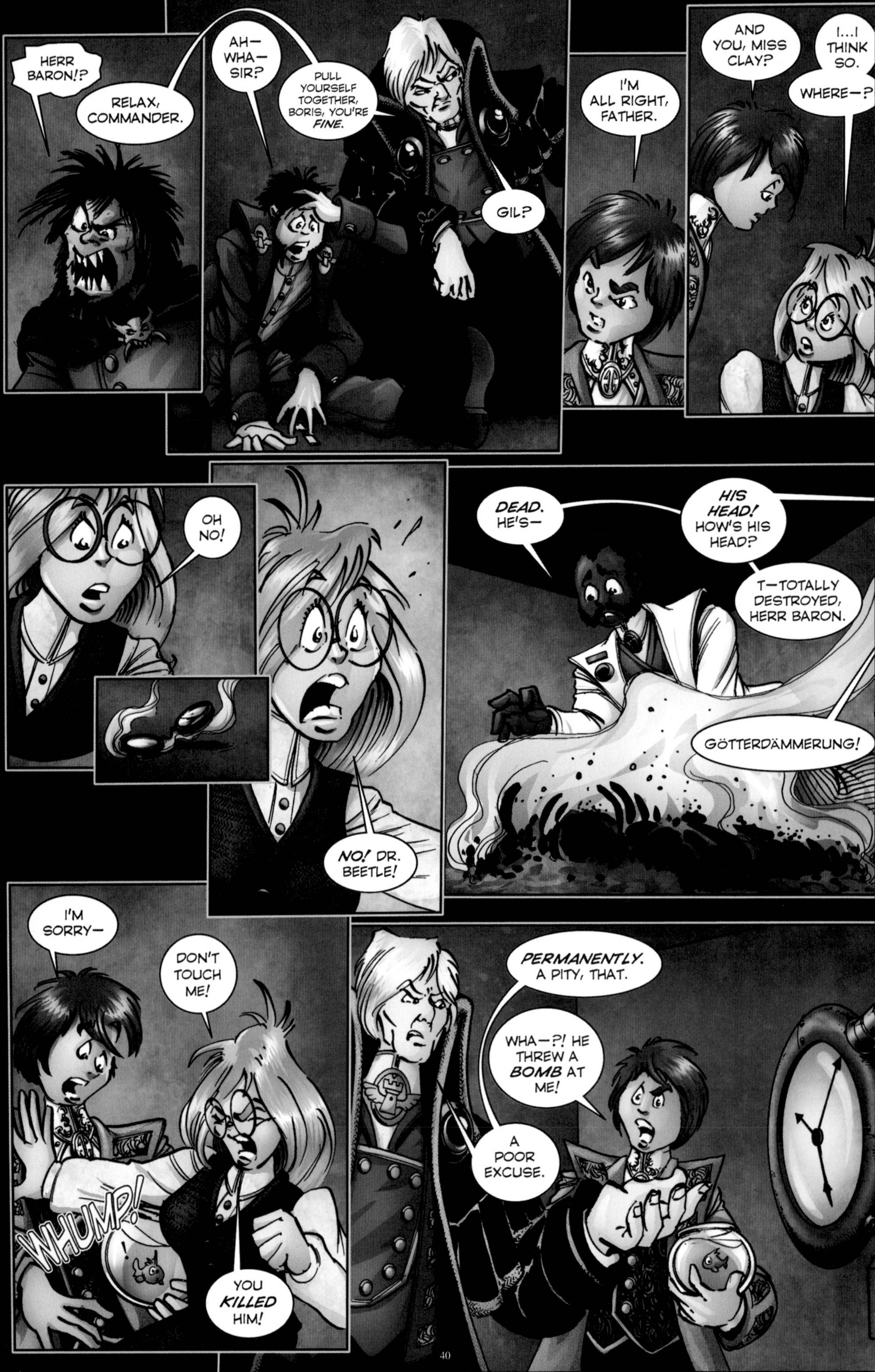

HERR BARON!?
RELAX, COMMANDER.
AH—WHA—SIR?
PULL YOURSELF TOGETHER, BORIS, YOU'RE FINE.
GIL?
I'M ALL RIGHT, FATHER.
AND YOU, MISS CLAY?
I...I THINK SO.
WHERE—?
OH NO!
NO! DR. BEETLE!
DEAD. HE'S—
HIS HEAD! HOW'S HIS HEAD?
T—TOTALLY DESTROYED, HERR BARON.
GÖTTERDÄMMERUNG!
I'M SORRY—
DON'T TOUCH ME!
WHUMP!
YOU KILLED HIM!
PERMANENTLY. A PITY, THAT.
WHA—?! HE THREW A BOMB AT ME!
A POOR EXCUSE.

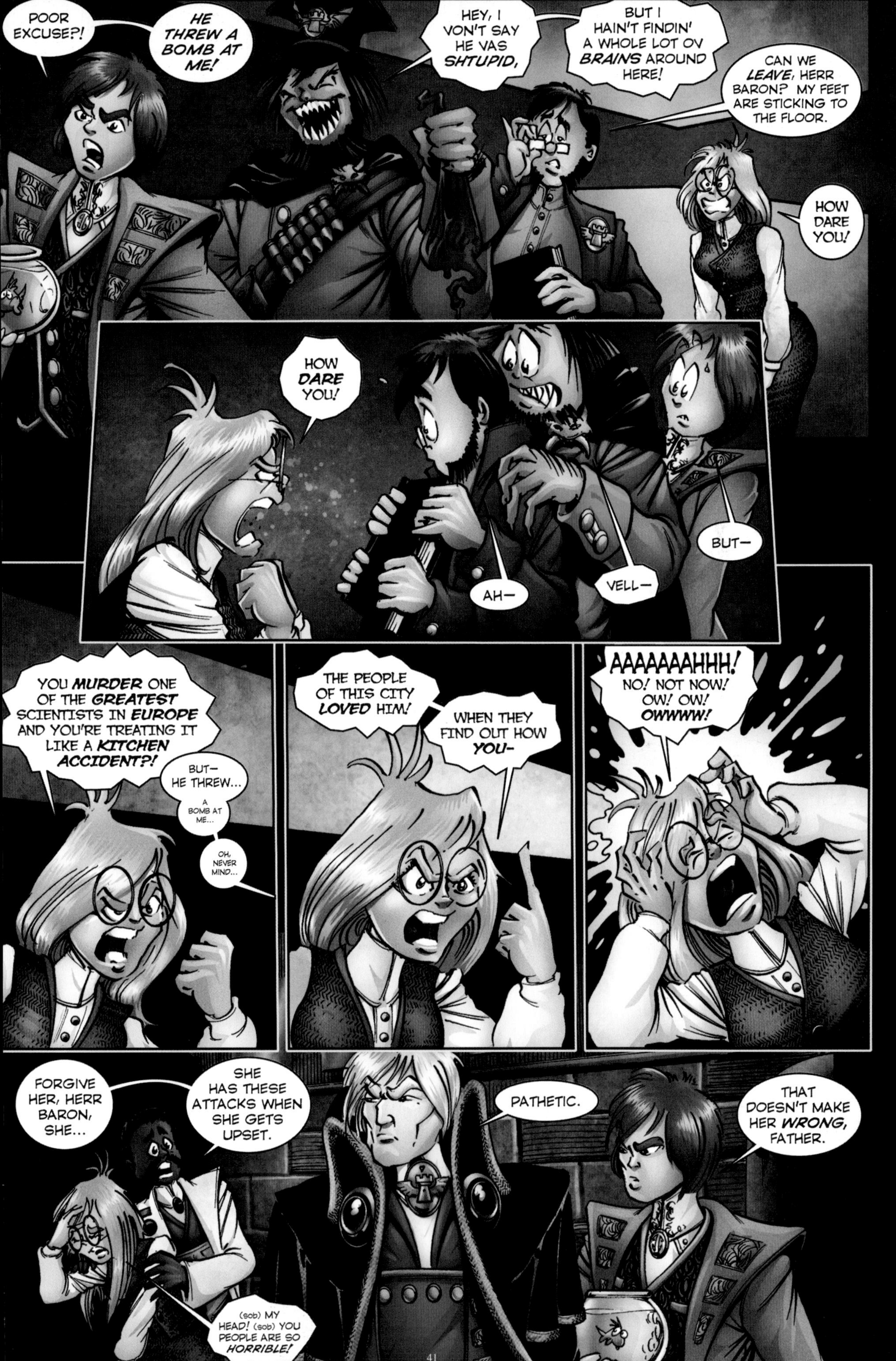

POOR EXCUSE?!
HE THREW A BOMB AT ME!
HEY, I VON'T SAY HE VAS SHTUPID,
BUT I HAIN'T FINDIN' A WHOLE LOT OV BRAINS AROUND HERE!
CAN WE LEAVE, HERR BARON? MY FEET ARE STICKING TO THE FLOOR.
HOW DARE YOU!
HOW DARE YOU!
AH—
VELL—
BUT—
YOU MURDER ONE OF THE GREATEST SCIENTISTS IN EUROPE AND YOU'RE TREATING IT LIKE A KITCHEN ACCIDENT?!
BUT— HE THREW...
A BOMB AT ME...
OH, NEVER MIND...
THE PEOPLE OF THIS CITY LOVED HIM!
WHEN THEY FIND OUT HOW YOU-
AAAAAAAHHH! NO! NOT NOW! OW! OW! OWWWW!
FORGIVE HER, HERR BARON, SHE...
SHE HAS THESE ATTACKS WHEN SHE GETS UPSET.
PATHETIC.
THAT DOESN'T MAKE HER WRONG, FATHER.
(sob) MY HEAD! (sob) YOU PEOPLE ARE SO HORRIBLE!

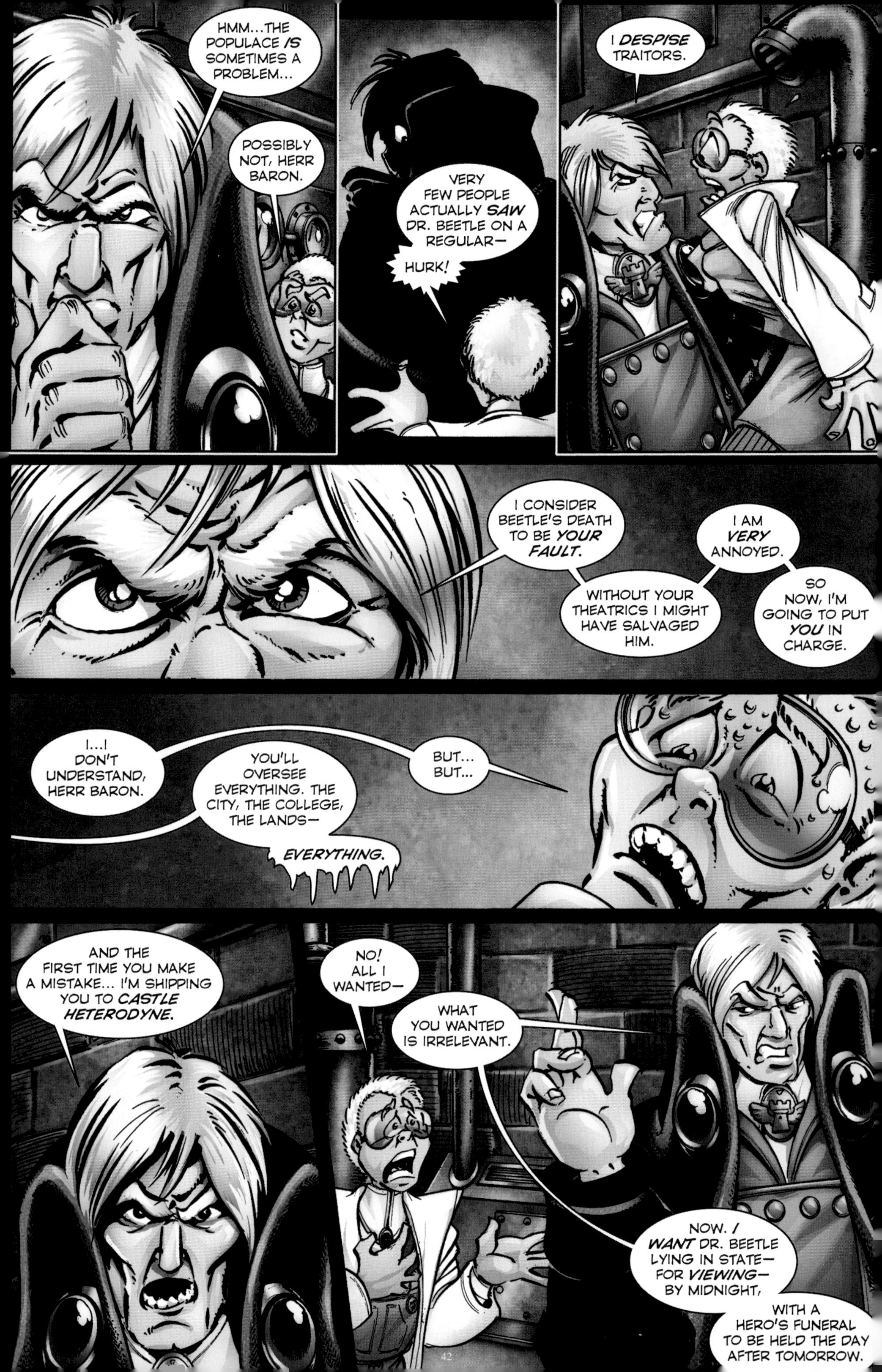
HMM...THE POPULACE *IS* SOMETIMES A PROBLEM...
POSSIBLY NOT, HERR BARON.
VERY FEW PEOPLE ACTUALLY *SAW* DR. BEETLE ON A REGULAR—
HURK!
I *DESPISE* TRAITORS.
I CONSIDER BEETLE'S DEATH TO BE *YOUR FAULT.*
WITHOUT YOUR THEATRICS I MIGHT HAVE SALVAGED HIM.
I AM *VERY* ANNOYED.
SO NOW, I'M GOING TO PUT *YOU* IN CHARGE.
BUT... BUT...
I...I DON'T UNDERSTAND, HERR BARON.
YOU'LL OVERSEE EVERYTHING. THE CITY, THE COLLEGE, THE LANDS—
EVERYTHING.
AND THE FIRST TIME YOU MAKE A MISTAKE... I'M SHIPPING YOU TO *CASTLE HETERODYNE.*
NO! ALL I WANTED—
WHAT YOU WANTED IS IRRELEVANT.
NOW. *I WANT* DR. BEETLE LYING IN STATE— FOR *VIEWING*— BY MIDNIGHT,
WITH A HERO'S FUNERAL TO BE HELD THE DAY AFTER TOMORROW.

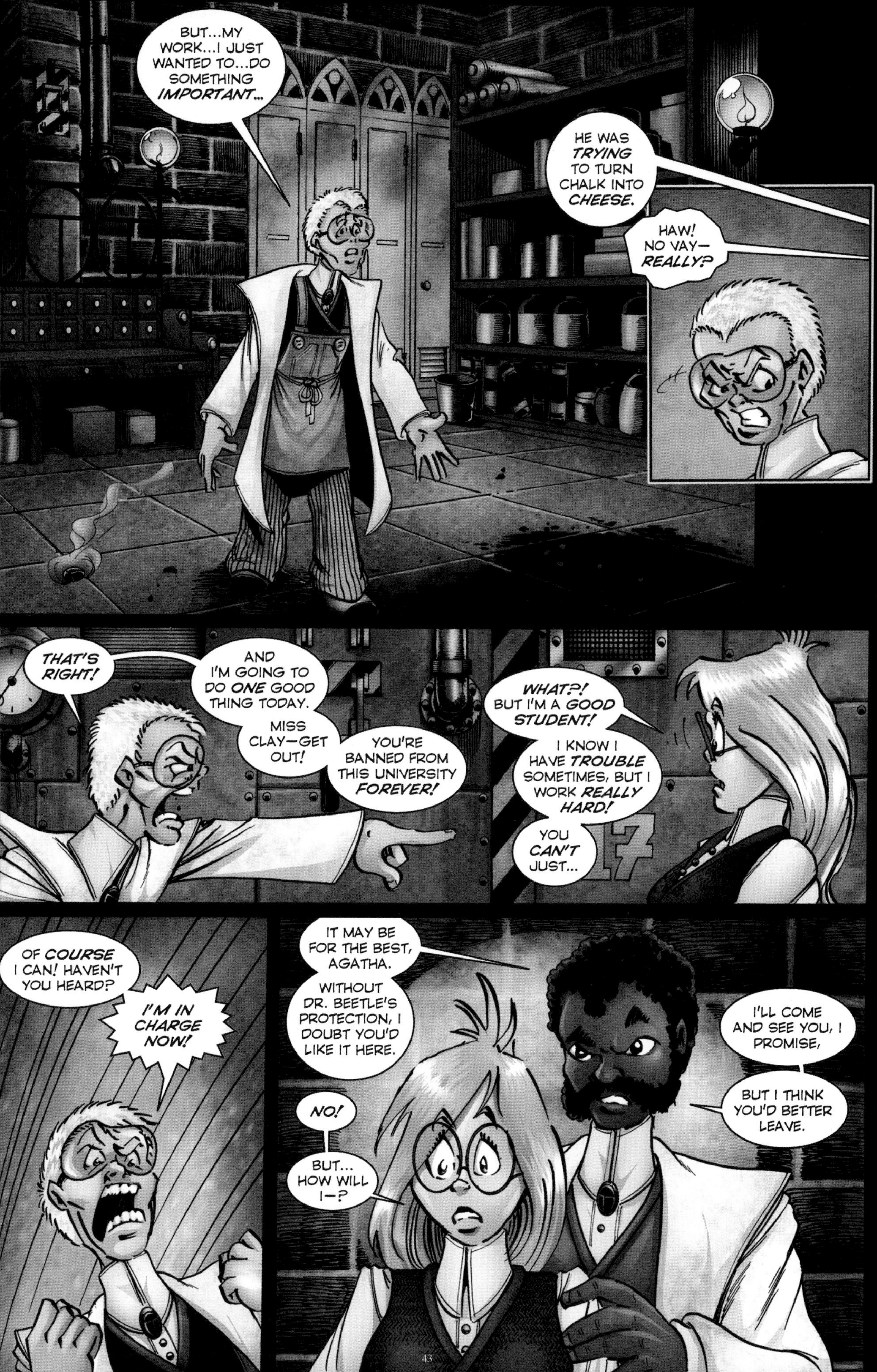
BUT...MY WORK...I JUST WANTED TO...DO SOMETHING IMPORTANT...
HE WAS TRYING TO TURN CHALK INTO CHEESE.
HAW! NO VAY— REALLY?
THAT'S RIGHT!
AND I'M GOING TO DO ONE GOOD THING TODAY.
MISS CLAY—GET OUT!
YOU'RE BANNED FROM THIS UNIVERSITY FOREVER!
WHAT?! BUT I'M A GOOD STUDENT!
I KNOW I HAVE TROUBLE SOMETIMES, BUT I WORK REALLY HARD!
YOU CAN'T JUST...
17
OF COURSE I CAN! HAVEN'T YOU HEARD?
I'M IN CHARGE NOW!
IT MAY BE FOR THE BEST, AGATHA.
WITHOUT DR. BEETLE'S PROTECTION, I DOUBT YOU'D LIKE IT HERE.
NO!
BUT... HOW WILL I—?
I'LL COME AND SEE YOU, I PROMISE,
BUT I THINK YOU'D BETTER LEAVE.

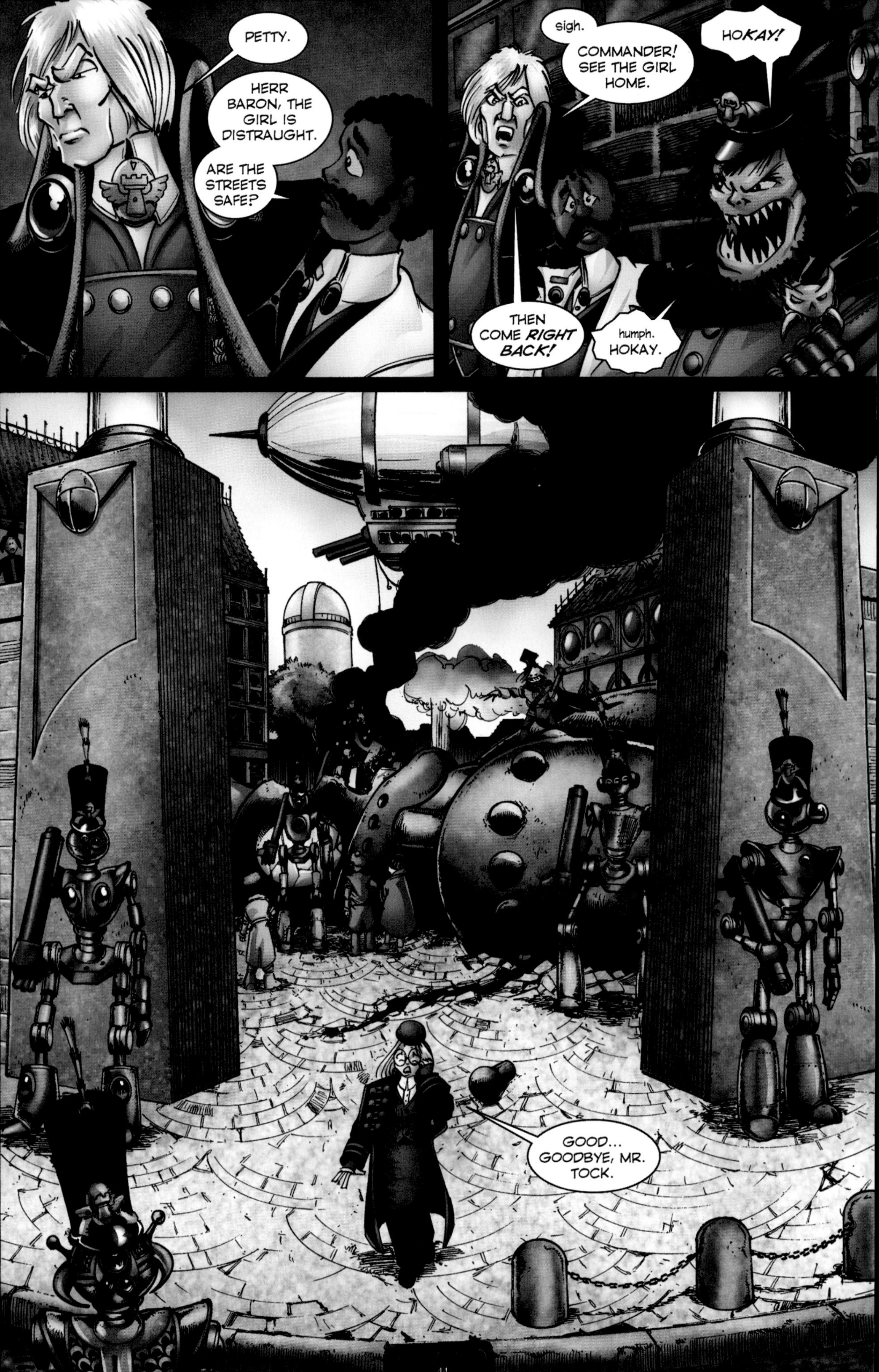
PETTY.
HERR BARON, THE GIRL IS DISTRAUGHT.
ARE THE STREETS SAFE?
sigh.
COMMANDER! SEE THE GIRL HOME.
HOKAY!
THEN COME RIGHT BACK!
humph. HOKAY.
GOOD... GOODBYE, MR. TOCK.

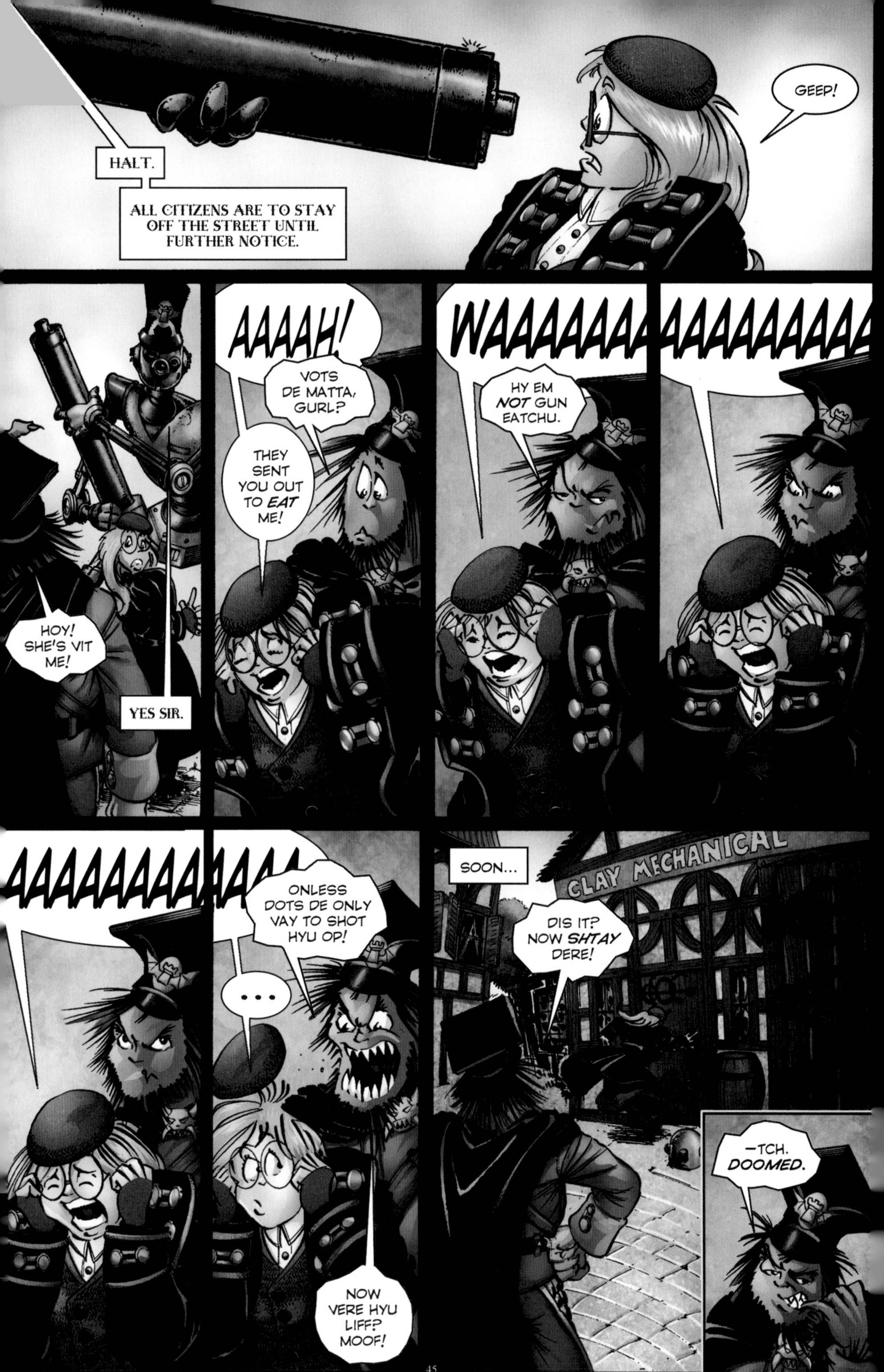
HALT.
ALL CITIZENS ARE TO STAY OFF THE STREET UNTIL FURTHER NOTICE.
GEEP!
HOY! SHE'S VIT ME!
YES SIR.
AAAAH!
VOTS DE MATTA, GURL?
THEY SENT YOU OUT TO EAT ME!
WAAAAAAAAAAAAAAAAAA
HY EM NOT GUN EATCHU.
AAAAAAAAAAAAA
ONLESS DOTS DE ONLY VAY TO SHOT HYU OP!
...
NOW VERE HYU LIFF? MOOF!
SOON...
CLAY MECHANICAL
DIS IT? NOW SHTAY DERE!
—TCH. DOOMED.

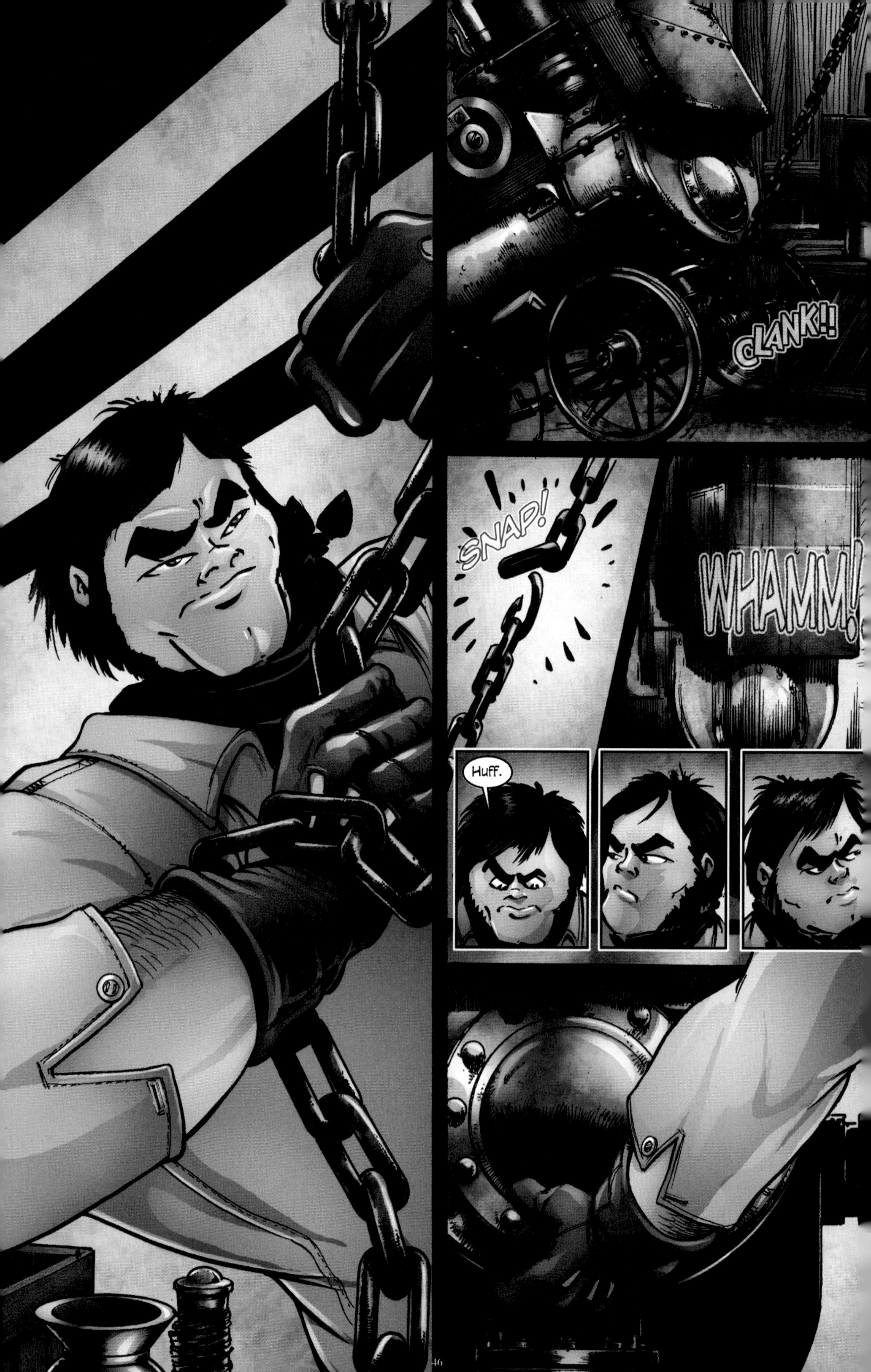
CLANK!!
SNAP!
WHAMM!
Huff.

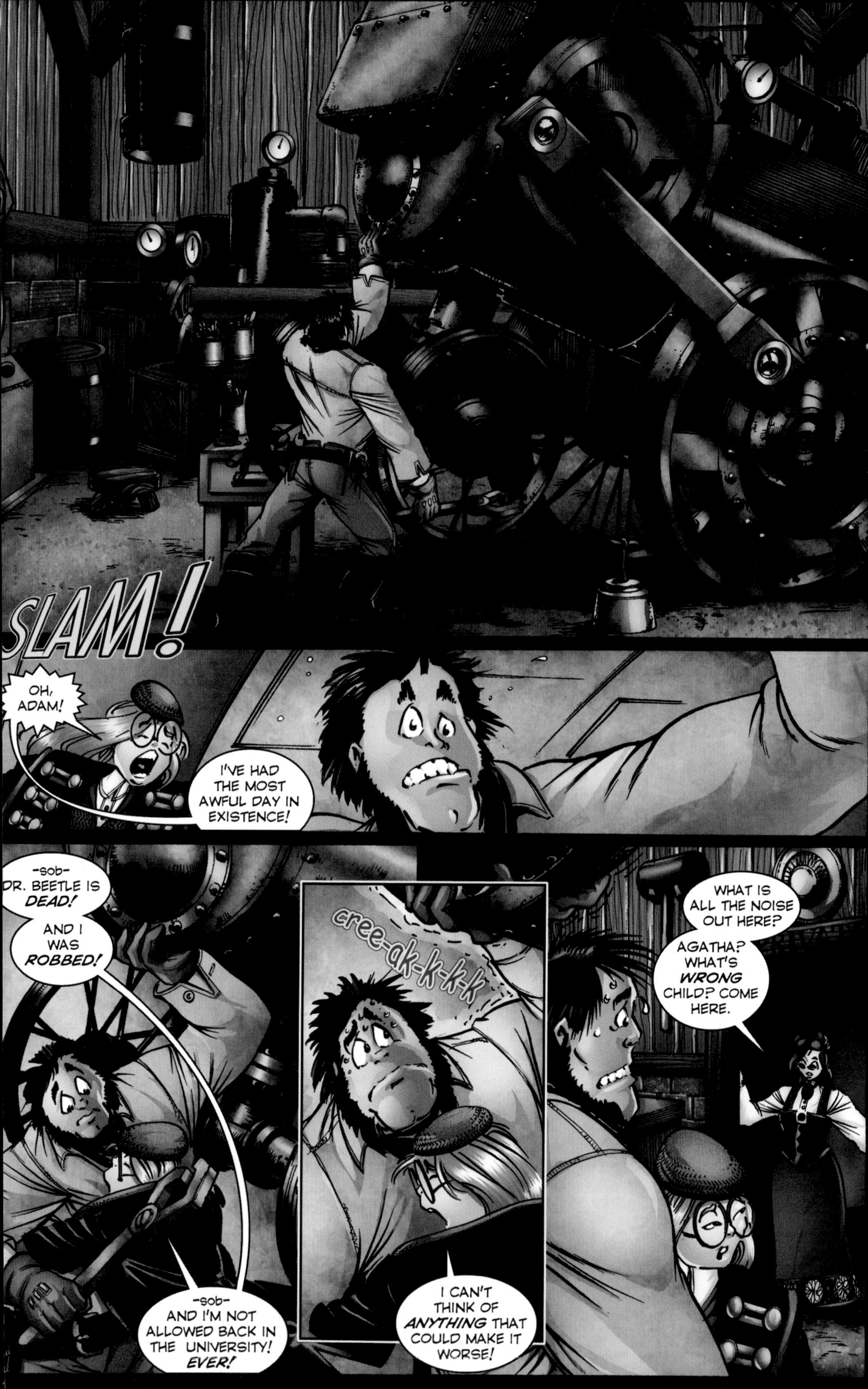
SLAM!
OH, ADAM!
I'VE HAD THE MOST AWFUL DAY IN EXISTENCE!
-sob- DR. BEETLE IS *DEAD!*
AND I WAS *ROBBED!*
-sob- AND I'M NOT ALLOWED BACK IN THE UNIVERSITY! *EVER!*
cree-ak-k-k-k
I CAN'T THINK OF *ANYTHING* THAT COULD MAKE IT WORSE!
WHAT IS ALL THE NOISE OUT HERE?
AGATHA? WHAT'S *WRONG* CHILD? COME HERE.

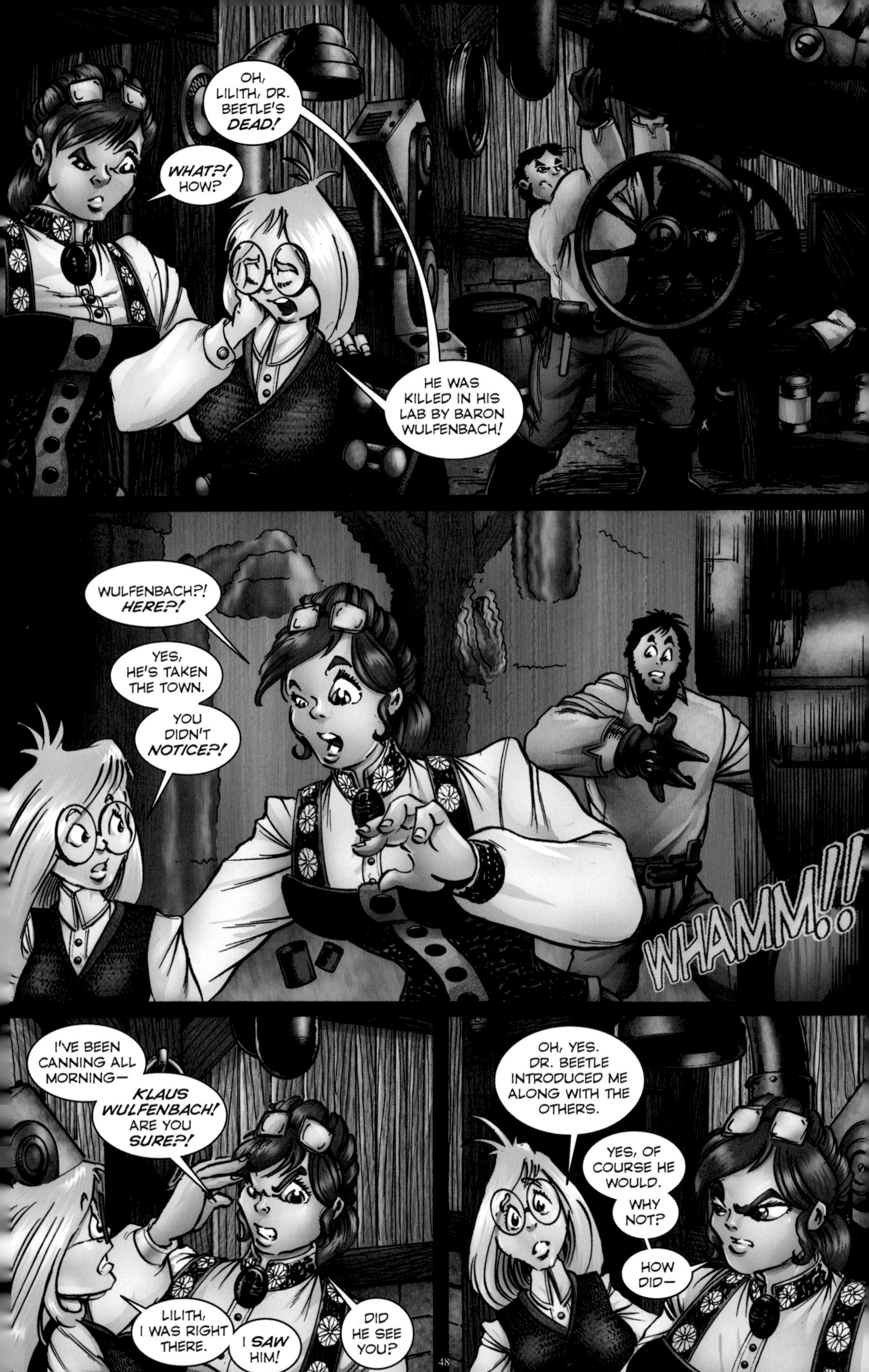
OH, LILITH, DR. BEETLE'S *DEAD!*
WHAT?! HOW?
HE WAS KILLED IN HIS LAB BY BARON WULFENBACH!
WULFENBACH?! *HERE?!*
YES, HE'S TAKEN THE TOWN.
YOU DIDN'T *NOTICE?!*
WHAMM!!
I'VE BEEN CANNING ALL MORNING—
KLAUS WULFENBACH! ARE YOU *SURE?!*
LILITH, I WAS RIGHT THERE.
I *SAW* HIM!
DID HE SEE YOU?
OH, YES. DR. BEETLE INTRODUCED ME ALONG WITH THE OTHERS.
YES, OF COURSE HE WOULD.
WHY NOT?
HOW DID—

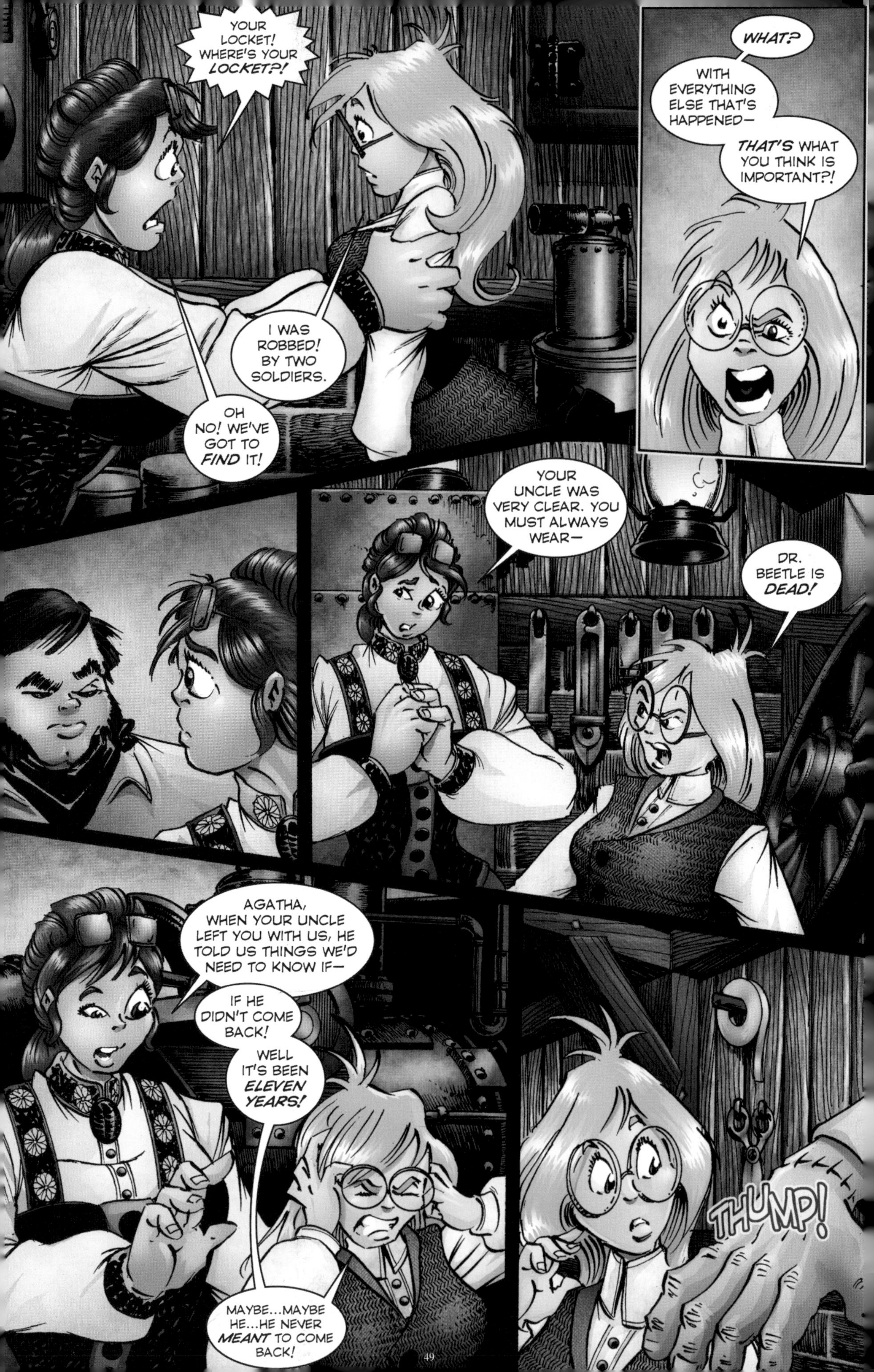

YOUR LOCKET! WHERE'S YOUR *LOCKET?!*
I WAS ROBBED*!* BY TWO SOLDIERS.
OH NO*!* WE'VE GOT TO *FIND* IT*!*
WHAT?
WITH EVERYTHING ELSE THAT'S HAPPENED—
THAT'S WHAT YOU THINK IS IMPORTANT?!
YOUR UNCLE WAS VERY CLEAR. YOU MUST ALWAYS WEAR—
DR. BEETLE IS *DEAD!*
AGATHA, WHEN YOUR UNCLE LEFT YOU WITH US, HE TOLD US THINGS WE'D NEED TO KNOW IF—
IF HE DIDN'T COME BACK*!*
WELL IT'S BEEN *ELEVEN YEARS!*
MAYBE...MAYBE HE...HE NEVER *MEANT* TO COME BACK*!*
THUMP!

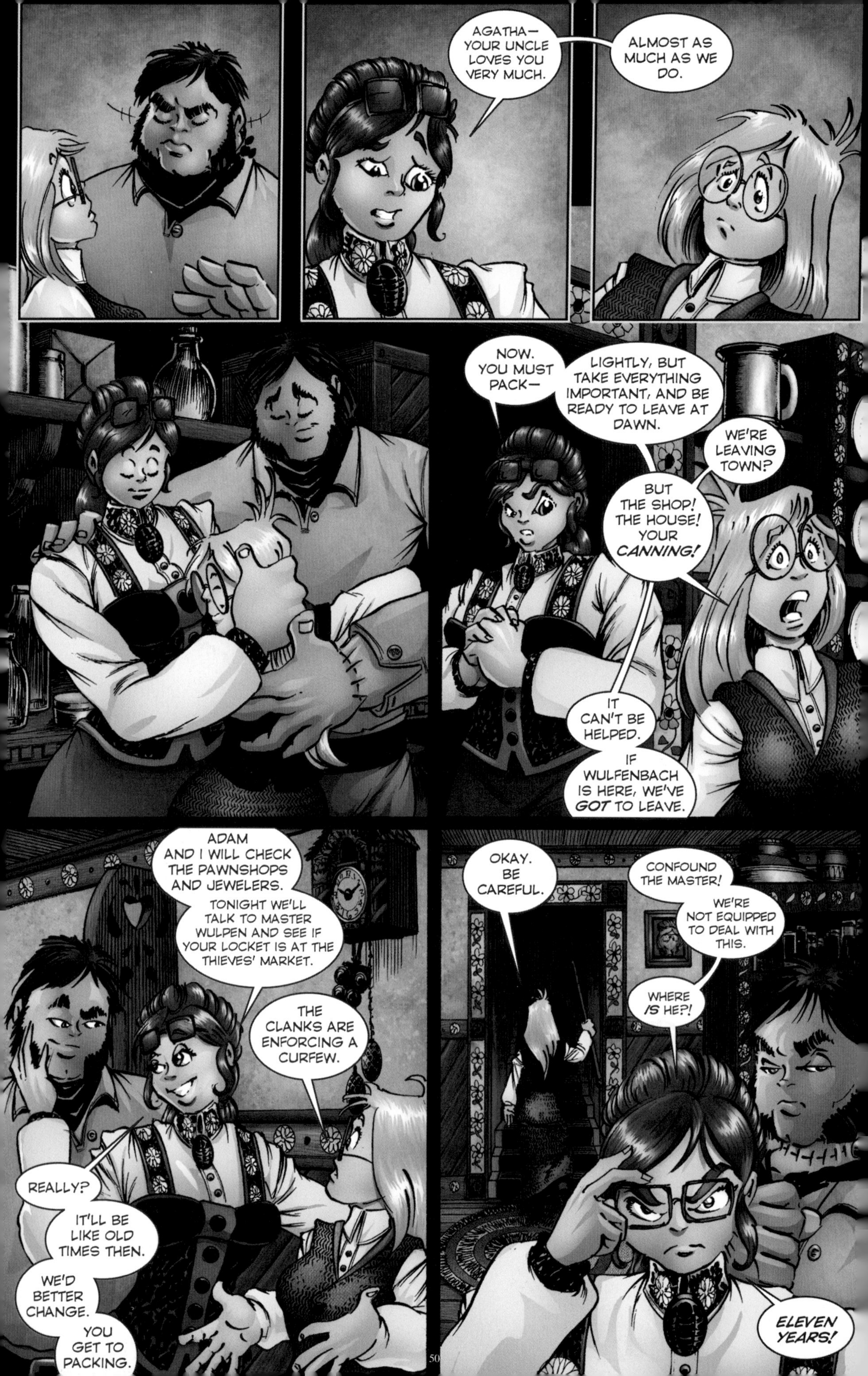
AGATHA— YOUR UNCLE LOVES YOU VERY MUCH.
ALMOST AS MUCH AS WE DO.
NOW. YOU MUST PACK—
LIGHTLY, BUT TAKE EVERYTHING IMPORTANT, AND BE READY TO LEAVE AT DAWN.
WE'RE LEAVING TOWN?
BUT THE SHOP! THE HOUSE! YOUR CANNING!
IT CAN'T BE HELPED.
IF WULFENBACH IS HERE, WE'VE GOT TO LEAVE.
ADAM AND I WILL CHECK THE PAWNSHOPS AND JEWELERS.
TONIGHT WE'LL TALK TO MASTER WULPEN AND SEE IF YOUR LOCKET IS AT THE THIEVES' MARKET.
THE CLANKS ARE ENFORCING A CURFEW.
REALLY?
IT'LL BE LIKE OLD TIMES THEN.
WE'D BETTER CHANGE.
YOU GET TO PACKING.
OKAY. BE CAREFUL.
CONFOUND THE MASTER!
WE'RE NOT EQUIPPED TO DEAL WITH THIS.
WHERE IS HE?!
ELEVEN YEARS!

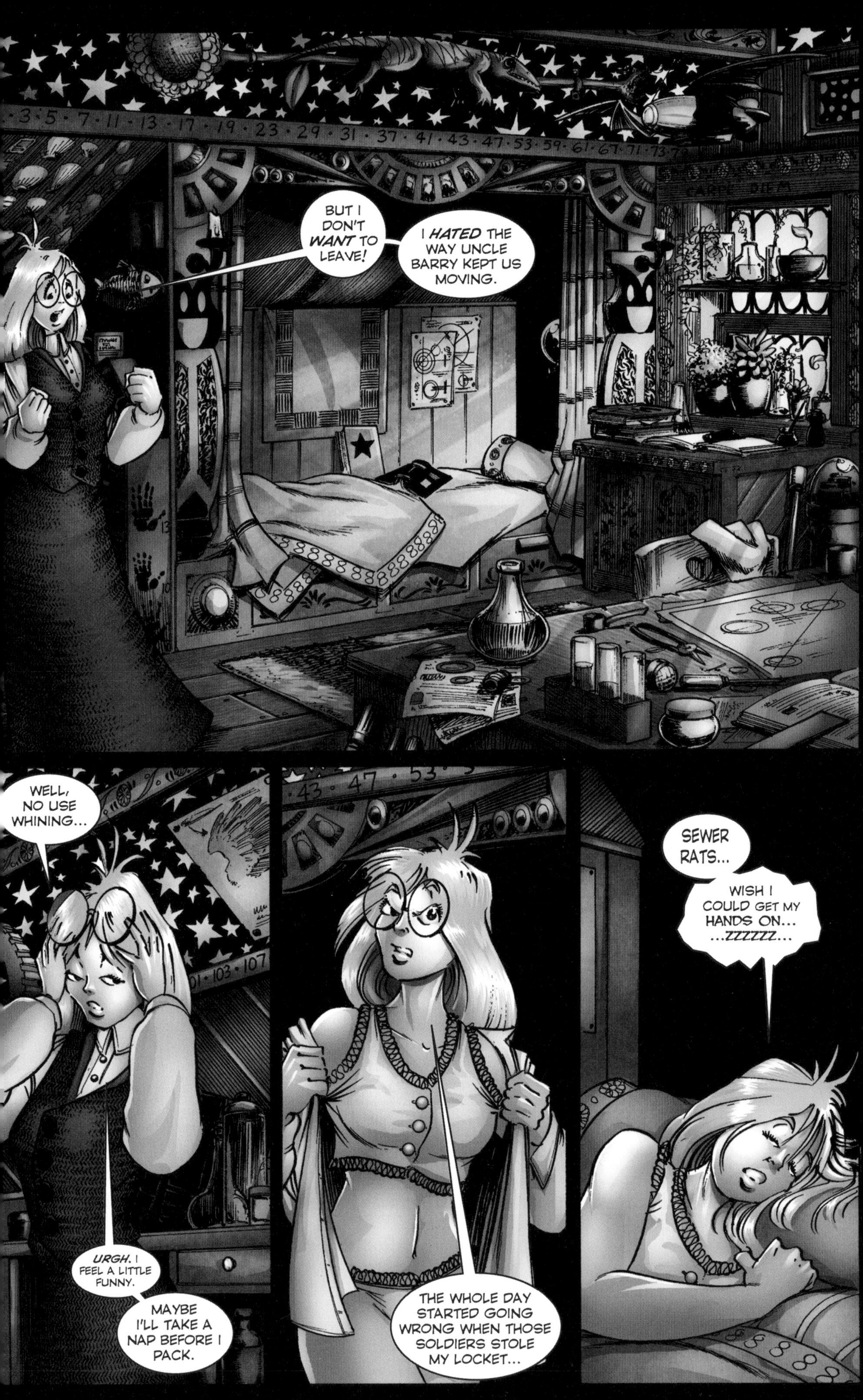

BUT I DON'T *WANT* TO LEAVE!
I *HATED* THE WAY UNCLE BARRY KEPT US MOVING.
CARPE DIEM
WELL, NO USE WHINING...
URGH. I FEEL A LITTLE FUNNY.
MAYBE I'LL TAKE A NAP BEFORE I PACK.
THE WHOLE DAY STARTED GOING WRONG WHEN THOSE SOLDIERS STOLE MY LOCKET...
SEWER RATS...
WISH I COULD GET MY HANDS ON... ...ZZZZZZ...

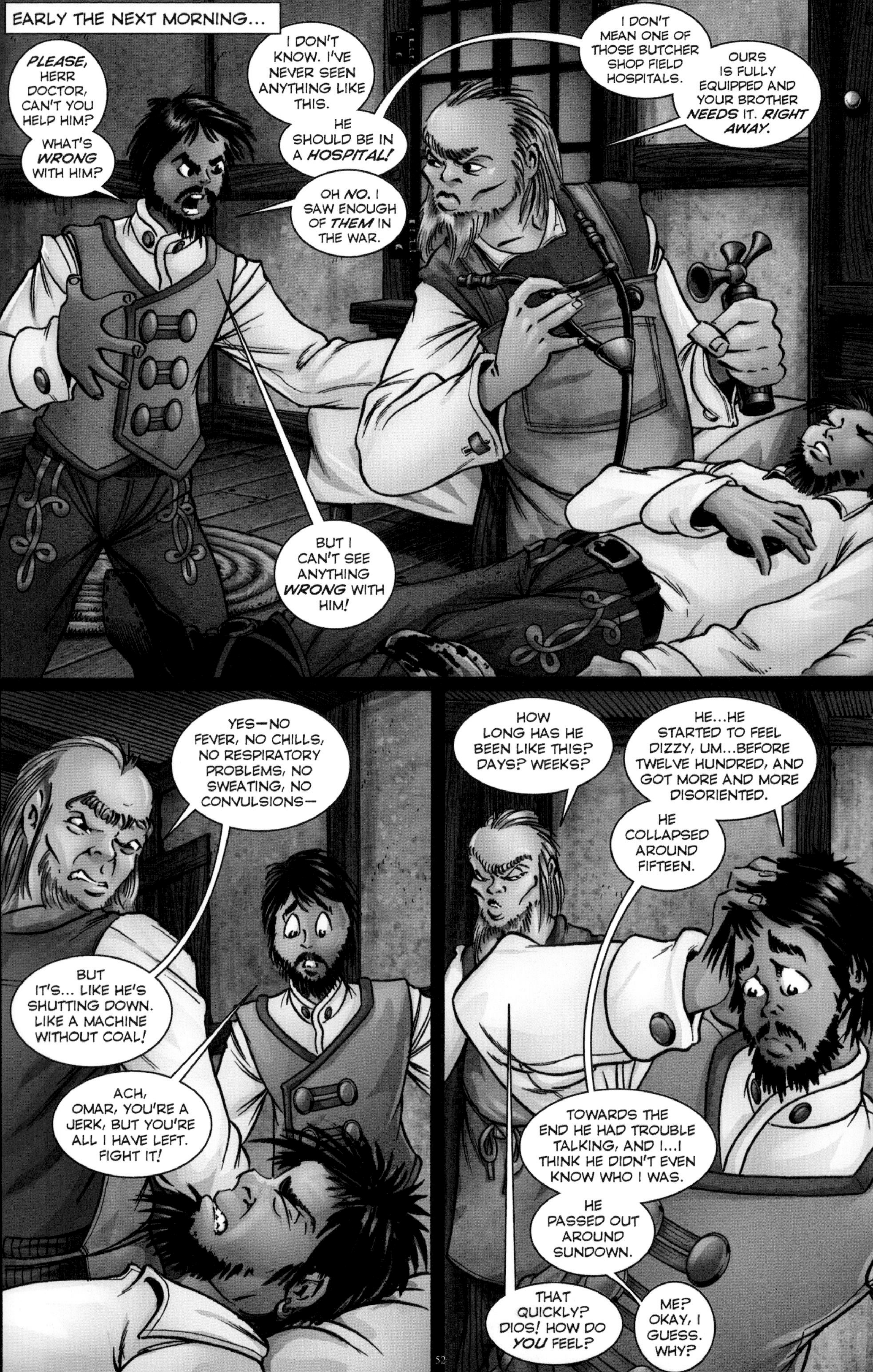
EARLY THE NEXT MORNING...
PLEASE, HERR DOCTOR, CAN'T YOU HELP HIM?
WHAT'S WRONG WITH HIM?
I DON'T KNOW. I'VE NEVER SEEN ANYTHING LIKE THIS.
HE SHOULD BE IN A HOSPITAL!
OH NO. I SAW ENOUGH OF THEM IN THE WAR.
I DON'T MEAN ONE OF THOSE BUTCHER SHOP FIELD HOSPITALS.
OURS IS FULLY EQUIPPED AND YOUR BROTHER NEEDS IT. RIGHT AWAY.
BUT I CAN'T SEE ANYTHING WRONG WITH HIM!
YES—NO FEVER, NO CHILLS, NO RESPIRATORY PROBLEMS, NO SWEATING, NO CONVULSIONS—
BUT IT'S... LIKE HE'S SHUTTING DOWN. LIKE A MACHINE WITHOUT COAL!
ACH, OMAR, YOU'RE A JERK, BUT YOU'RE ALL I HAVE LEFT. FIGHT IT!
HOW LONG HAS HE BEEN LIKE THIS? DAYS? WEEKS?
HE...HE STARTED TO FEEL DIZZY, UM...BEFORE TWELVE HUNDRED, AND GOT MORE AND MORE DISORIENTED.
HE COLLAPSED AROUND FIFTEEN.
TOWARDS THE END HE HAD TROUBLE TALKING, AND I...I THINK HE DIDN'T EVEN KNOW WHO I WAS.
HE PASSED OUT AROUND SUNDOWN.
THAT QUICKLY? DIOS! HOW DO YOU FEEL?
ME? OKAY, I GUESS. WHY?

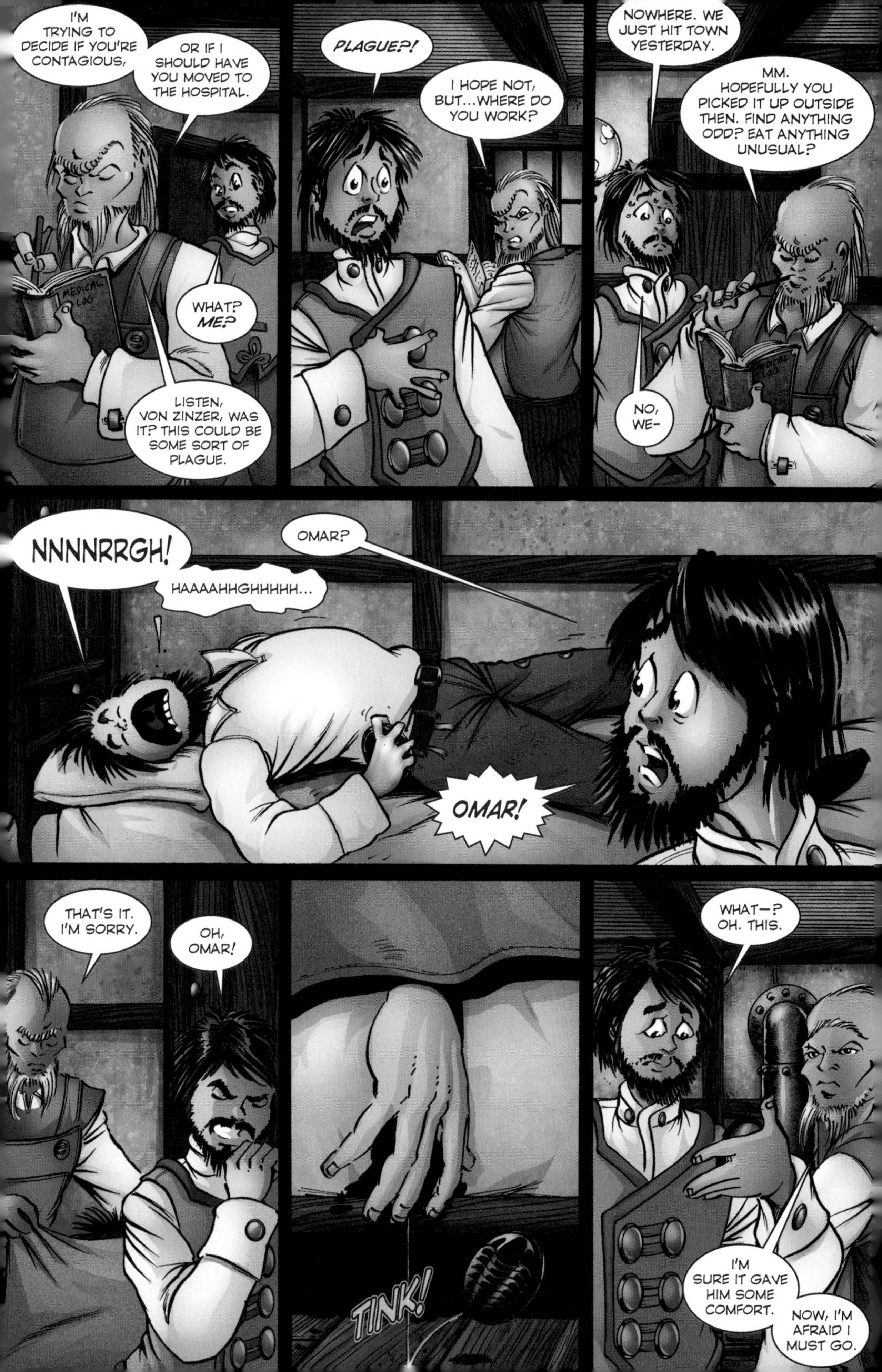
I'M TRYING TO DECIDE IF YOU'RE CONTAGIOUS,
OR IF I SHOULD HAVE YOU MOVED TO THE HOSPITAL.
MEDICAL LOG
WHAT? ME?
LISTEN, VON ZINZER, WAS IT? THIS COULD BE SOME SORT OF PLAGUE.
PLAGUE?!
I HOPE NOT, BUT...WHERE DO YOU WORK?
NOWHERE. WE JUST HIT TOWN YESTERDAY.
MM. HOPEFULLY YOU PICKED IT UP OUTSIDE THEN. FIND ANYTHING ODD? EAT ANYTHING UNUSUAL?
NO, WE-
NNNNRRGH!
HAAAAHHGHHHHH...
OMAR?
!
OMAR!
THAT'S IT. I'M SORRY.
OH, OMAR!
TINK!
WHAT—? OH. THIS.
I'M SURE IT GAVE HIM SOME COMFORT.
NOW, I'M AFRAID I MUST GO.

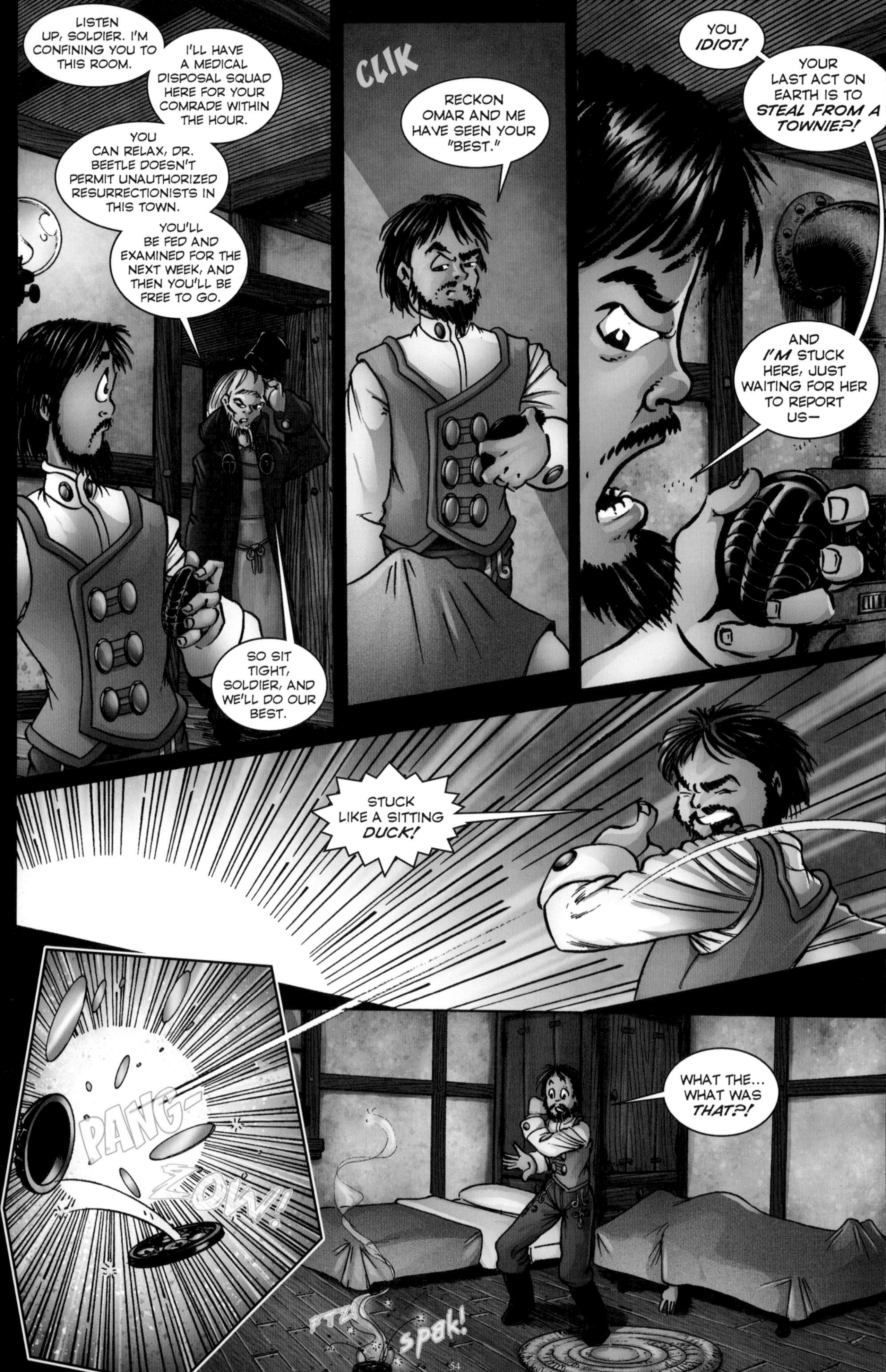

LISTEN UP, SOLDIER. I'M CONFINING YOU TO THIS ROOM.
I'LL HAVE A MEDICAL DISPOSAL SQUAD HERE FOR YOUR COMRADE WITHIN THE HOUR.
YOU CAN RELAX, DR. BEETLE DOESN'T PERMIT UNAUTHORIZED RESURRECTIONISTS IN THIS TOWN.
YOU'LL BE FED AND EXAMINED FOR THE NEXT WEEK, AND THEN YOU'LL BE FREE TO GO.
SO SIT TIGHT, SOLDIER, AND WE'LL DO OUR BEST.
CLIK
RECKON OMAR AND ME HAVE SEEN YOUR "BEST."
YOU *IDIOT!*
YOUR LAST ACT ON EARTH IS TO ***STEAL FROM A TOWNIE?!***
AND *I'M* STUCK HERE, JUST WAITING FOR HER TO REPORT US—
STUCK LIKE A SITTING *DUCK!*
PANG-
ZOW!
WHAT THE... WHAT WAS *THAT?!*
FTZ!
spak!

HUH. THIS LOCKET HAD SOME SORT OF MECHANISM INSIDE IT.
TOO COMPLICATED TO BE A WATCH.
I'VE NEVER SEEN ANYTHING LIKE THIS.
WHAT DID IT DO?!
DAUGHTER OF THUNDER...
THIS THING KILLED OMAR!
THERE'S NO PLAGUE!
YEAH, HE STARTED ACTING STRANGE AFTER THAT GIRL—
BEETLE BEER
THE GIRL! SHE WAS WEARING IT AND IT WASN'T KILLING HER.
SHE MUST HAVE... TURNED IT ON SOMEHOW.
SHE KNEW IT'D DO FOR HIM, THE BLACK-HEARTED—
WAIT! WASN'T THERE—
A LABEL! YES!
"IF FOUND, RETURN TO AGATHA CLAY, CLAY MECHANICAL, FORGE STREET, BEETLEBURG. REWARD."
Agatha Clay
Clay Mechanical
Forge Street Beetleburg
REWARD
7B
A REWARD, HUH? I'LL GIVE HER A REWARD A'RIGHT, AND SHE'LL MAKE NO REPORTS WHEN I'M DONE WITH HER.

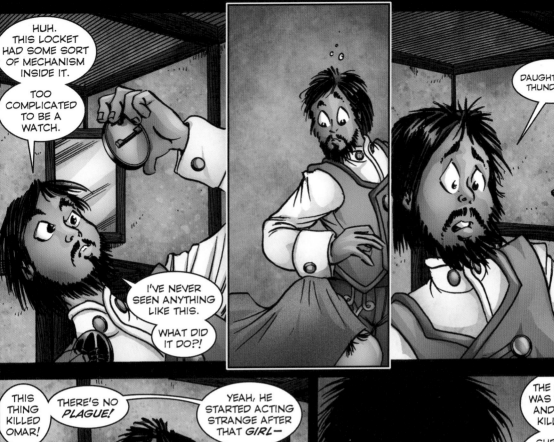

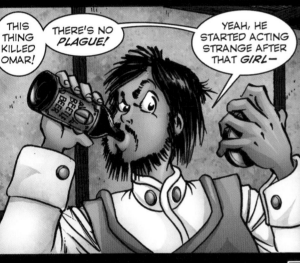

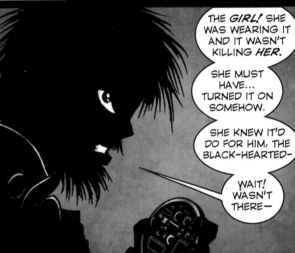

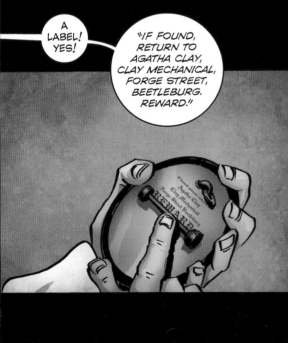

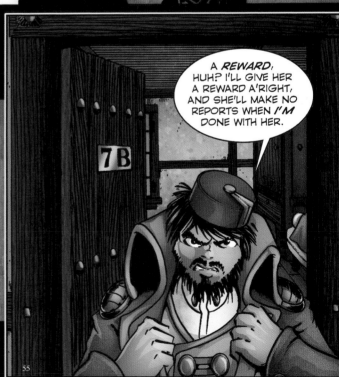

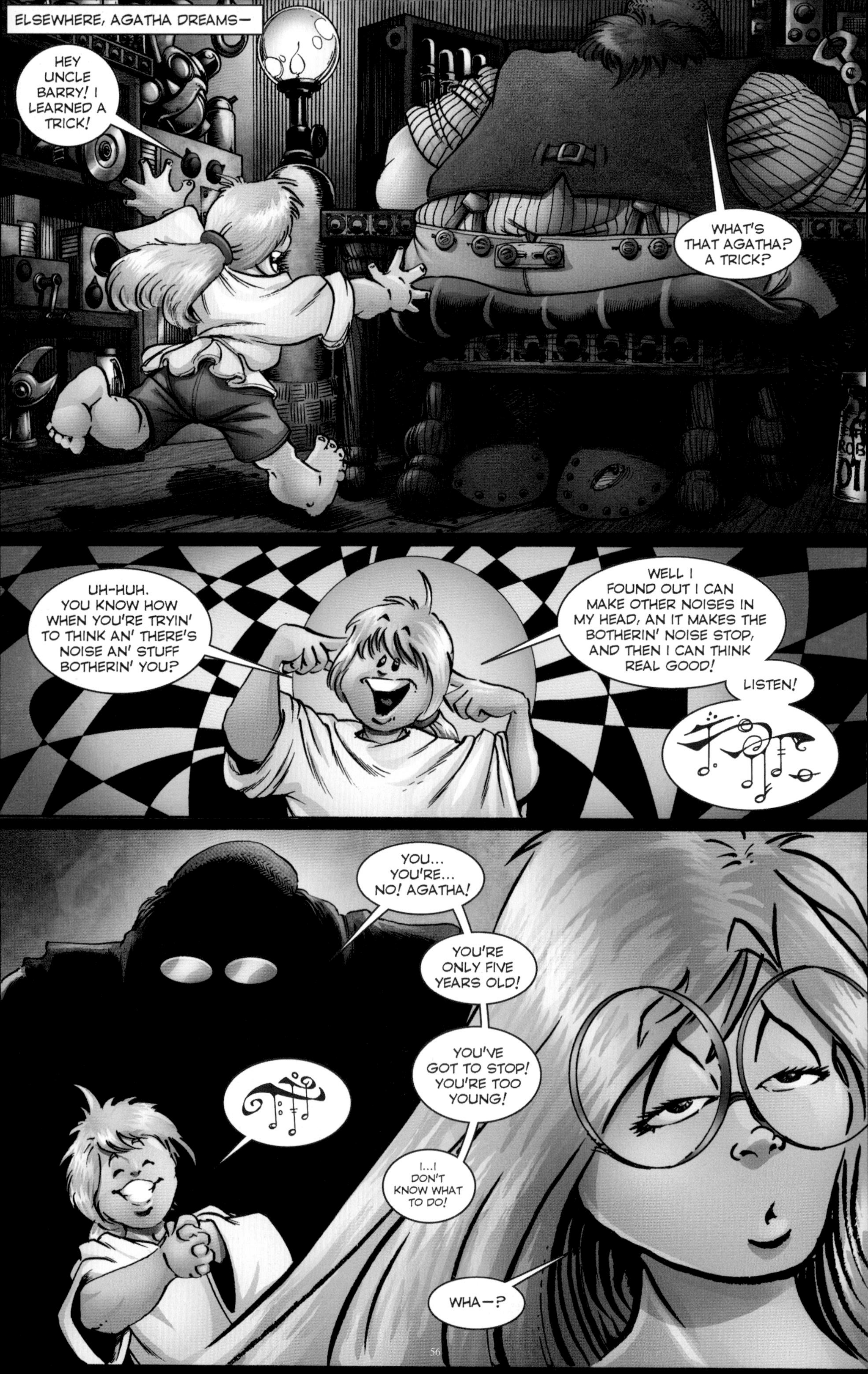
ELSEWHERE, AGATHA DREAMS—
HEY UNCLE BARRY! I LEARNED A TRICK!
WHAT'S THAT AGATHA? A TRICK?
UH-HUH. YOU KNOW HOW WHEN YOU'RE TRYIN' TO THINK AN' THERE'S NOISE AN' STUFF BOTHERIN' YOU?
WELL I FOUND OUT I CAN MAKE OTHER NOISES IN MY HEAD, AN IT MAKES THE BOTHERIN' NOISE STOP, AND THEN I CAN THINK REAL GOOD!
LISTEN!
YOU... YOU'RE... NO! AGATHA!
YOU'RE ONLY FIVE YEARS OLD!
YOU'VE GOT TO STOP! YOU'RE TOO YOUNG!
I...I DON'T KNOW WHAT TO DO!
WHA—?

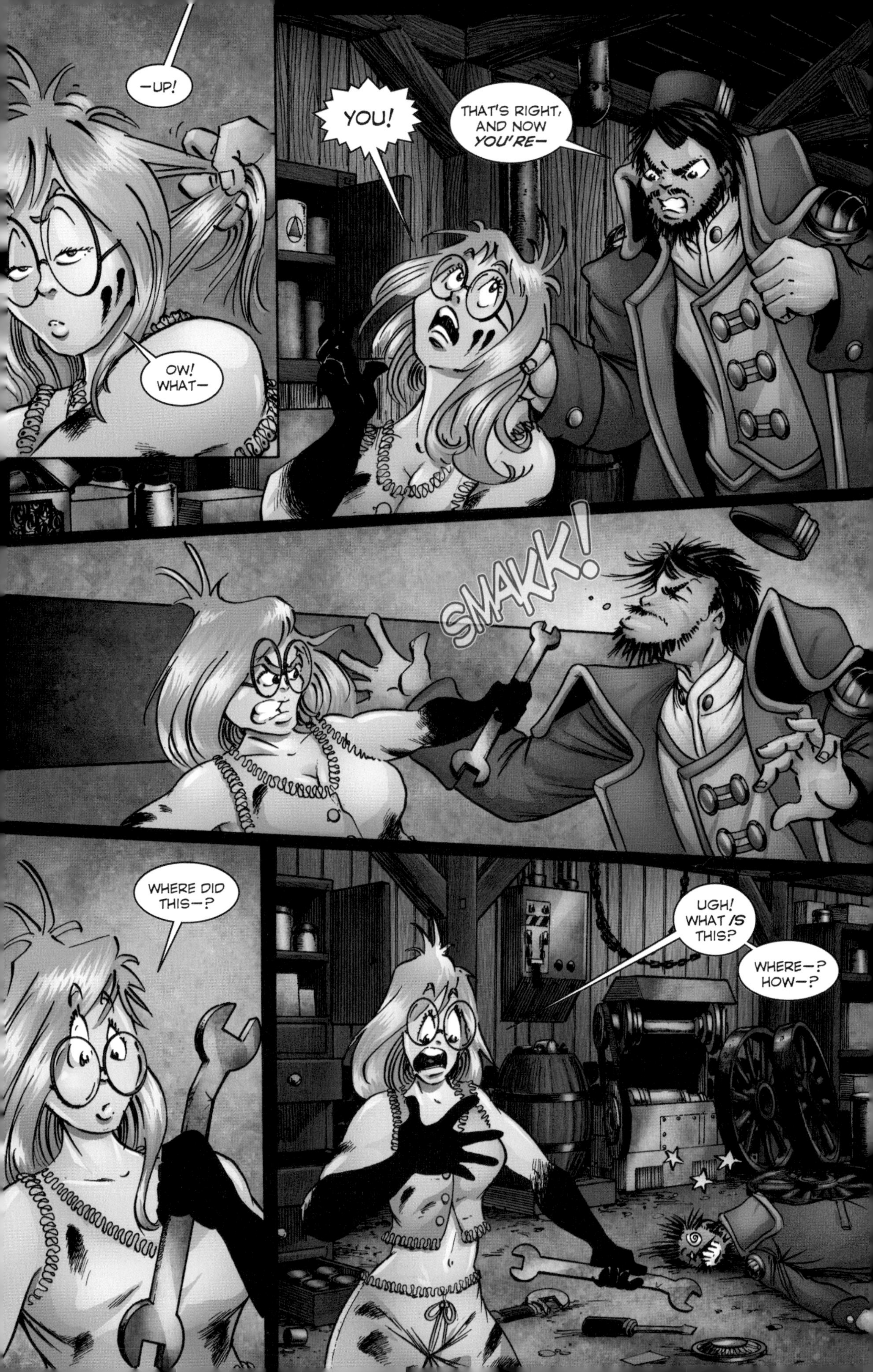

—UP!
OW! WHAT—
YOU!
THAT'S RIGHT, AND NOW *YOU'RE*—
SMAKK!
WHERE DID THIS—?
UGH! WHAT *IS* THIS?
WHERE—? HOW—?

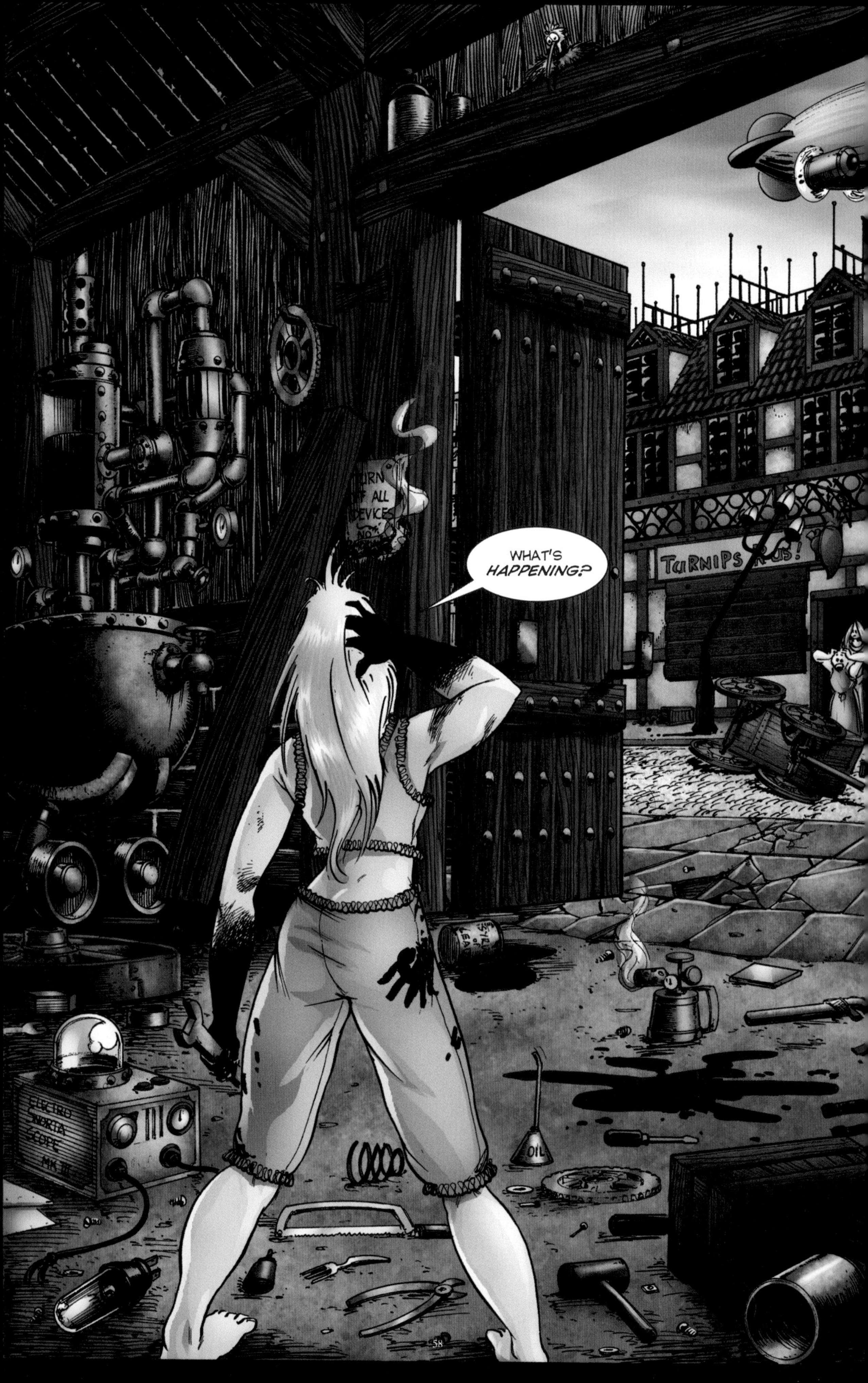
WHAT'S HAPPENING?
TURNIPS R US!
OIL

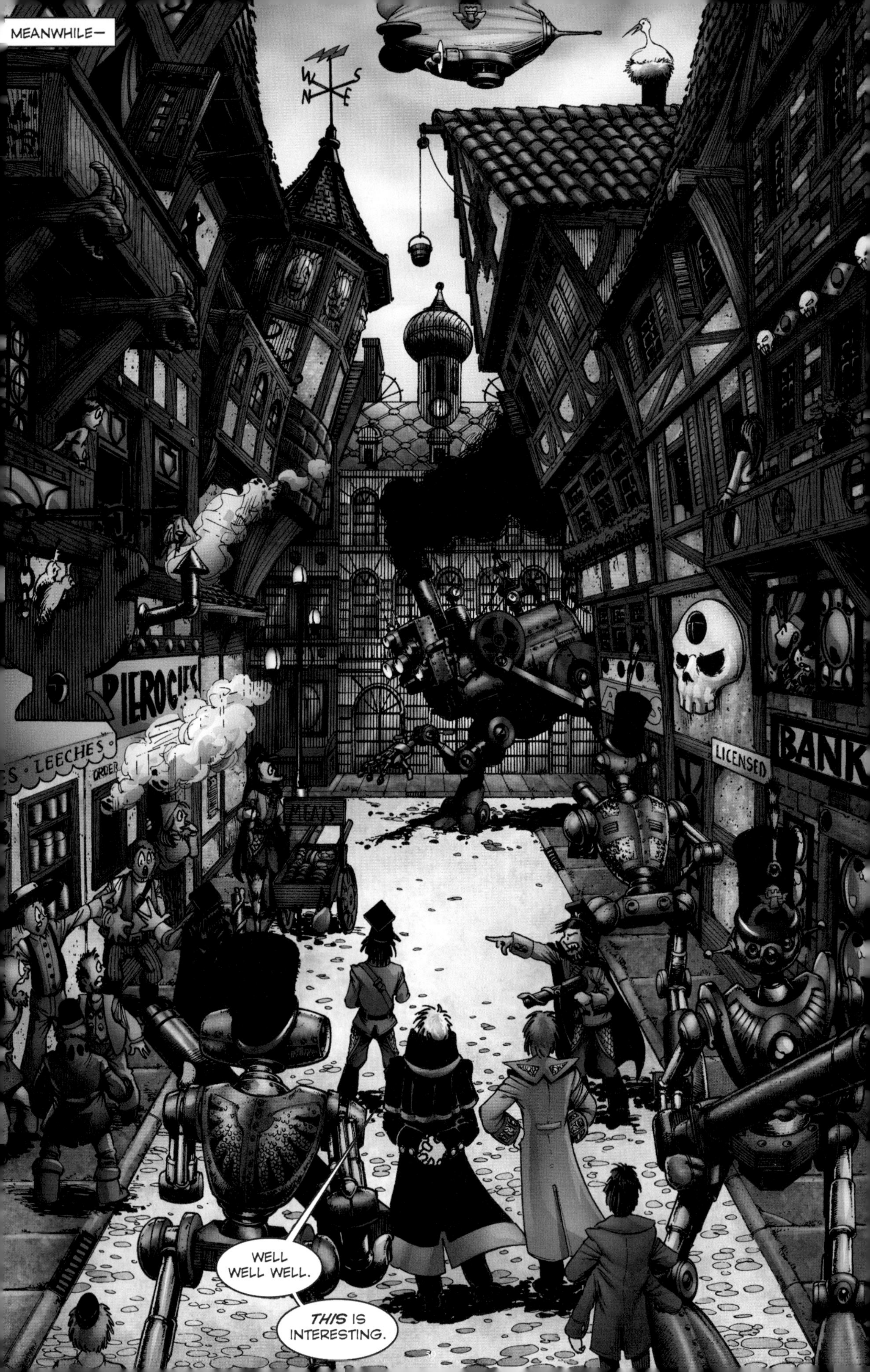

MEANWHILE—
W S N E
PIEROGIES
LEECHES
ORDER
LICENSED
BANK
WELL WELL WELL.
THIS IS INTERESTING.

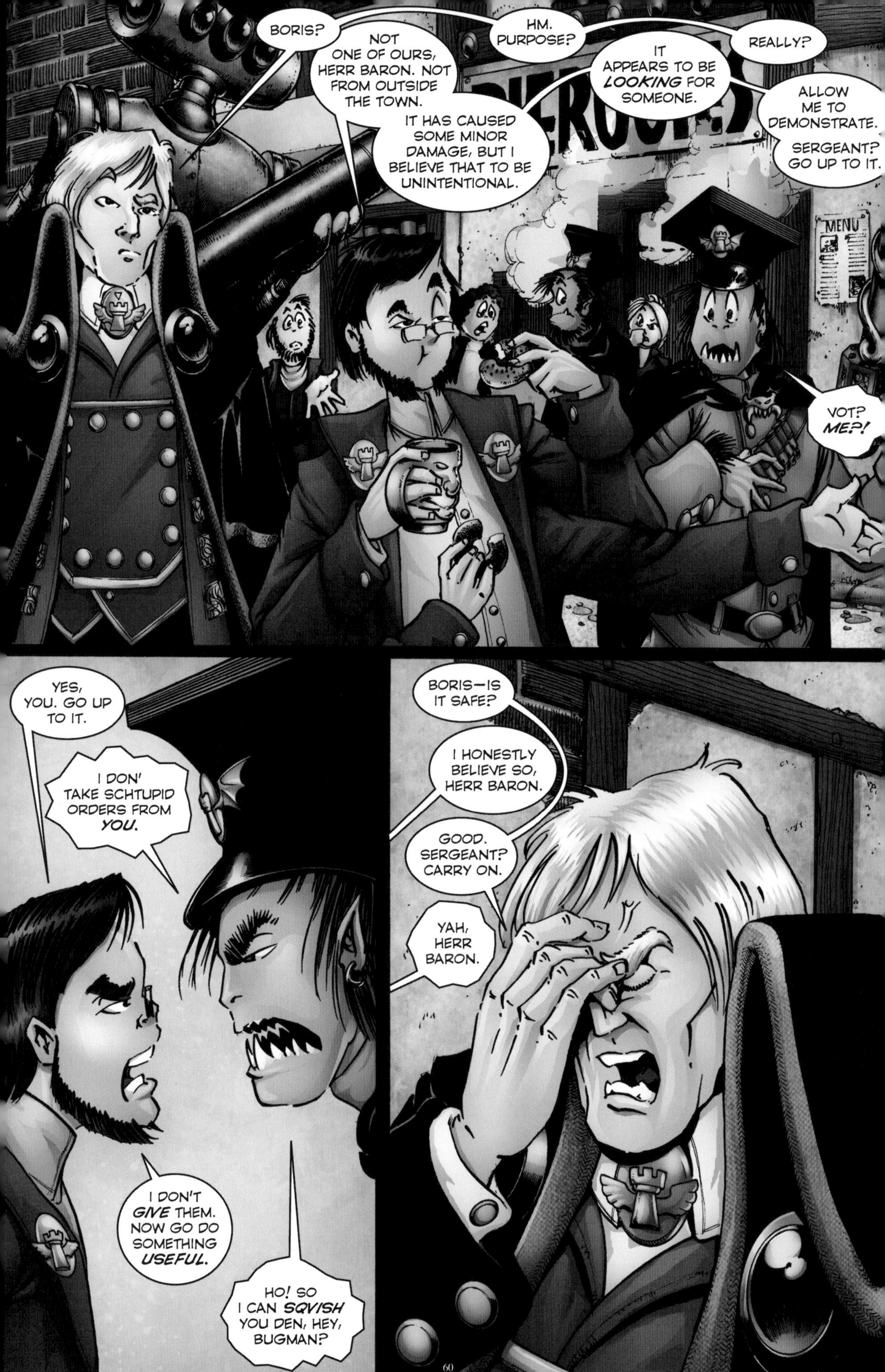
BORIS?
NOT ONE OF OURS, HERR BARON. NOT FROM OUTSIDE THE TOWN.
IT HAS CAUSED SOME MINOR DAMAGE, BUT I BELIEVE THAT TO BE UNINTENTIONAL.
HM. PURPOSE?
IT APPEARS TO BE *LOOKING* FOR SOMEONE.
REALLY?
ALLOW ME TO DEMONSTRATE.
SERGEANT? GO UP TO IT.
MENU
VOT? *ME?!*
YES, YOU. GO UP TO IT.
I DON' TAKE SCHTUPID ORDERS FROM *YOU*.
I DON'T *GIVE* THEM. NOW GO DO SOMETHING *USEFUL*.
HO! SO I CAN *SQVISH* YOU DEN, HEY, BUGMAN?
BORIS—IS IT SAFE?
I HONESTLY BELIEVE SO, HERR BARON.
GOOD. SERGEANT? CARRY ON.
YAH, HERR BARON.

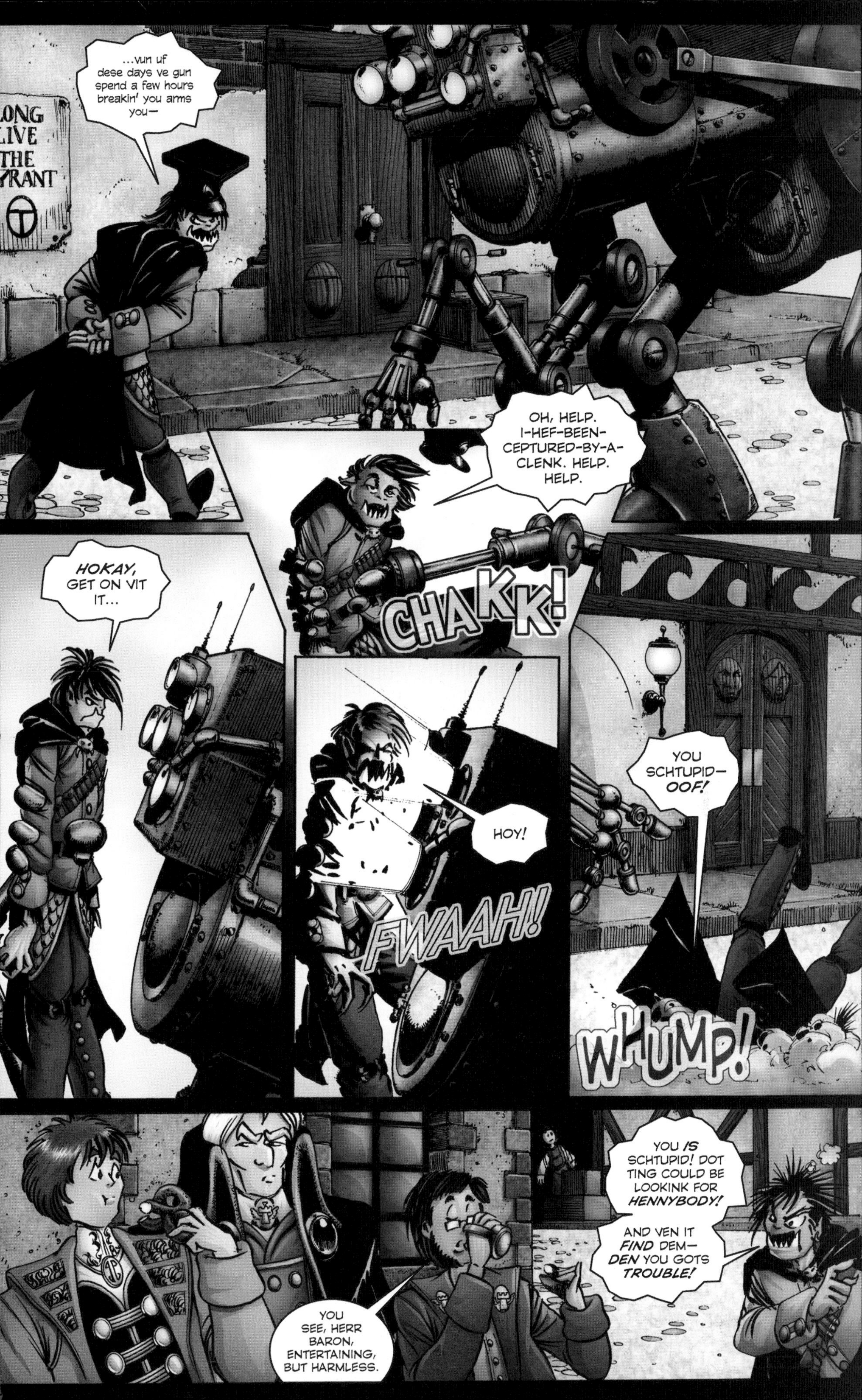
LONG LIVE THE TYRANT
...vun uf dese days ve gun spend a few hours breakin' you arms you—
OH, HELP. I-HEF-BEEN-CEPTURED-BY-A-CLENK. HELP. HELP.
HOKAY, GET ON VIT IT...
CHAKK!
HOY!
FWAAH!
YOU SCHTUPID—OOF!
WHUMP!
YOU IS SCHTUPID! DOT TING COULD BE LOOKINK FOR HENNYBODY!
AND VEN IT FIND DEM—DEN YOU GOTS TROUBLE!
YOU SEE, HERR BARON, ENTERTAINING, BUT HARMLESS.

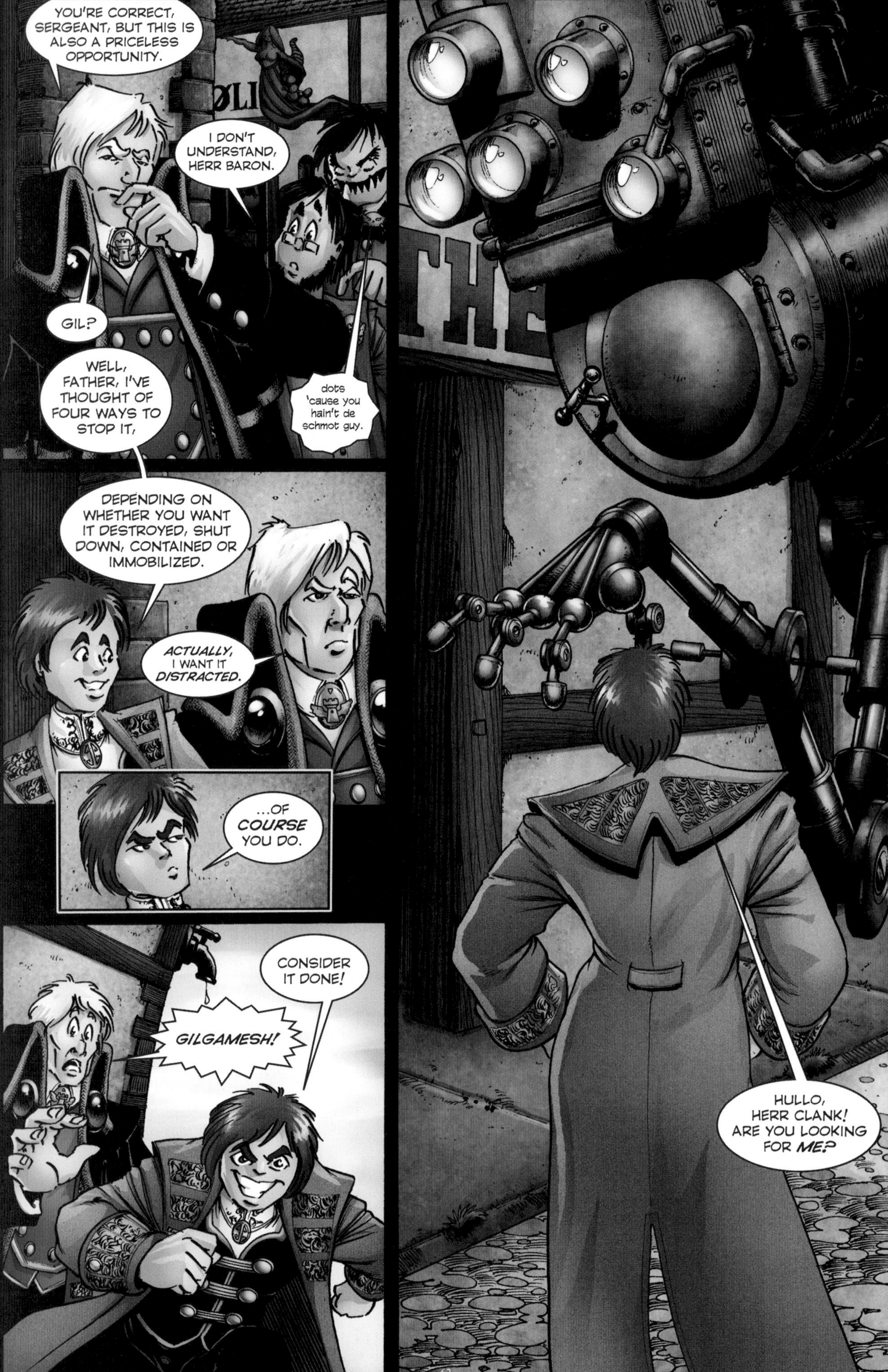
YOU'RE CORRECT, SERGEANT, BUT THIS IS ALSO A PRICELESS OPPORTUNITY.
I DON'T UNDERSTAND, HERR BARON.
GIL?
WELL, FATHER, I'VE THOUGHT OF FOUR WAYS TO STOP IT,
dots 'cause you hain't de schmot guy.
DEPENDING ON WHETHER YOU WANT IT DESTROYED, SHUT DOWN, CONTAINED OR IMMOBILIZED.
ACTUALLY, I WANT IT *DISTRACTED.*
...OF **COURSE** YOU DO.
CONSIDER IT DONE!
GILGAMESH!
HULLO, HERR CLANK! ARE YOU LOOKING FOR *ME?*

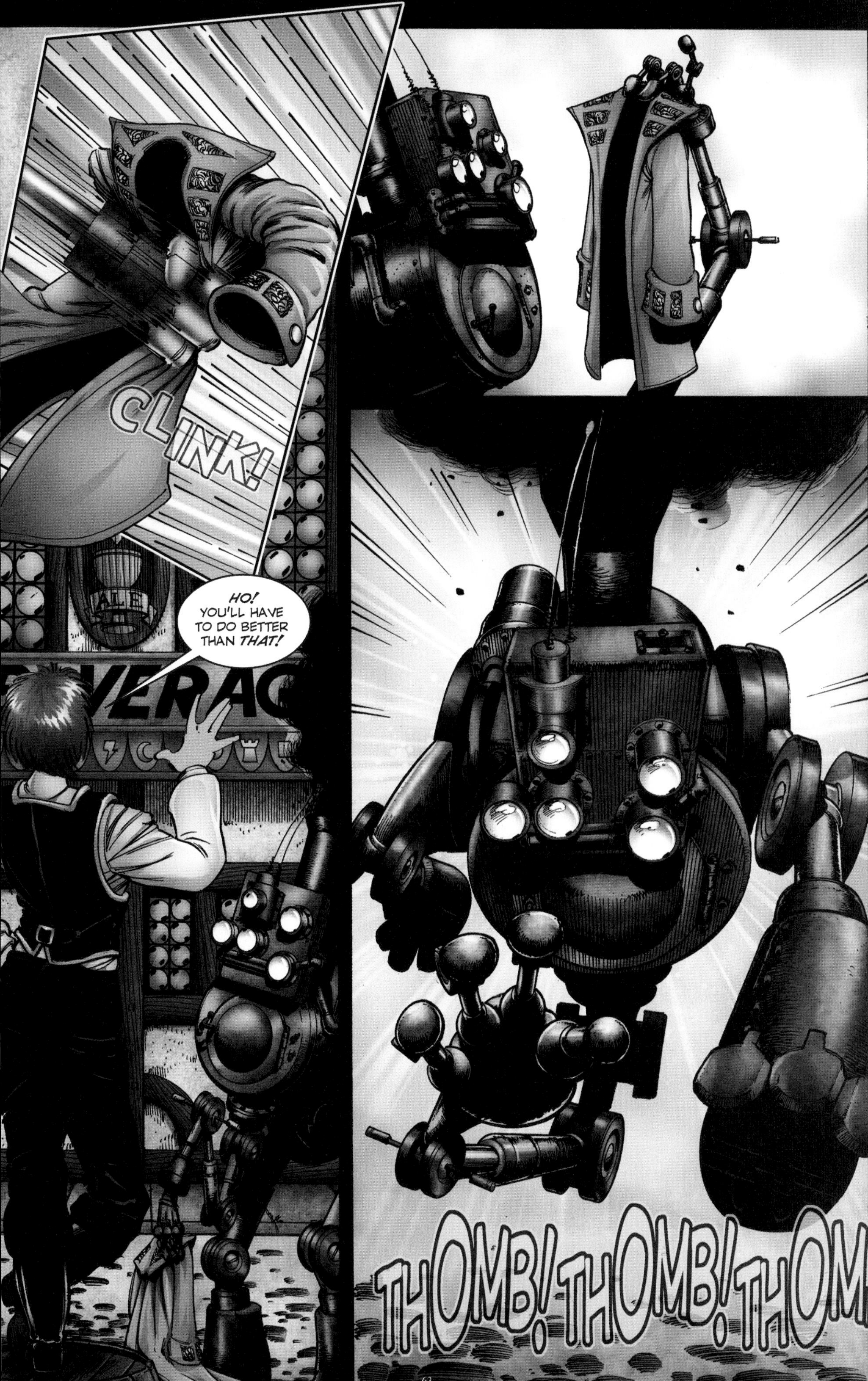
CLINK!
HO! YOU'LL HAVE TO DO BETTER THAN *THAT!*
THOMB! THOMB! THOM

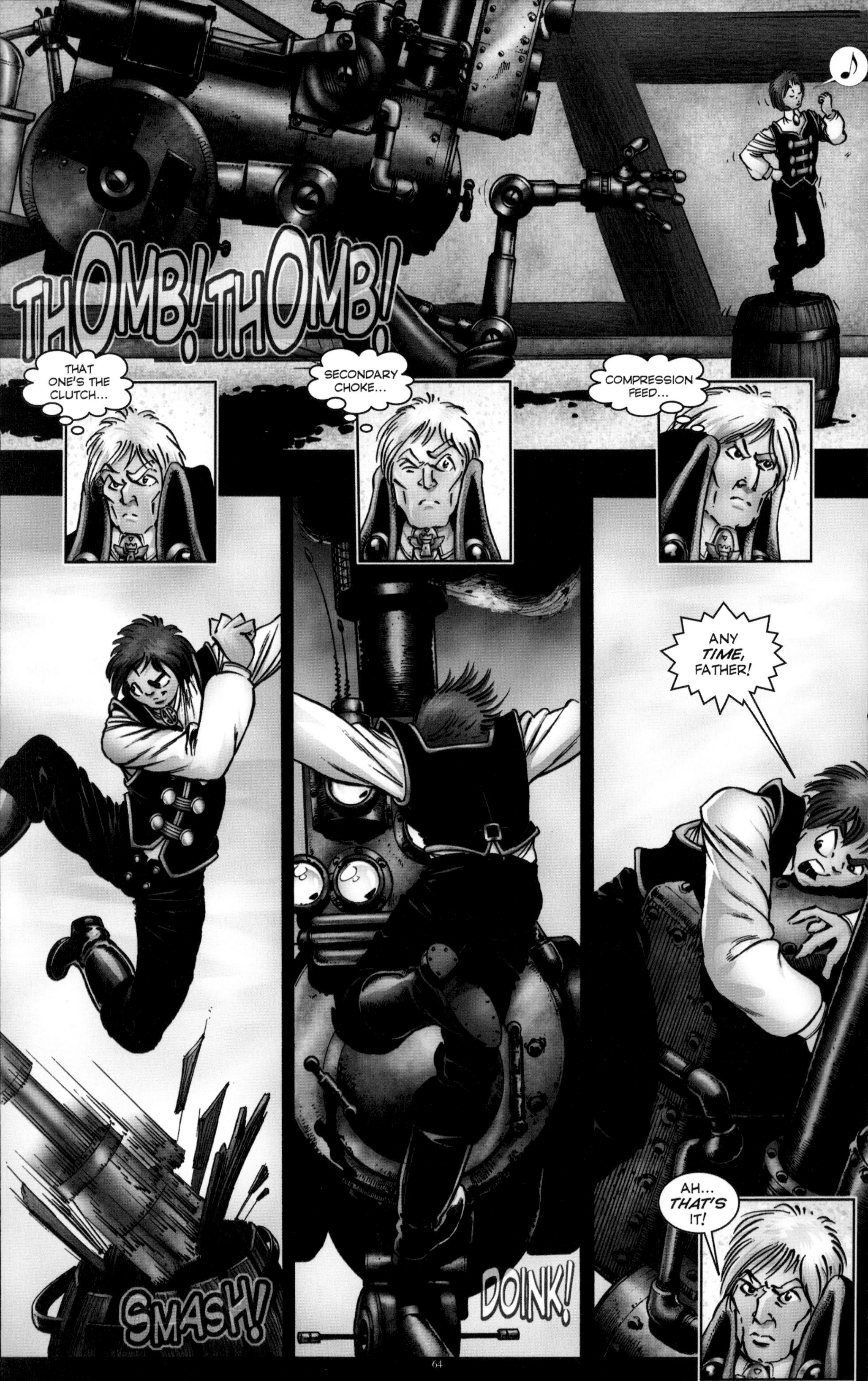
♪
THOMB! THOMB!
THAT ONE'S THE CLUTCH...
SECONDARY CHOKE...
COMPRESSION FEED...
SMASH!
DOINK!
ANY *TIME,* FATHER!
AH... *THAT'S* IT!

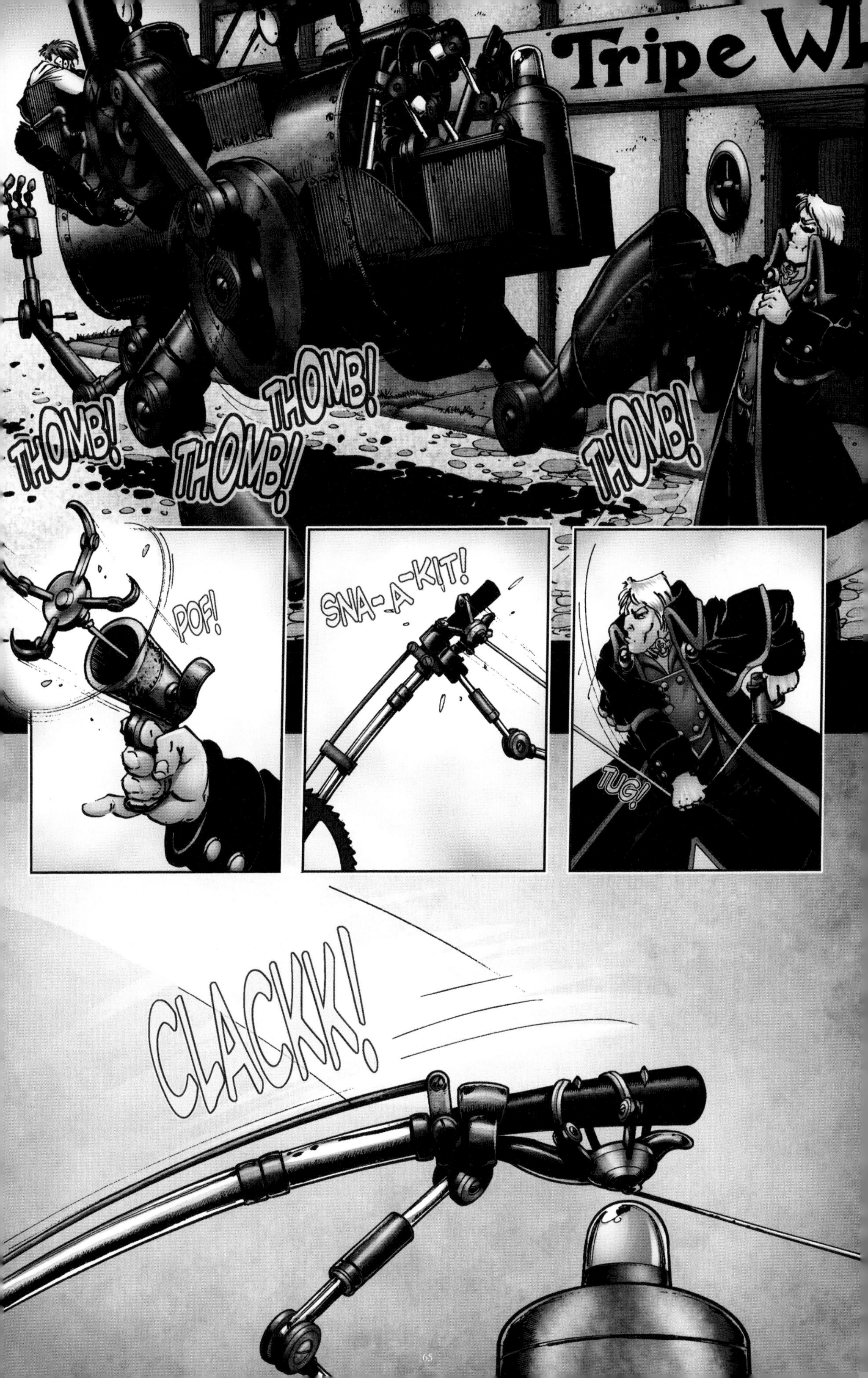
Tripe W
THOMB!
THOMB!
THOMB!
THOMB!
POF!
SNA-A-KIT!
TUG!
CLACKK!

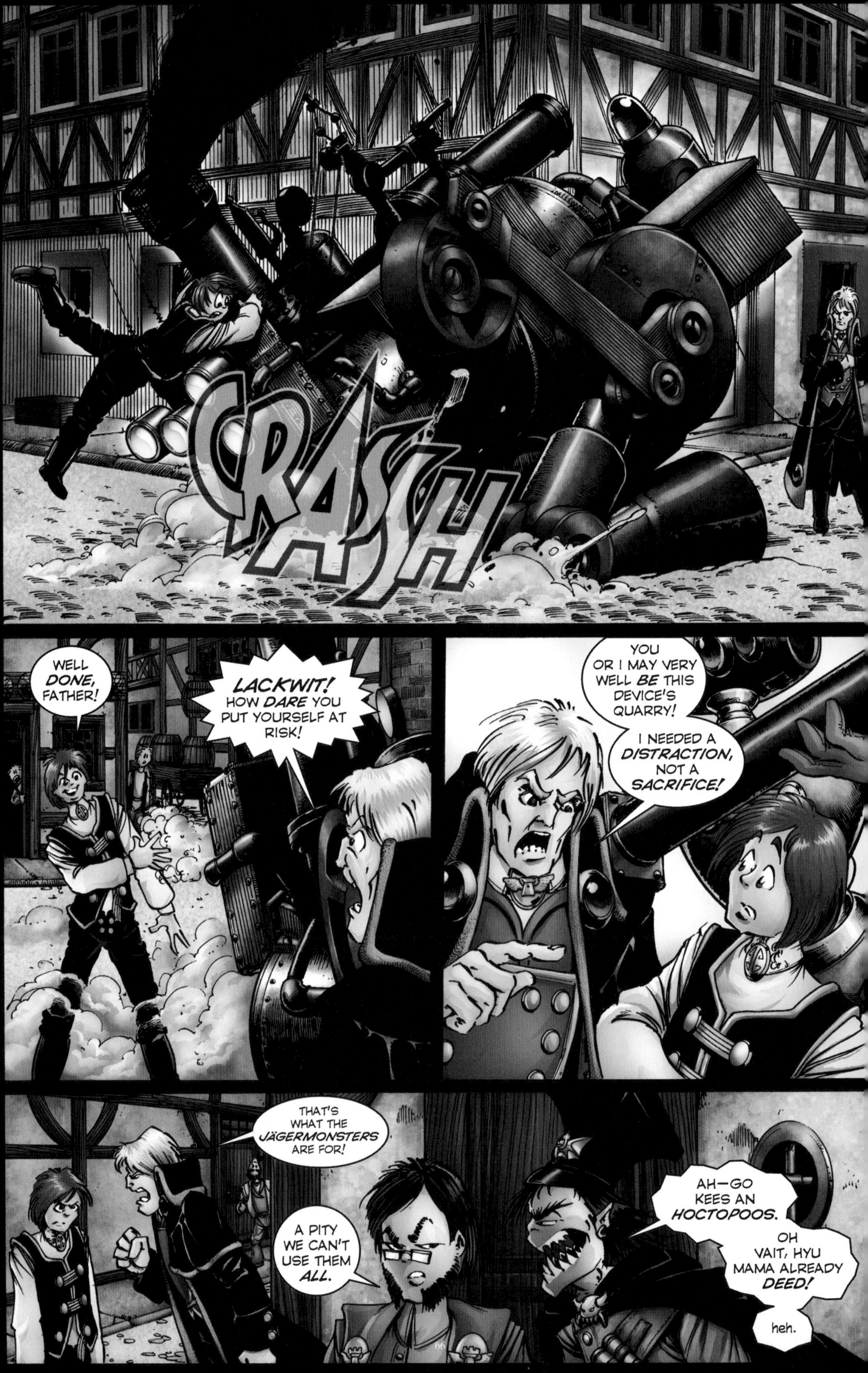
CRASH
WELL DONE, FATHER!
LACKWIT! HOW DARE YOU PUT YOURSELF AT RISK!
YOU OR I MAY VERY WELL BE THIS DEVICE'S QUARRY!
I NEEDED A DISTRACTION, NOT A SACRIFICE!
THAT'S WHAT THE JÄGERMONSTERS ARE FOR!
A PITY WE CAN'T USE THEM ALL.
AH—GO KEES AN HOCTOPOOS.
OH VAIT, HYU MAMA ALREADY DEED!
heh.

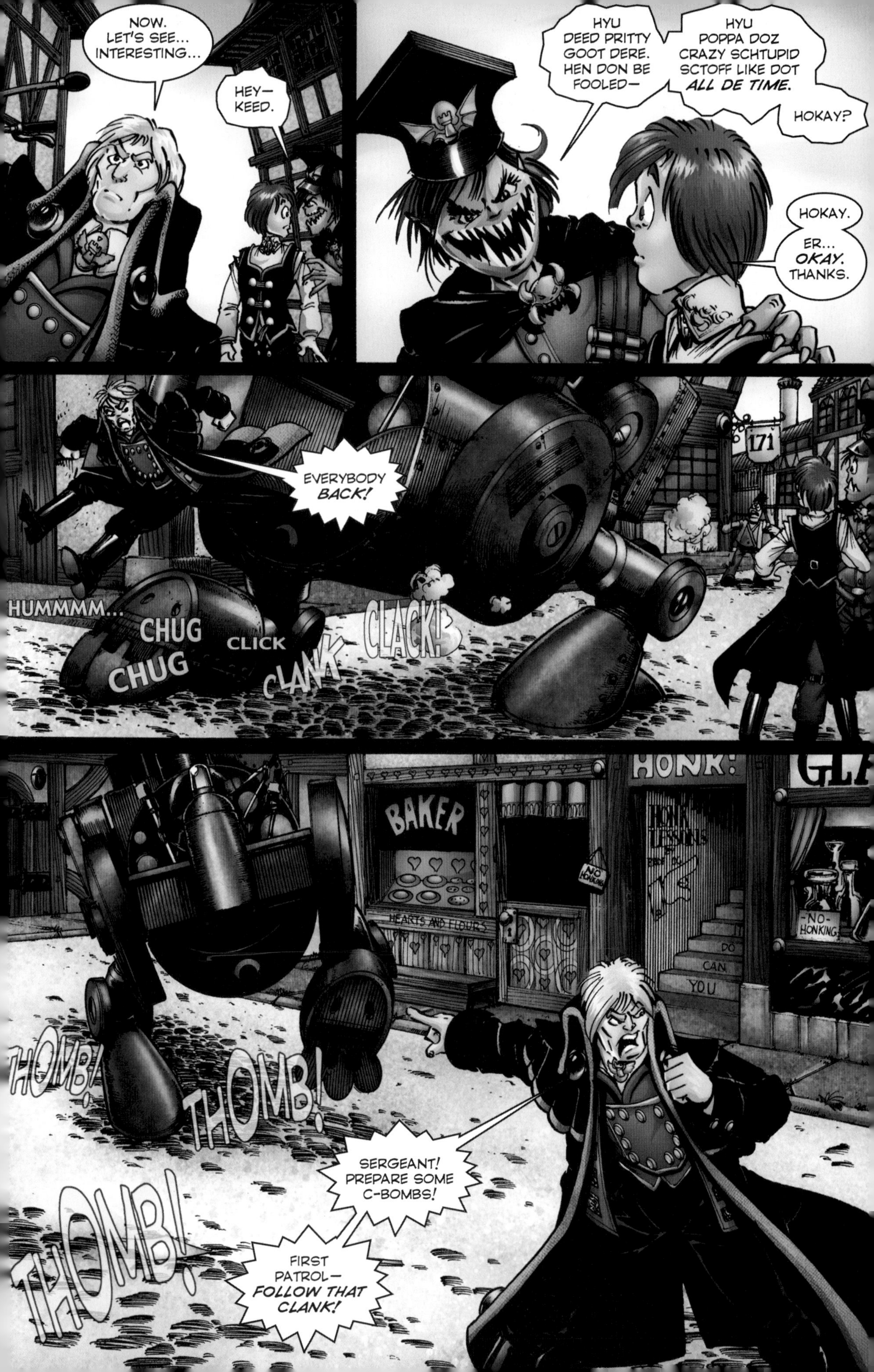
NOW. LET'S SEE... INTERESTING...
HEY— KEED.
HYU DEED PRITTY GOOT DERE. HEN DON BE FOOLED—
HYU POPPA DOZ CRAZY SCHTUPID SCTOFF LIKE DOT ALL DE TIME.
HOKAY?
HOKAY.
ER... OKAY. THANKS.
EVERYBODY BACK!
171
HUMMMM...
CHUG
CHUG
CLICK
CLANK
CLACK!
BAKER
HEARTS AND FLOURS
HONK!
NO HONKING
-NO- HONKING
DO
CAN
YOU
THOMB!
THOMB!
THOMB!
SERGEANT! PREPARE SOME C-BOMBS!
FIRST PATROL— FOLLOW THAT CLANK!

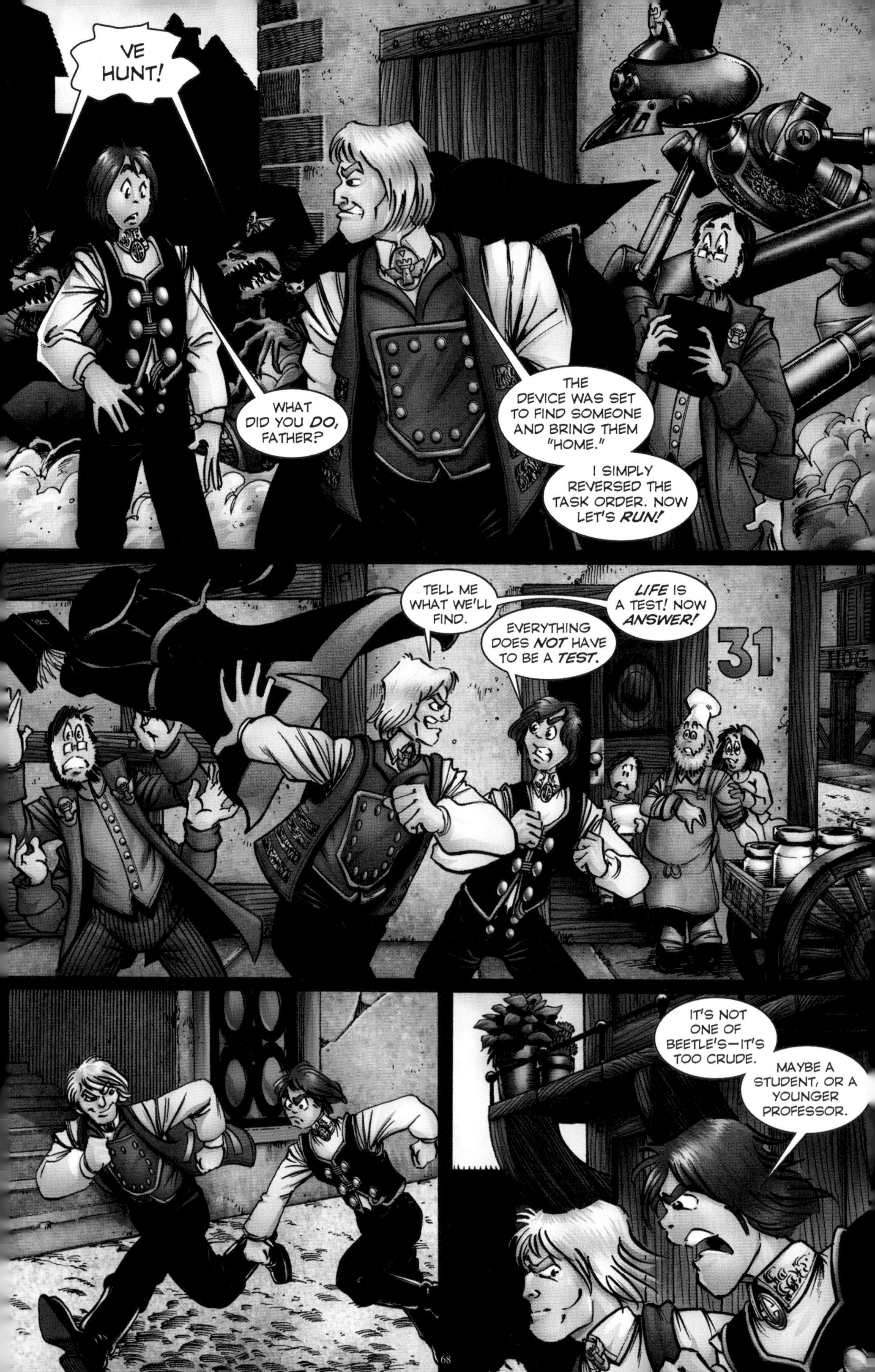
VE HUNT!
WHAT DID YOU DO, FATHER?
THE DEVICE WAS SET TO FIND SOMEONE AND BRING THEM "HOME."
I SIMPLY REVERSED THE TASK ORDER. NOW LET'S RUN!
TELL ME WHAT WE'LL FIND.
LIFE IS A TEST! NOW ANSWER!
EVERYTHING DOES NOT HAVE TO BE A TEST.
31
HOG
MILK
IT'S NOT ONE OF BEETLE'S—IT'S TOO CRUDE.
MAYBE A STUDENT, OR A YOUNGER PROFESSOR.

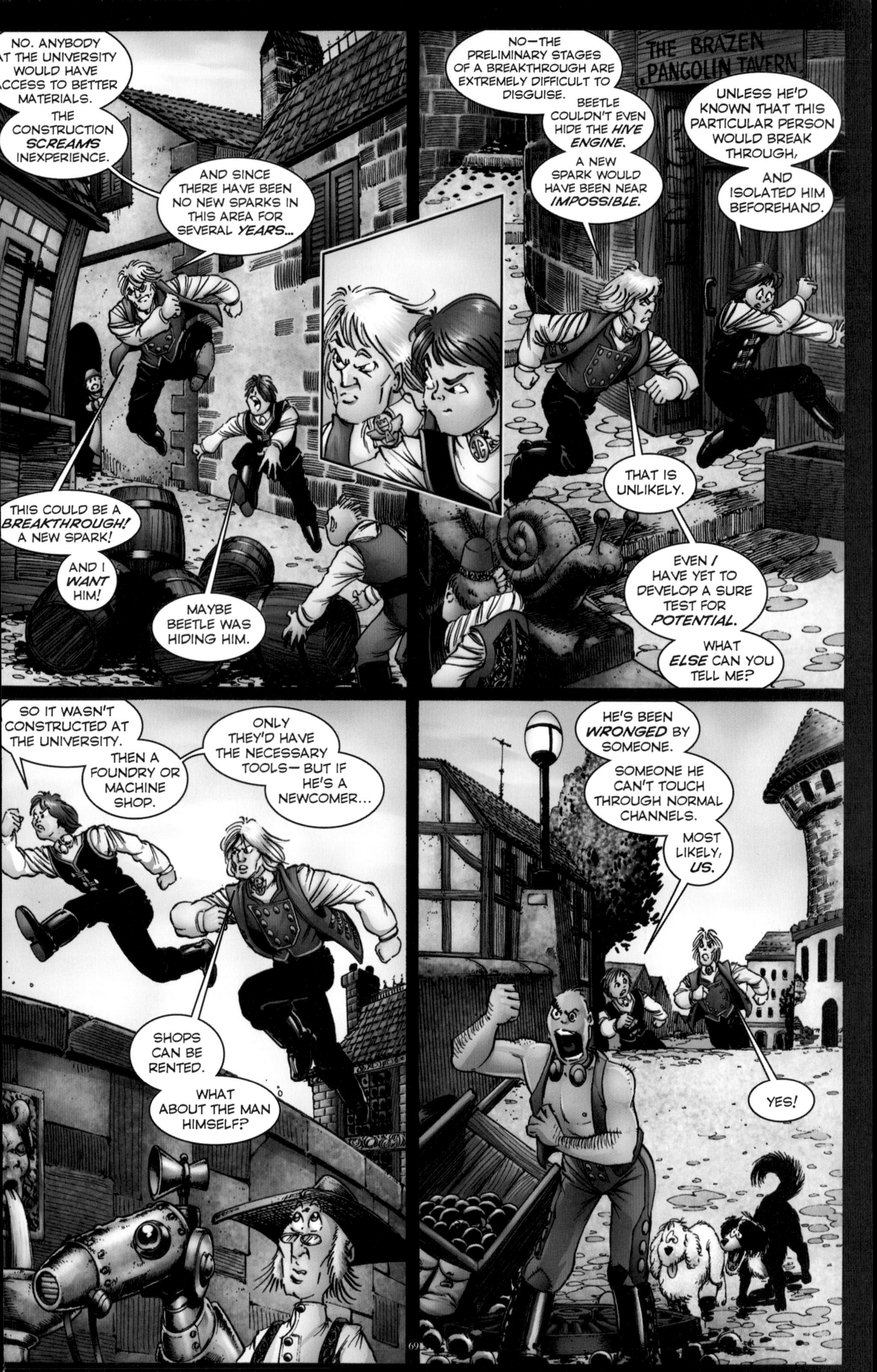
NO. ANYBODY AT THE UNIVERSITY WOULD HAVE ACCESS TO BETTER MATERIALS.
THE CONSTRUCTION SCREAMS INEXPERIENCE.
AND SINCE THERE HAVE BEEN NO NEW SPARKS IN THIS AREA FOR SEVERAL YEARS...
THIS COULD BE A BREAKTHROUGH! A NEW SPARK!
AND I WANT HIM!
MAYBE BEETLE WAS HIDING HIM.
THE BRAZEN PANGOLIN TAVERN
NO—THE PRELIMINARY STAGES OF A BREAKTHROUGH ARE EXTREMELY DIFFICULT TO DISGUISE.
BEETLE COULDN'T EVEN HIDE THE HIVE ENGINE.
A NEW SPARK WOULD HAVE BEEN NEAR IMPOSSIBLE.
UNLESS HE'D KNOWN THAT THIS PARTICULAR PERSON WOULD BREAK THROUGH,
AND ISOLATED HIM BEFOREHAND.
THAT IS UNLIKELY.
EVEN I HAVE YET TO DEVELOP A SURE TEST FOR POTENTIAL.
WHAT ELSE CAN YOU TELL ME?
SO IT WASN'T CONSTRUCTED AT THE UNIVERSITY.
THEN A FOUNDRY OR MACHINE SHOP.
ONLY THEY'D HAVE THE NECESSARY TOOLS—BUT IF HE'S A NEWCOMER...
SHOPS CAN BE RENTED.
WHAT ABOUT THE MAN HIMSELF?
HE'S BEEN WRONGED BY SOMEONE.
SOMEONE HE CAN'T TOUCH THROUGH NORMAL CHANNELS.
MOST LIKELY, US.
YES!

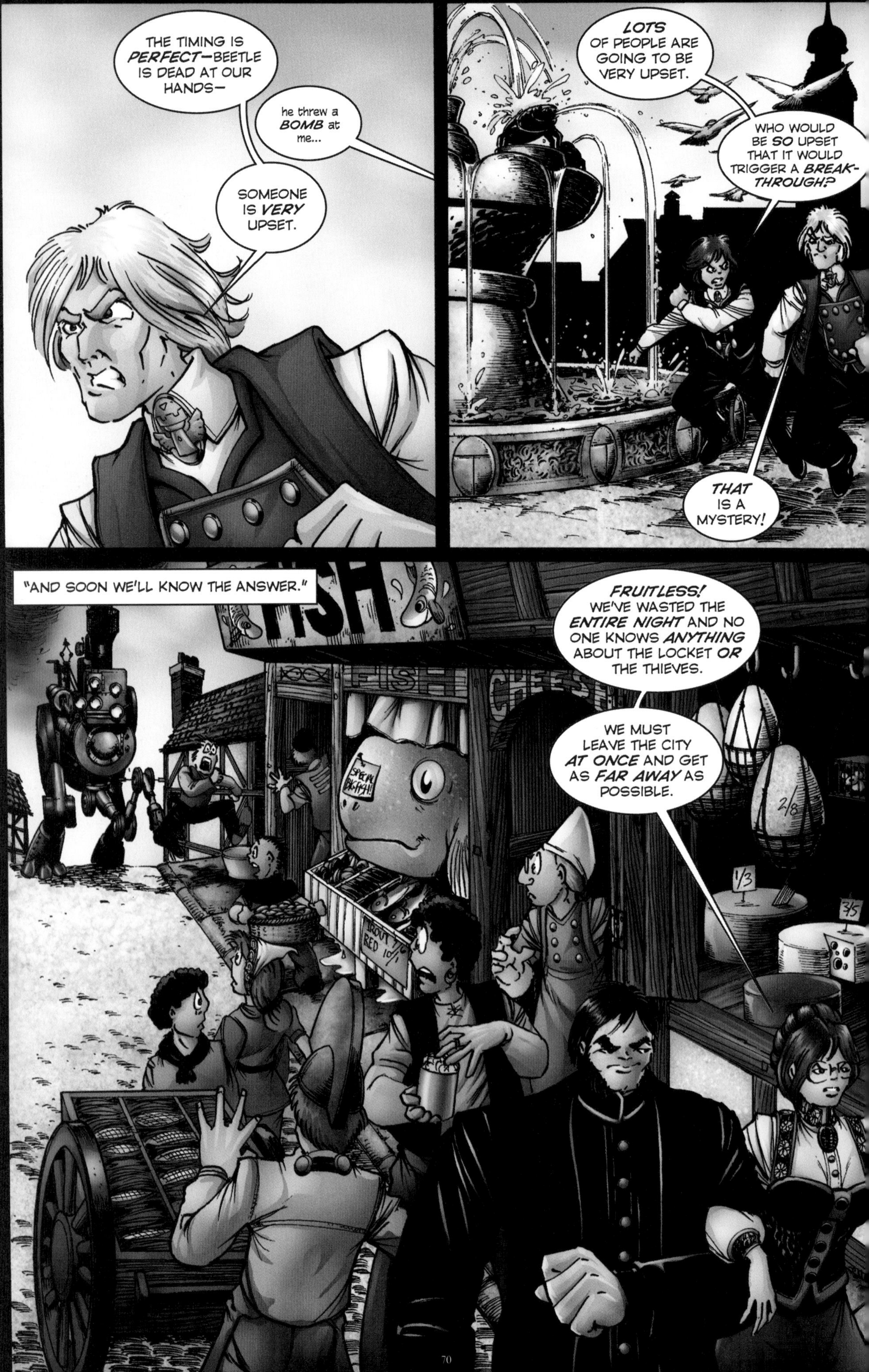
THE TIMING IS PERFECT—BEETLE IS DEAD AT OUR HANDS—
he threw a BOMB at me...
SOMEONE IS VERY UPSET.
LOTS OF PEOPLE ARE GOING TO BE VERY UPSET.
WHO WOULD BE SO UPSET THAT IT WOULD TRIGGER A BREAK-THROUGH?
THAT IS A MYSTERY!
"AND SOON WE'LL KNOW THE ANSWER."
FISH
FRUITLESS! WE'VE WASTED THE ENTIRE NIGHT AND NO ONE KNOWS ANYTHING ABOUT THE LOCKET OR THE THIEVES.
WE MUST LEAVE THE CITY AT ONCE AND GET AS FAR AWAY AS POSSIBLE.

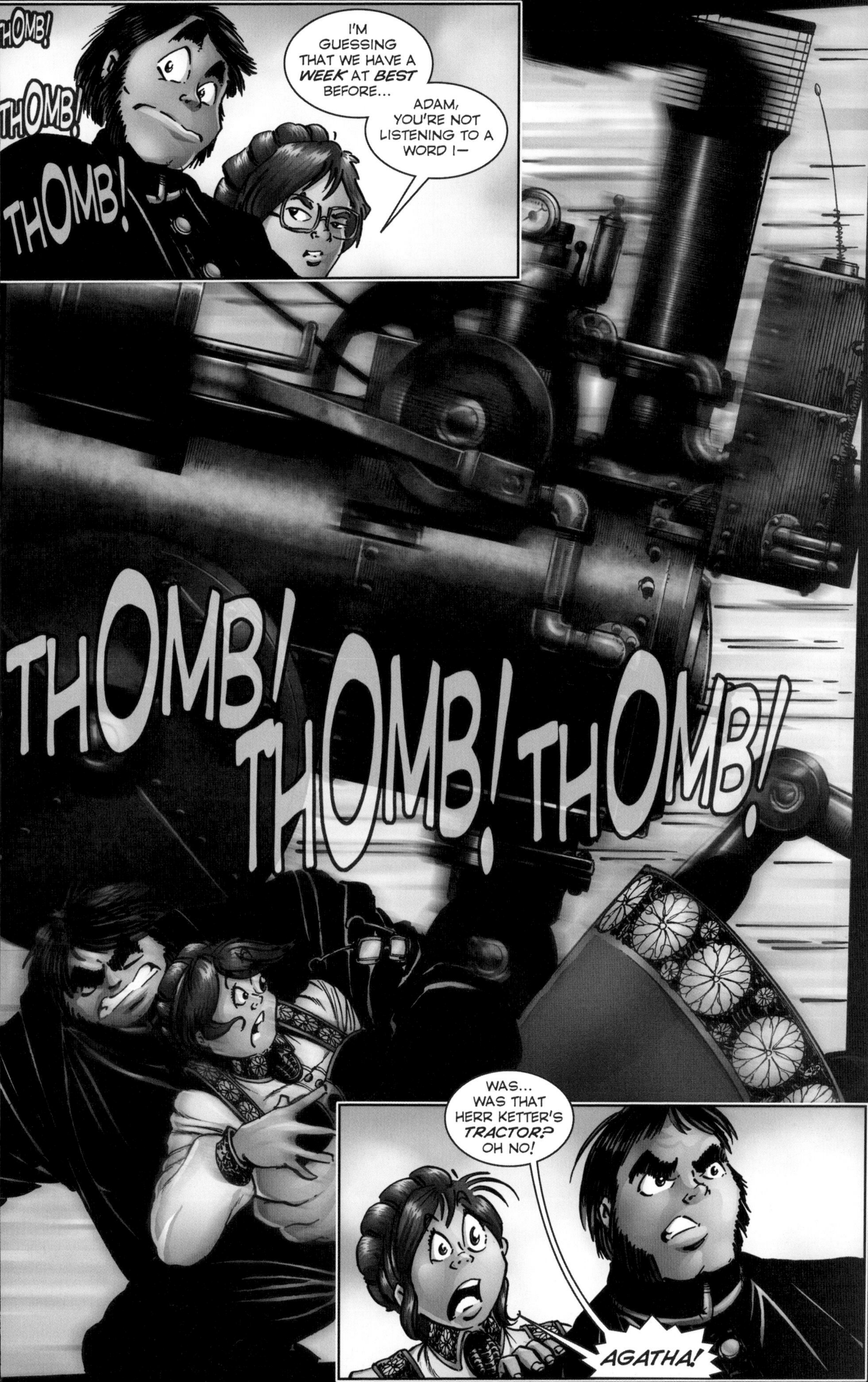
THOMB!
THOMB!
THOMB!
I'M GUESSING THAT WE HAVE A WEEK AT BEST BEFORE...
ADAM, YOU'RE NOT LISTENING TO A WORD !—
THOMB! THOMB! THOMB!
WAS... WAS THAT HERR KETTER'S TRACTOR? OH NO!
AGATHA!

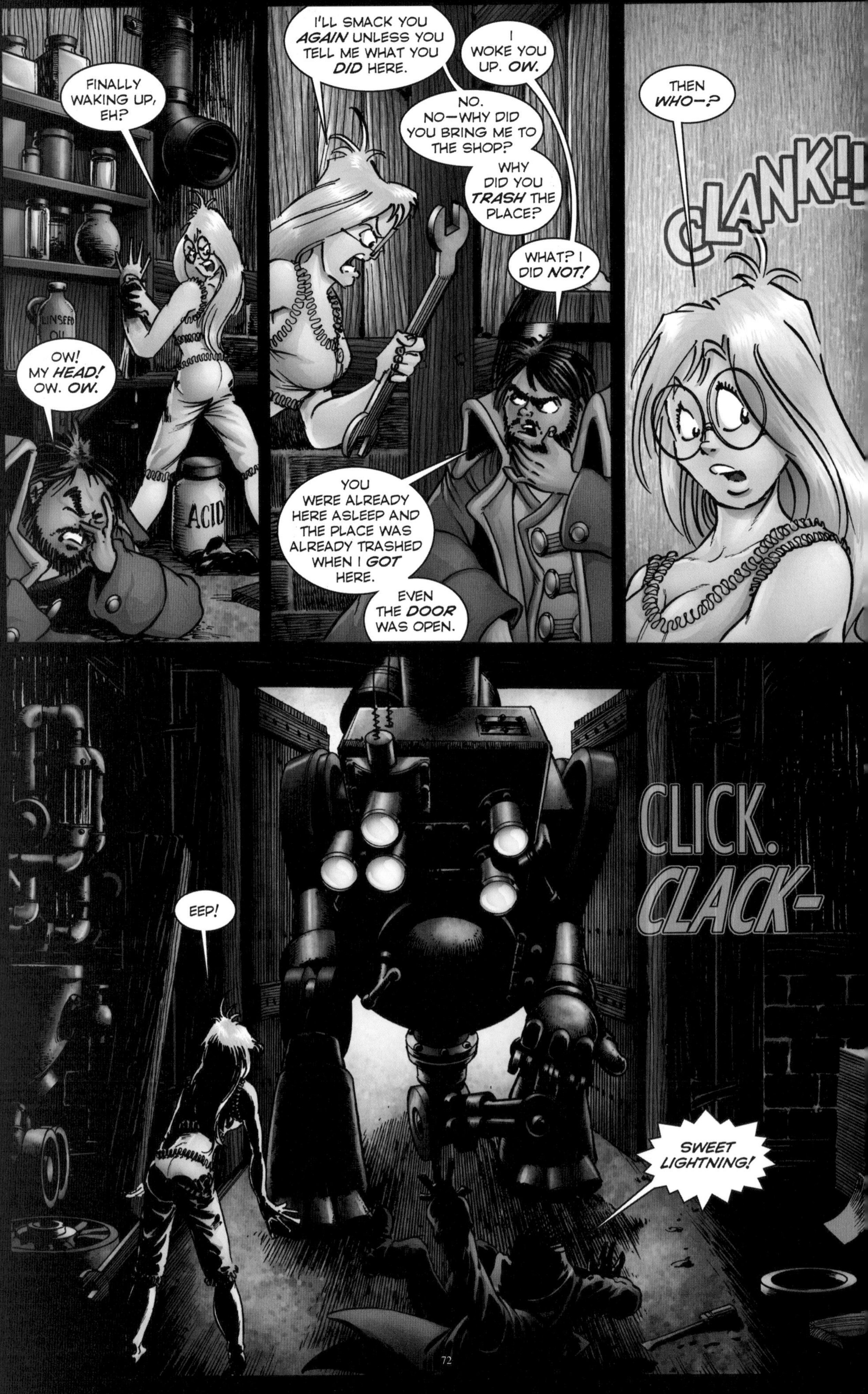
FINALLY WAKING UP, EH?
OW! MY HEAD! OW. OW.
ACID
I'LL SMACK YOU AGAIN UNLESS YOU TELL ME WHAT YOU DID HERE.
I WOKE YOU UP. OW.
NO. NO—WHY DID YOU BRING ME TO THE SHOP?
WHY DID YOU TRASH THE PLACE?
WHAT? I DID NOT!
YOU WERE ALREADY HERE ASLEEP AND THE PLACE WAS ALREADY TRASHED WHEN I GOT HERE.
EVEN THE DOOR WAS OPEN.
THEN WHO—?
CLANK!!
CLICK.
CLACK-
EEP!
SWEET LIGHTNING!

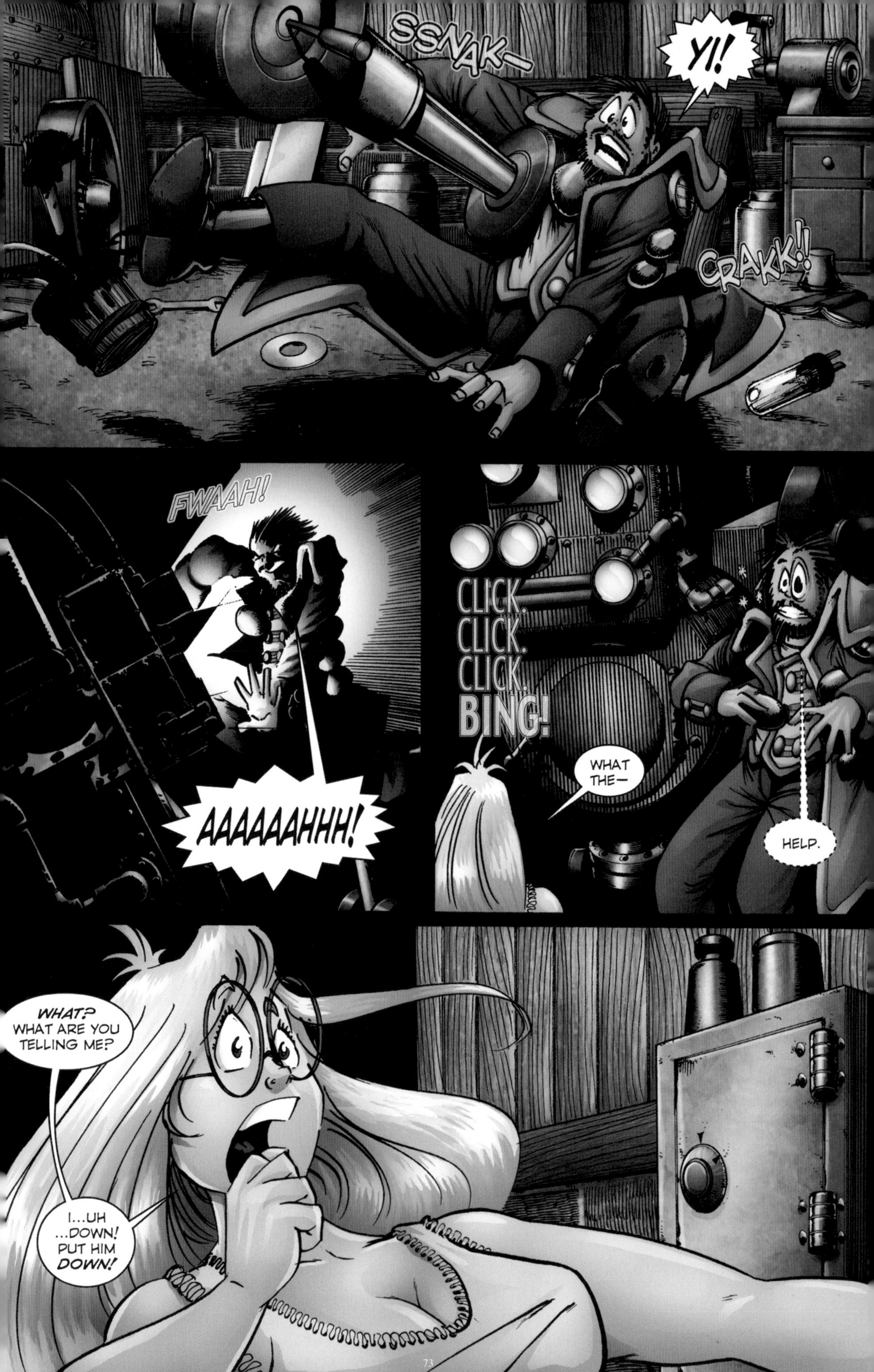
SSNAK—
YI!
CRAKK!!
FWAAH!
AAAAAAHHH!
CLICK.
CLICK.
CLICK.
BING!
WHAT THE—
HELP.
WHAT? WHAT ARE YOU TELLING ME?
I...UH ...DOWN! PUT HIM DOWN!

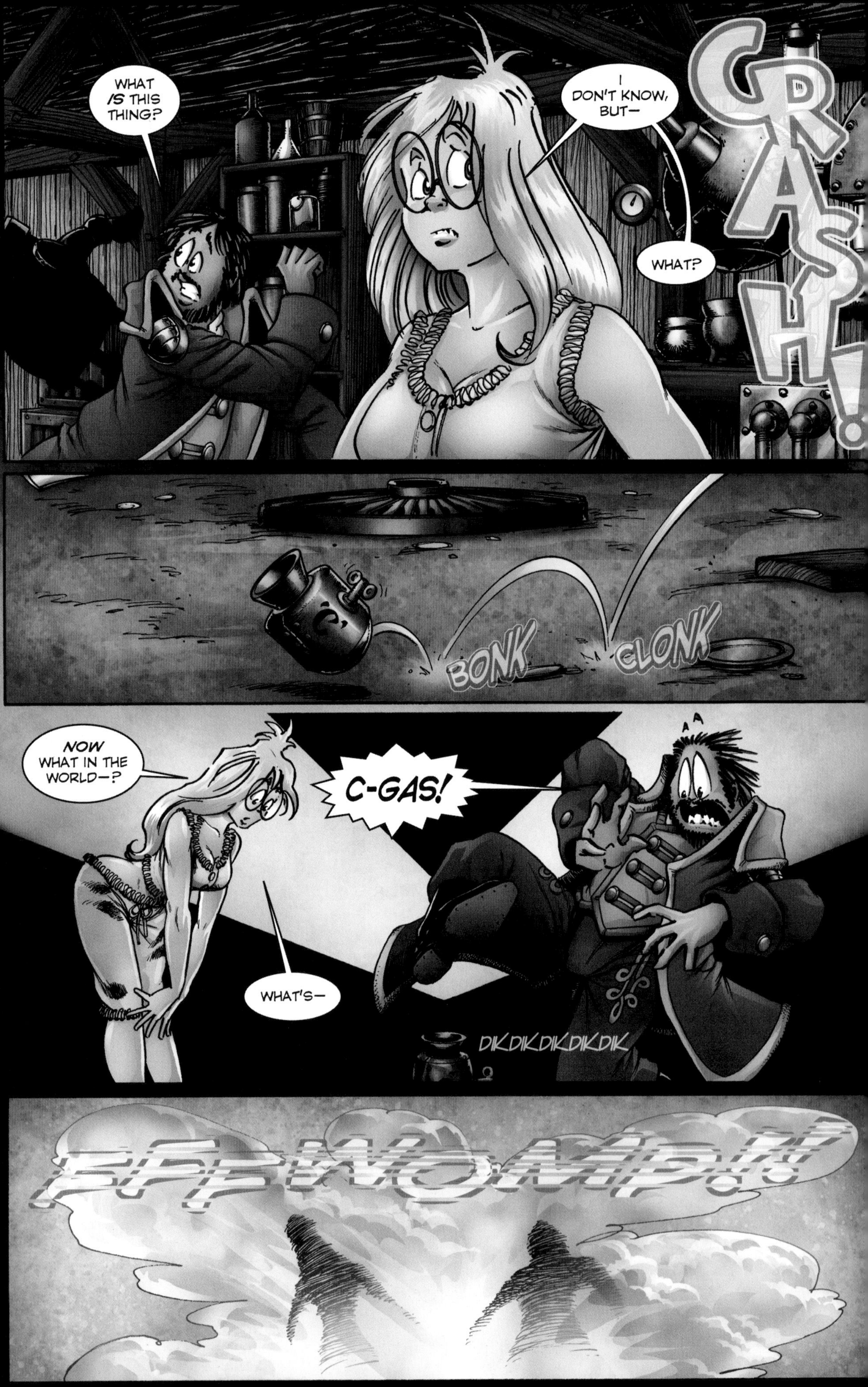
WHAT *IS* THIS THING?
I DON'T KNOW, BUT—
WHAT?
CRASH!
BONK
CLONK
NOW WHAT IN THE WORLD—?
C-GAS!
WHAT'S—
DIKDIKDIKDIKDIK
FFFWOMP!!

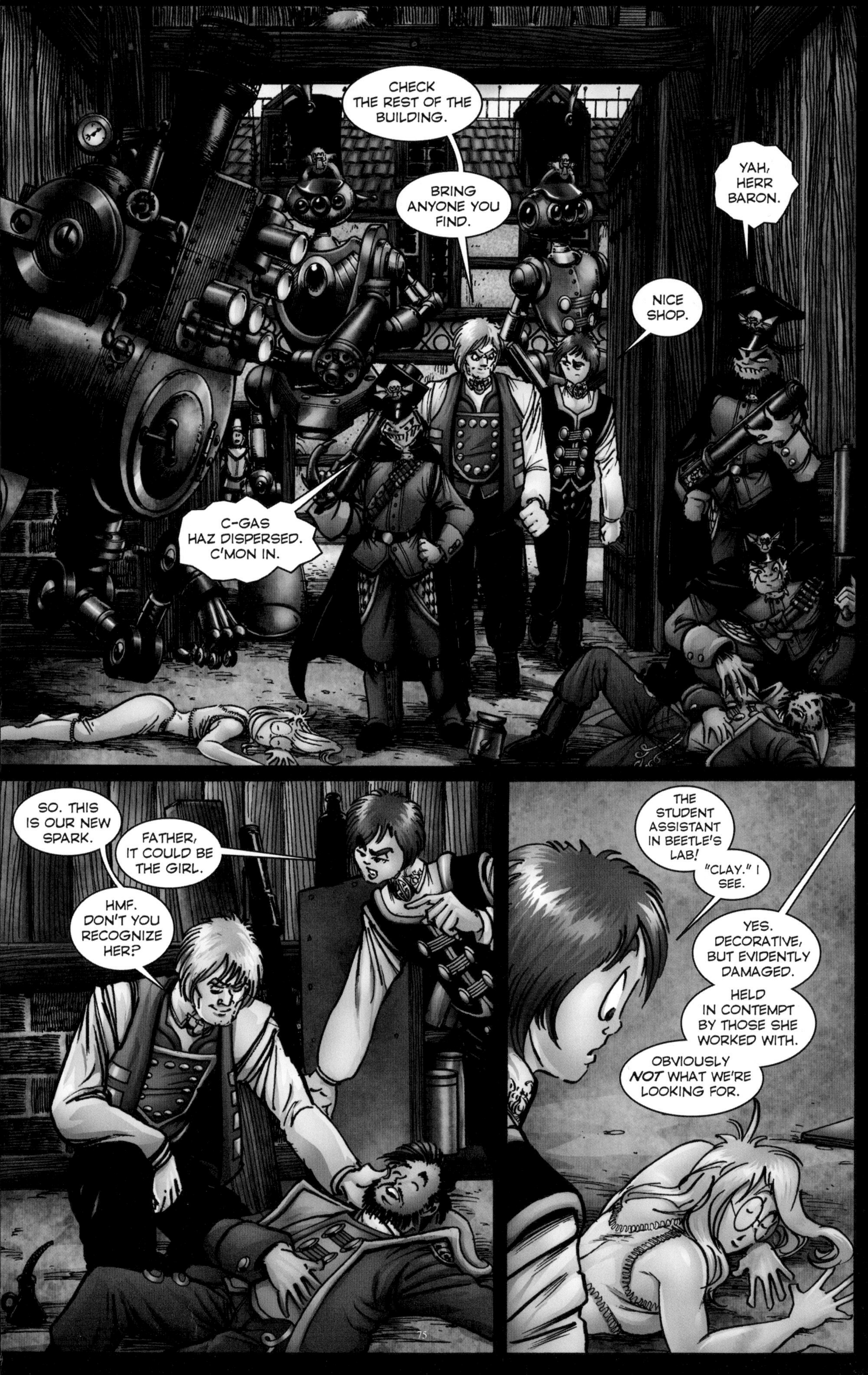
CHECK THE REST OF THE BUILDING.
BRING ANYONE YOU FIND.
YAH, HERR BARON.
NICE SHOP.
C-GAS HAZ DISPERSED. C'MON IN.
SO. THIS IS OUR NEW SPARK.
FATHER, IT COULD BE THE GIRL.
HMF. DON'T YOU RECOGNIZE HER?
THE STUDENT ASSISTANT IN BEETLE'S LAB!
"CLAY." I SEE.
YES. DECORATIVE, BUT EVIDENTLY DAMAGED.
HELD IN CONTEMPT BY THOSE SHE WORKED WITH.
OBVIOUSLY ***NOT*** WHAT WE'RE LOOKING FOR.

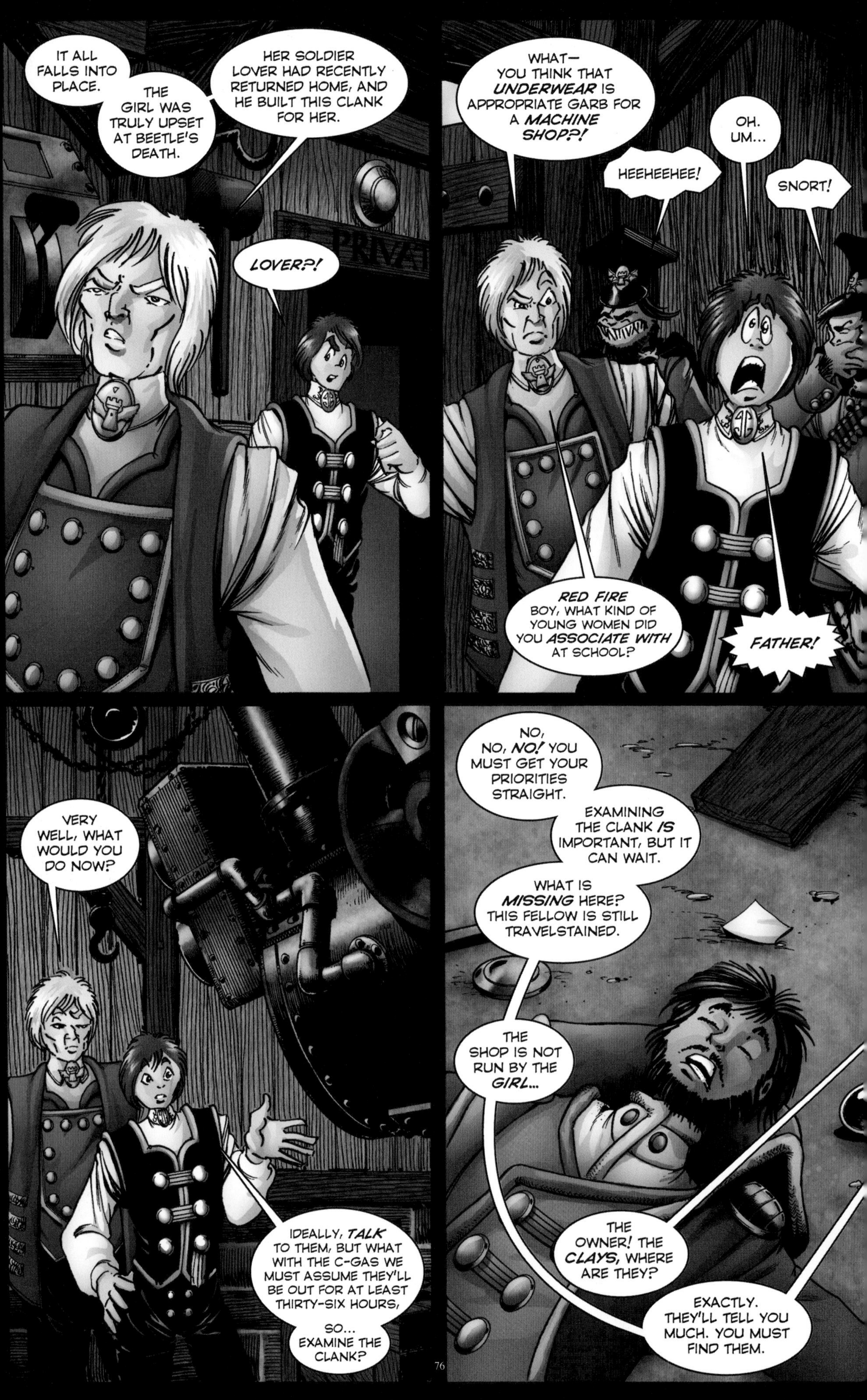

IT ALL FALLS INTO PLACE.
THE GIRL WAS TRULY UPSET AT BEETLE'S DEATH.
HER SOLDIER LOVER HAD RECENTLY RETURNED HOME, AND HE BUILT THIS CLANK FOR HER.
LOVER?!
WHAT— YOU THINK THAT UNDERWEAR IS APPROPRIATE GARB FOR A MACHINE SHOP?!
HEEHEEHEE!
OH. UM...
SNORT!
RED FIRE BOY, WHAT KIND OF YOUNG WOMEN DID YOU ASSOCIATE WITH AT SCHOOL?
FATHER!
VERY WELL, WHAT WOULD YOU DO NOW?
IDEALLY, TALK TO THEM, BUT WHAT WITH THE C-GAS WE MUST ASSUME THEY'LL BE OUT FOR AT LEAST THIRTY-SIX HOURS,
SO... EXAMINE THE CLANK?
NO, NO, NO! YOU MUST GET YOUR PRIORITIES STRAIGHT.
EXAMINING THE CLANK IS IMPORTANT, BUT IT CAN WAIT.
WHAT IS MISSING HERE? THIS FELLOW IS STILL TRAVELSTAINED.
THE SHOP IS NOT RUN BY THE GIRL...
THE OWNER! THE CLAYS, WHERE ARE THEY?
EXACTLY. THEY'LL TELL YOU MUCH. YOU MUST FIND THEM.

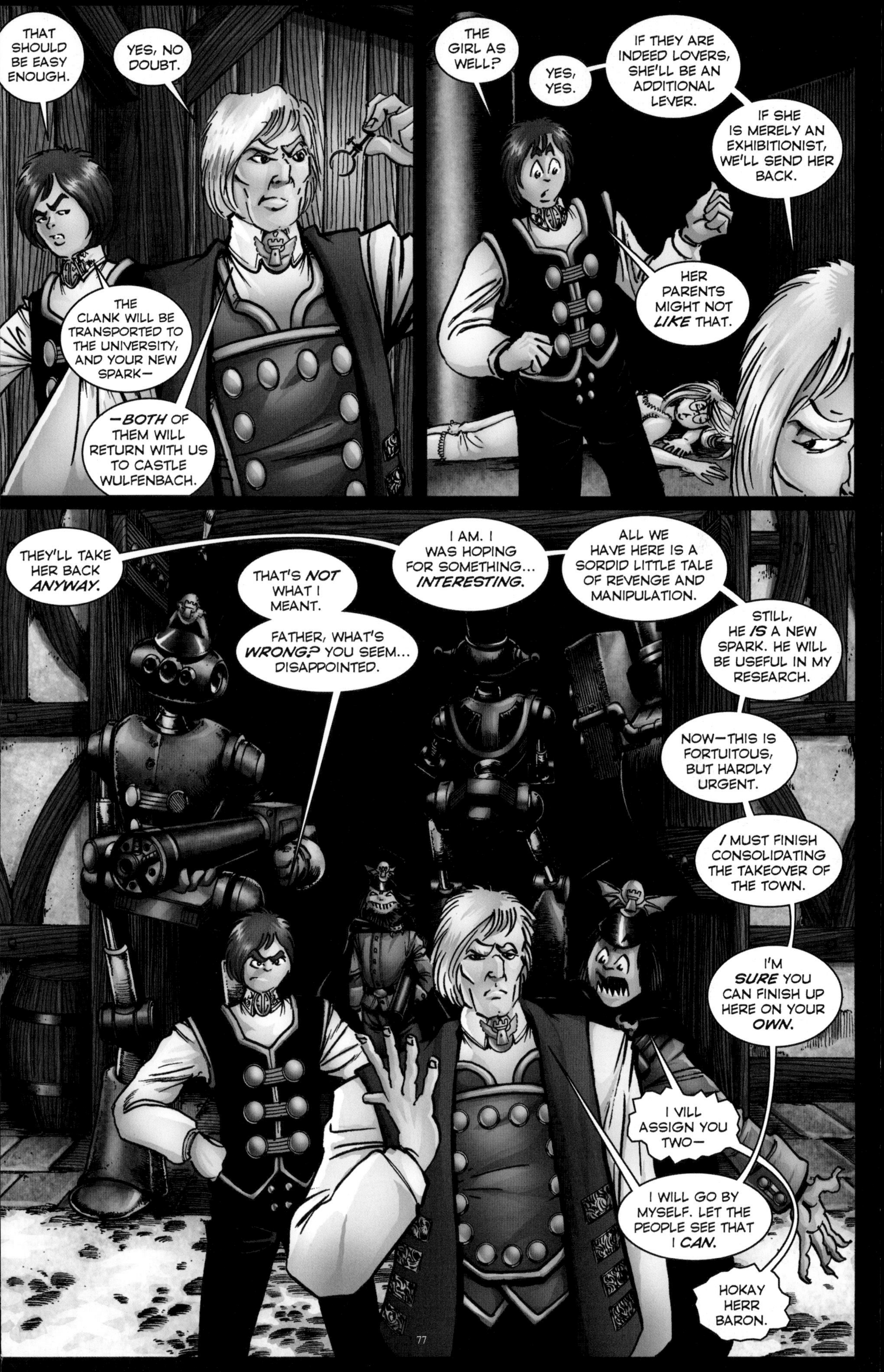
THAT SHOULD BE EASY ENOUGH.
YES, NO DOUBT.
THE CLANK WILL BE TRANSPORTED TO THE UNIVERSITY, AND YOUR NEW SPARK—
—*BOTH* OF THEM WILL RETURN WITH US TO CASTLE WULFENBACH.
THE GIRL AS WELL?
YES, YES.
IF THEY ARE INDEED LOVERS, SHE'LL BE AN ADDITIONAL LEVER.
IF SHE IS MERELY AN EXHIBITIONIST, WE'LL SEND HER BACK.
HER PARENTS MIGHT NOT *LIKE* THAT.
THEY'LL TAKE HER BACK *ANYWAY*.
THAT'S *NOT* WHAT I MEANT.
FATHER, WHAT'S *WRONG?* YOU SEEM... DISAPPOINTED.
I AM. I WAS HOPING FOR SOMETHING... *INTERESTING*.
ALL WE HAVE HERE IS A SORDID LITTLE TALE OF REVENGE AND MANIPULATION.
STILL, HE *IS* A NEW SPARK. HE WILL BE USEFUL IN MY RESEARCH.
NOW—THIS IS FORTUITOUS, BUT HARDLY URGENT.
I MUST FINISH CONSOLIDATING THE TAKEOVER OF THE TOWN.
I'M *SURE* YOU CAN FINISH UP HERE ON YOUR *OWN*.
I VILL ASSIGN YOU TWO—
I WILL GO BY MYSELF. LET THE PEOPLE SEE THAT I *CAN*.
HOKAY HERR BARON.

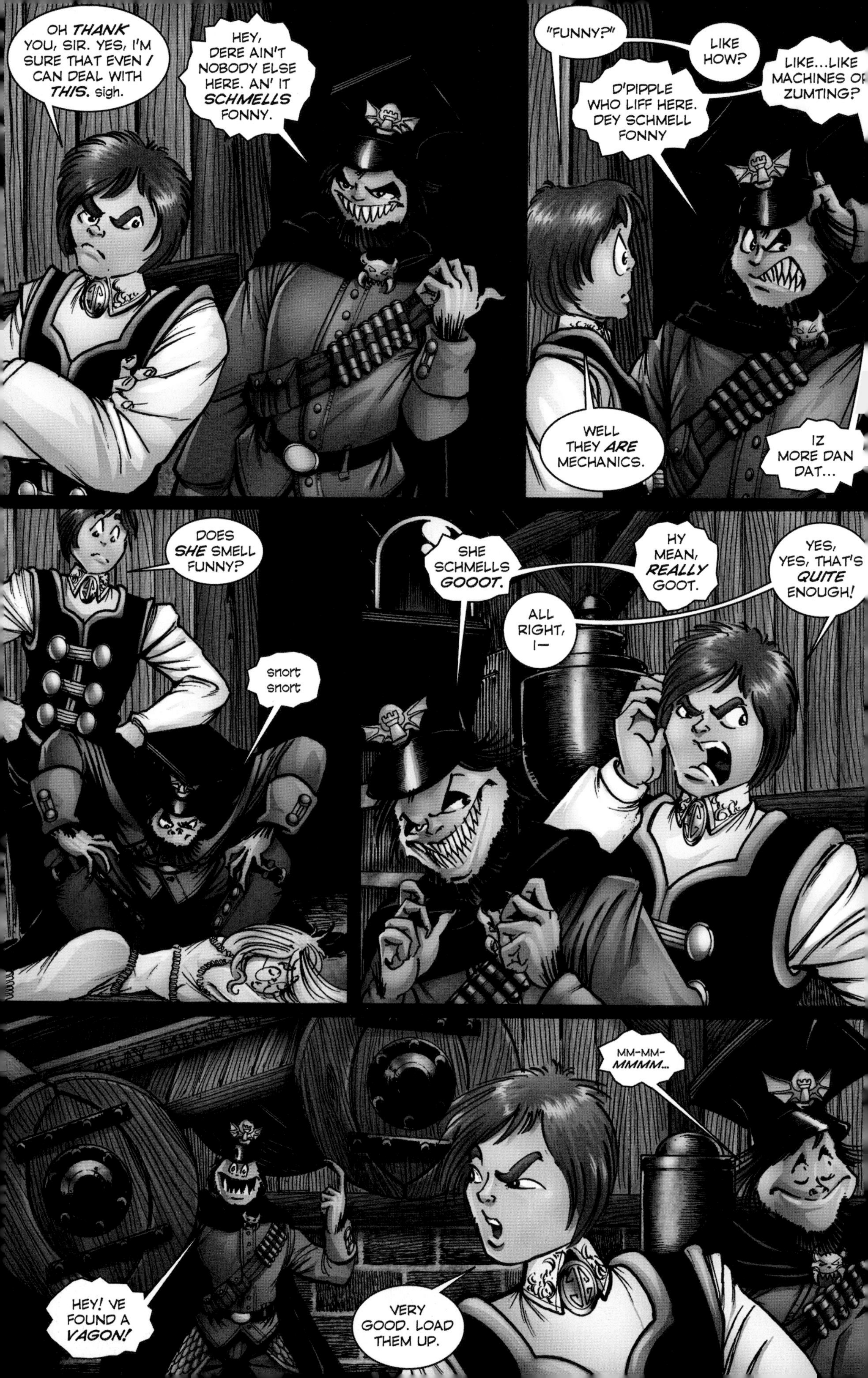
OH THANK YOU, SIR. YES, I'M SURE THAT EVEN I CAN DEAL WITH THIS. sigh.
HEY, DERE AIN'T NOBODY ELSE HERE. AN' IT SCHMELLS FONNY.
"FUNNY?"
LIKE HOW?
D'PIPPLE WHO LIFF HERE. DEY SCHMELL FONNY
LIKE...LIKE MACHINES OR ZUMTING?
WELL THEY ARE MECHANICS.
IZ MORE DAN DAT...
DOES SHE SMELL FUNNY?
snort snort
SHE SCHMELLS GOOOT.
HY MEAN, REALLY GOOT.
ALL RIGHT, I—
YES, YES, THAT'S QUITE ENOUGH!
MM-MM-MMMM...
HEY! VE FOUND A VAGON!
VERY GOOD. LOAD THEM UP.

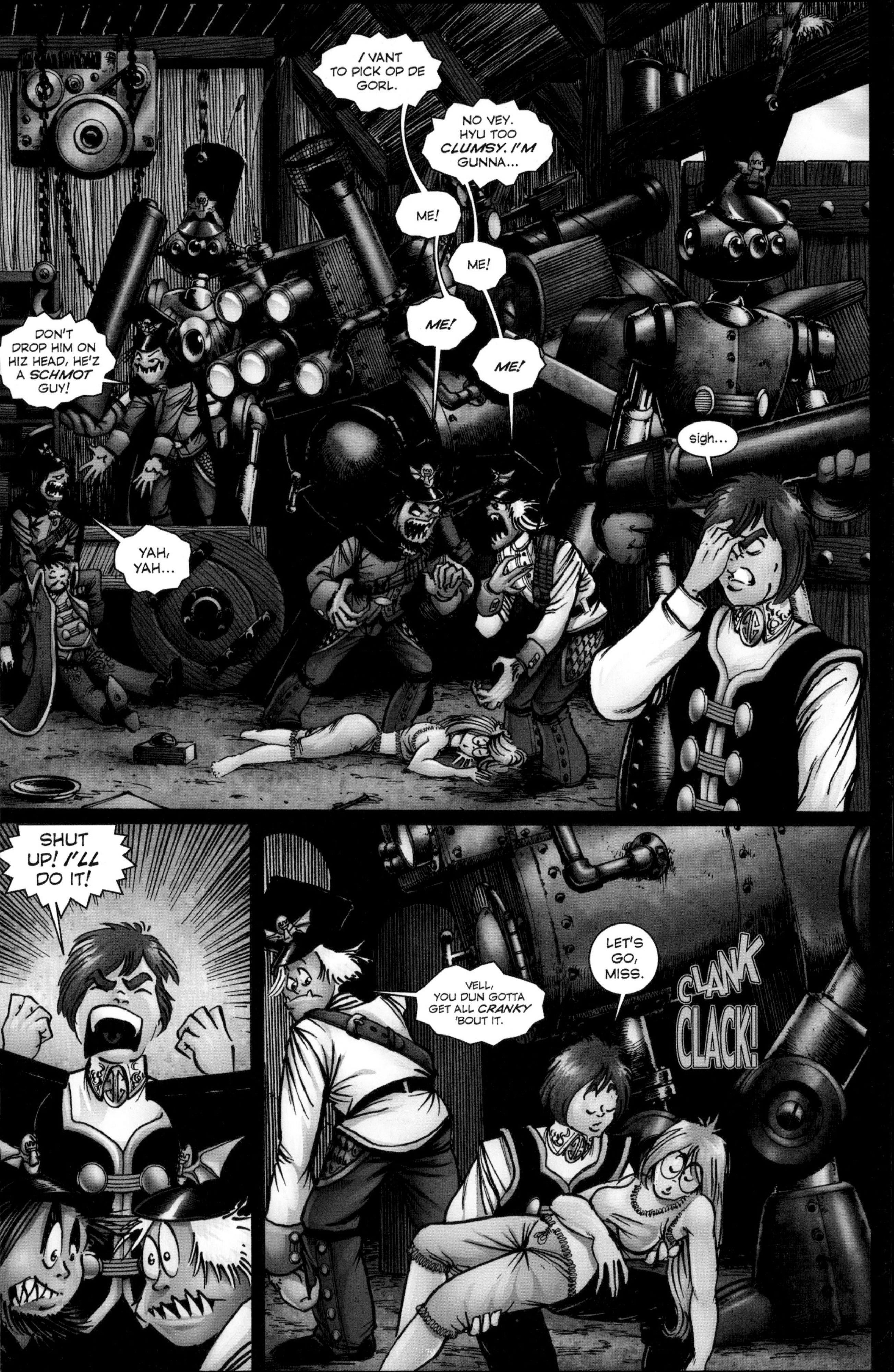
I VANT TO PICK OP DE GORL.
NO VEY. HYU TOO CLUMSY. I'M GUNNA...
ME!
ME!
ME!
ME!
DON'T DROP HIM ON HIZ HEAD, HE'Z A SCHMOT GUY!
YAH, YAH...
sigh...
SHUT UP! I'LL DO IT!
VELL, YOU DUN GOTTA GET ALL CRANKY 'BOUT IT.
LET'S GO, MISS.
CLANK
CLACK!

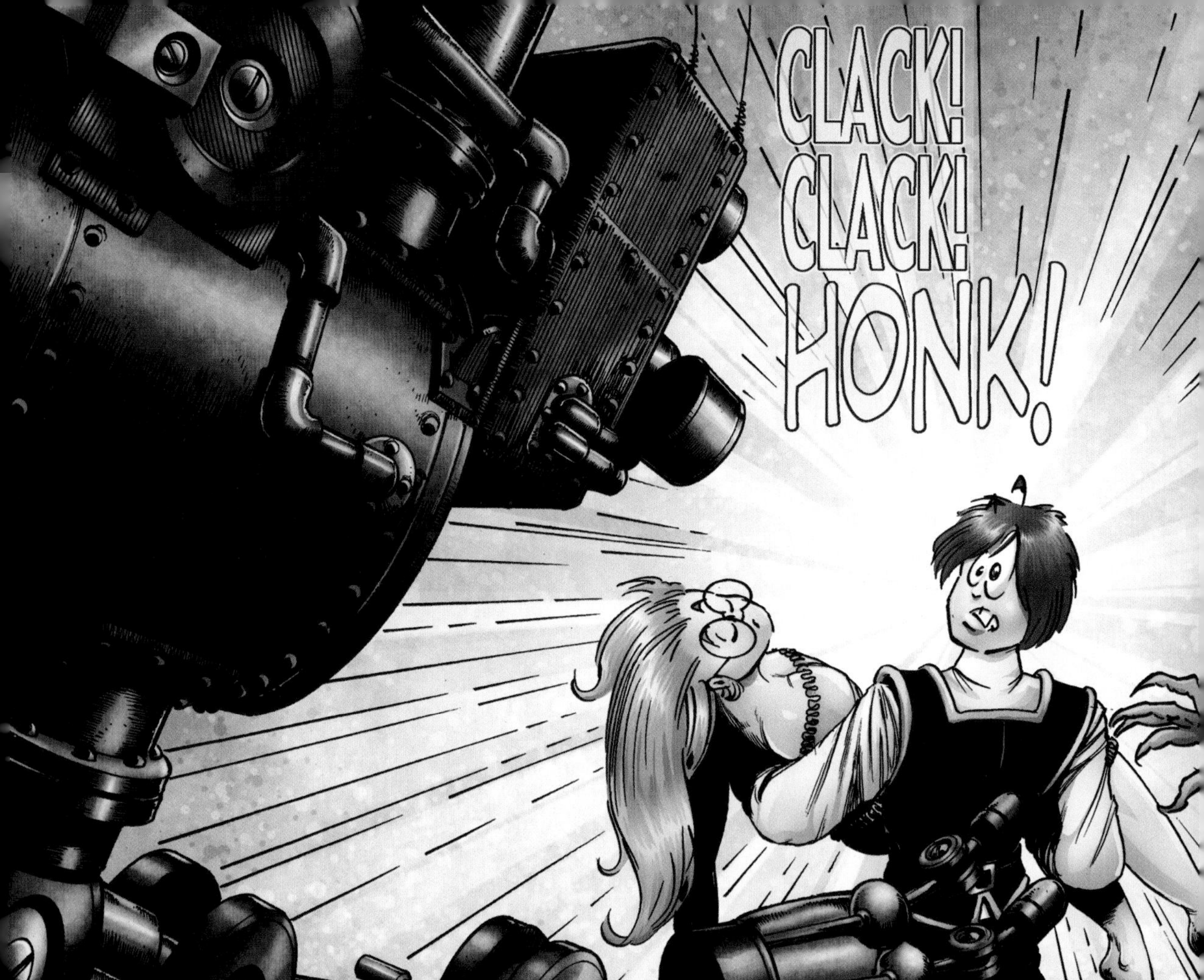
CLACK!
CLACK!
HONK!
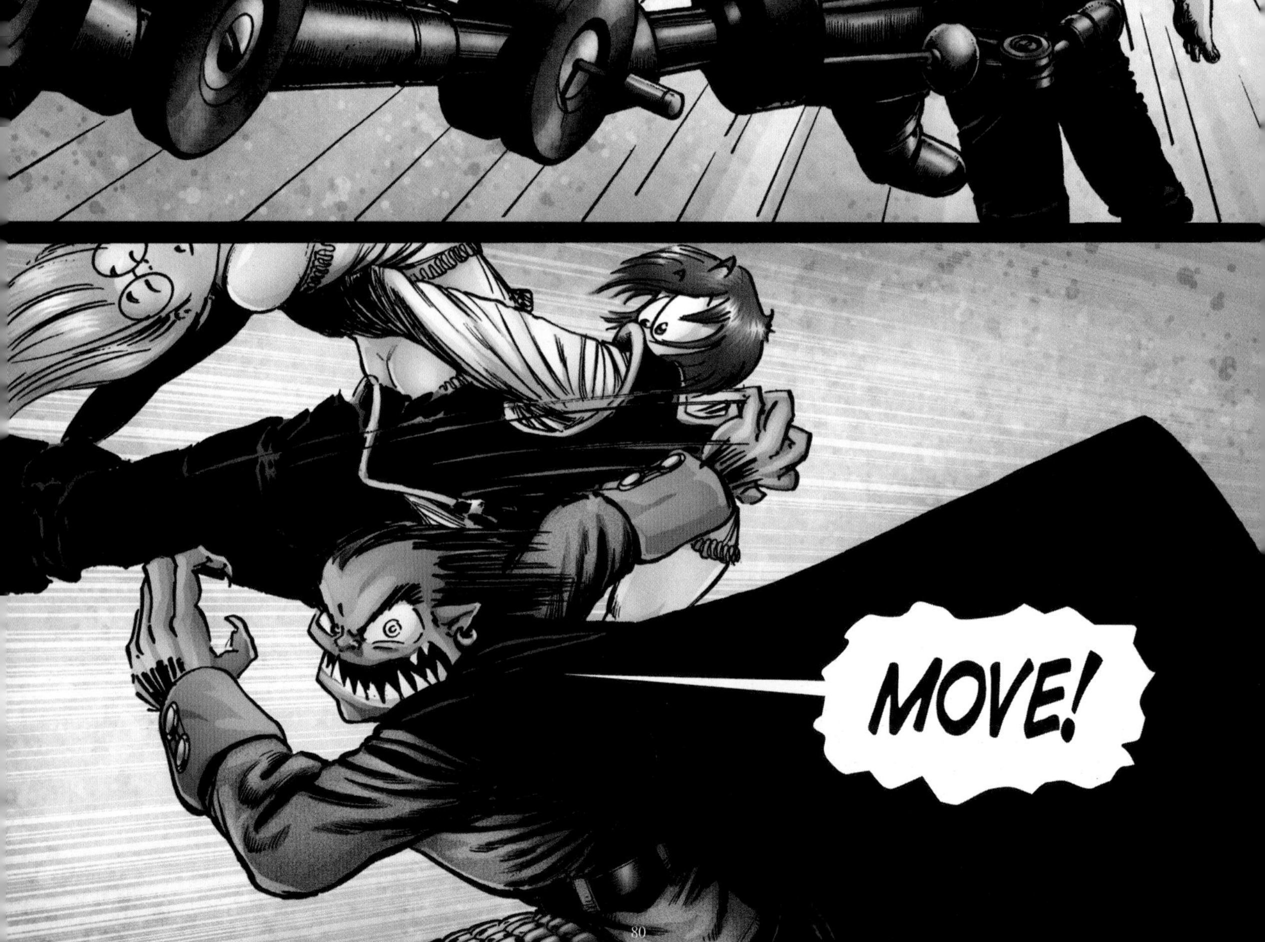
MOVE!

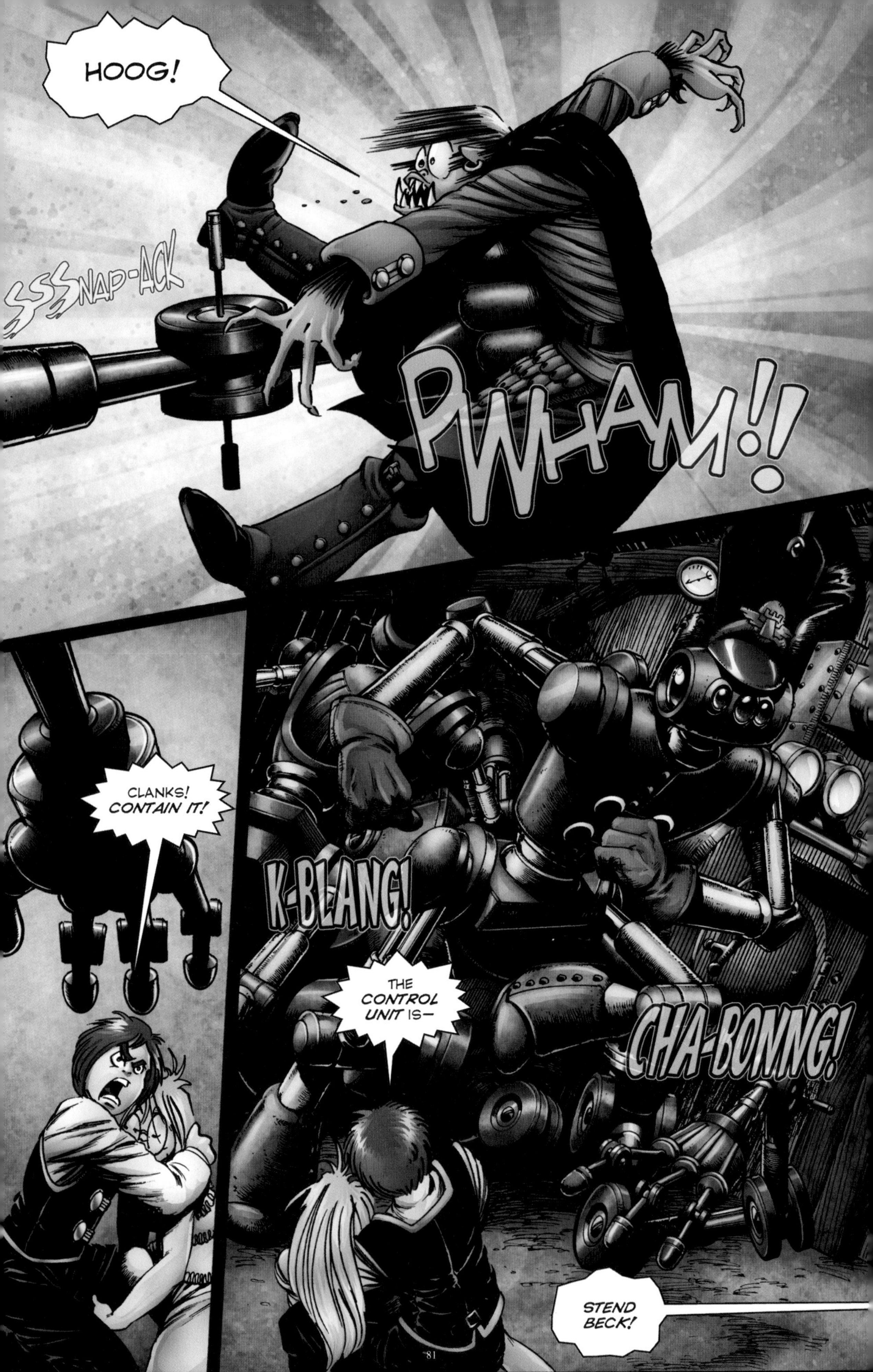
HOOG!
SSSNAP-ACK
PWHAM!!
CLANKS! CONTAIN IT!
K-BLANG!
THE CONTROL UNIT IS—
CHA-BONNG!
STEND BECK!

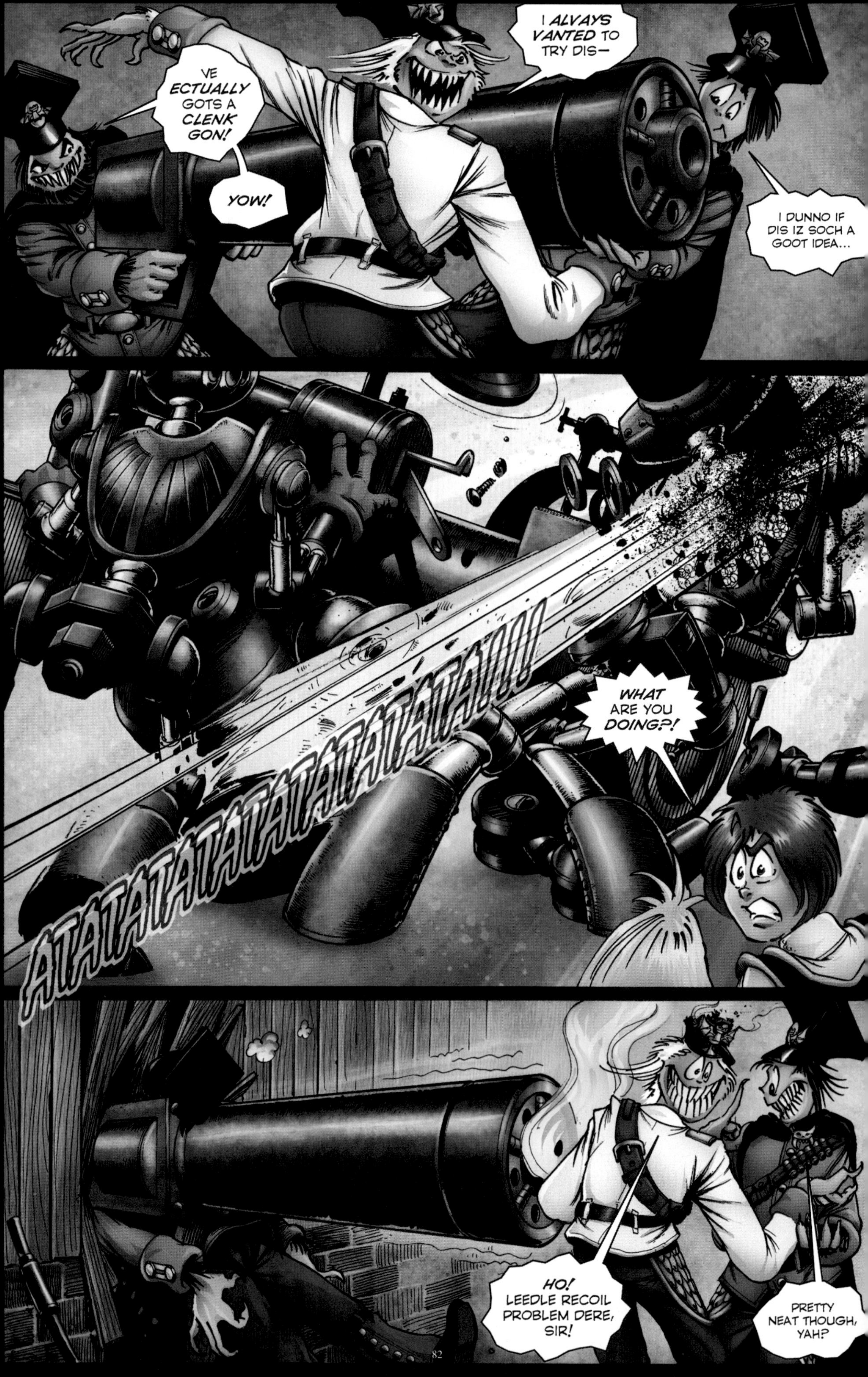
VE *ECTUALLY* GOTS A *CLENK GON!*
YOW!
I *ALVAYS VANTED* TO TRY DIS—
I DUNNO IF DIS IZ SOCH A GOOT IDEA...
WHAT ARE YOU *DOING?!*
HO! LEEDLE RECOIL PROBLEM DERE, *SIR!*
PRETTY NEAT THOUGH, YAH?

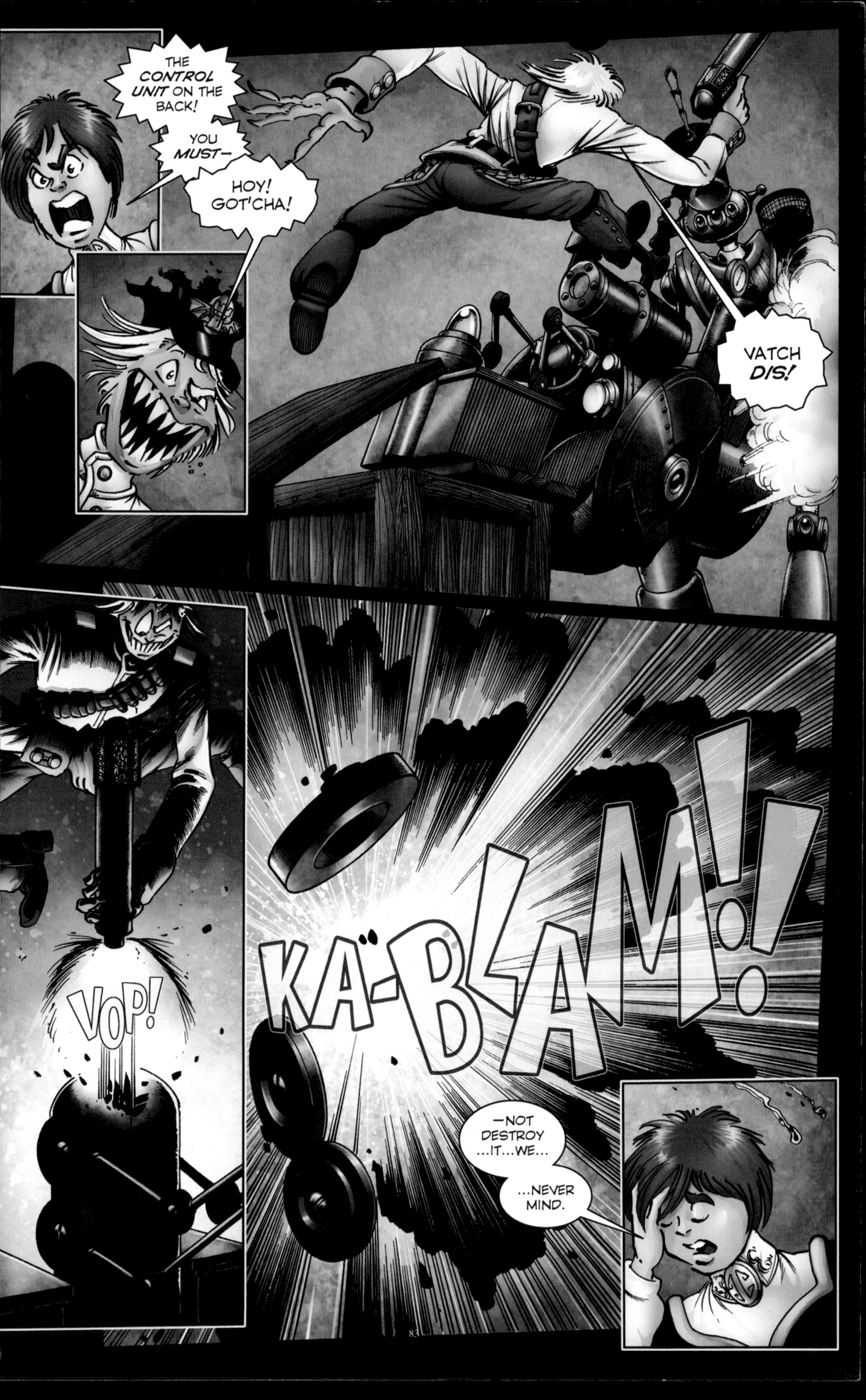
THE CONTROL UNIT ON THE BACK!
YOU MUST—
HOY! GOT'CHA!
VATCH DIS!
VOP!
KA-BLAM!!
—NOT DESTROY ...IT...WE...
...NEVER MIND.

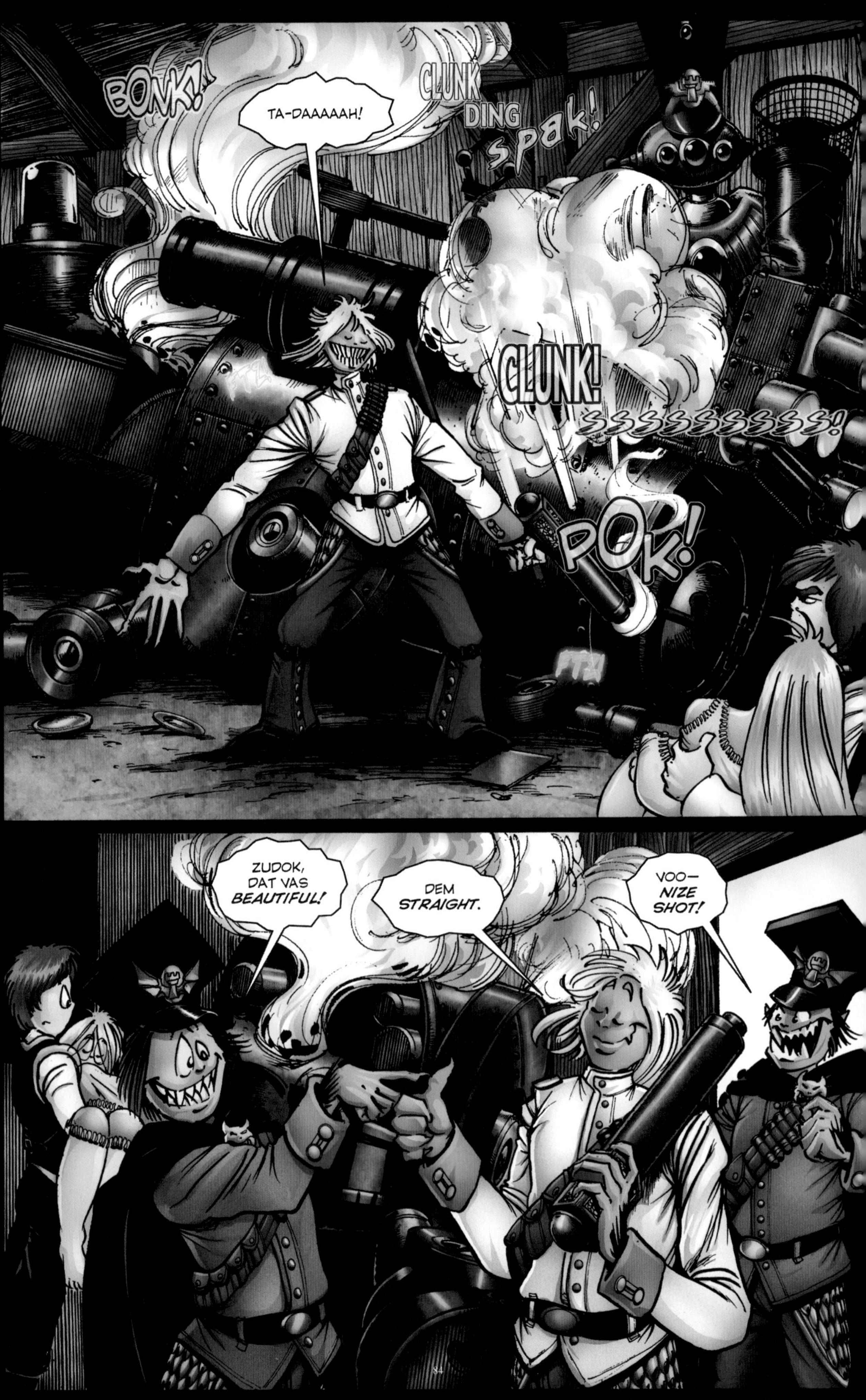
BONK!
TA-DAAAAAH!
CLUNK
DING
spak!
CLUNK!
SSSSSSSSSS!
POK!
ZUDOK, DAT VAS BEAUTIFUL!
DEM STRAIGHT.
VOO-NIZE SHOT!

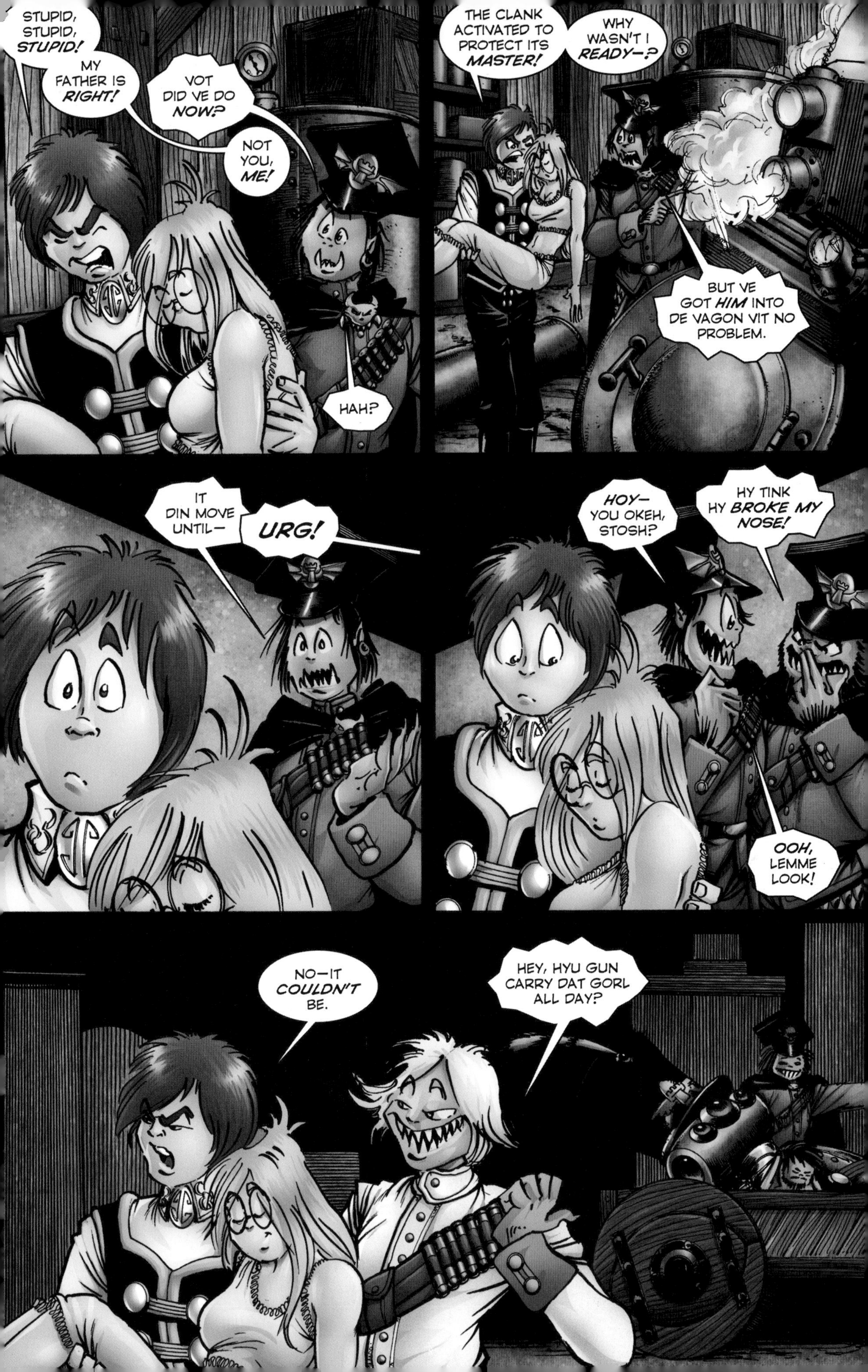
STUPID, STUPID, *STUPID!*
MY FATHER IS *RIGHT!*
VOT DID VE DO *NOW?*
NOT YOU, *ME!*
HAH?
THE CLANK ACTIVATED TO PROTECT ITS *MASTER!*
WHY WASN'T I *READY—?*
BUT VE GOT *HIM* INTO DE VAGON VIT NO PROBLEM.
IT DIN MOVE UNTIL—
URG!
HOY— YOU OKEH, STOSH?
HY TINK HY *BROKE MY NOSE!*
OOH, LEMME LOOK!
NO—IT *COULDN'T* BE.
HEY, HYU GUN CARRY DAT GORL ALL DAY?

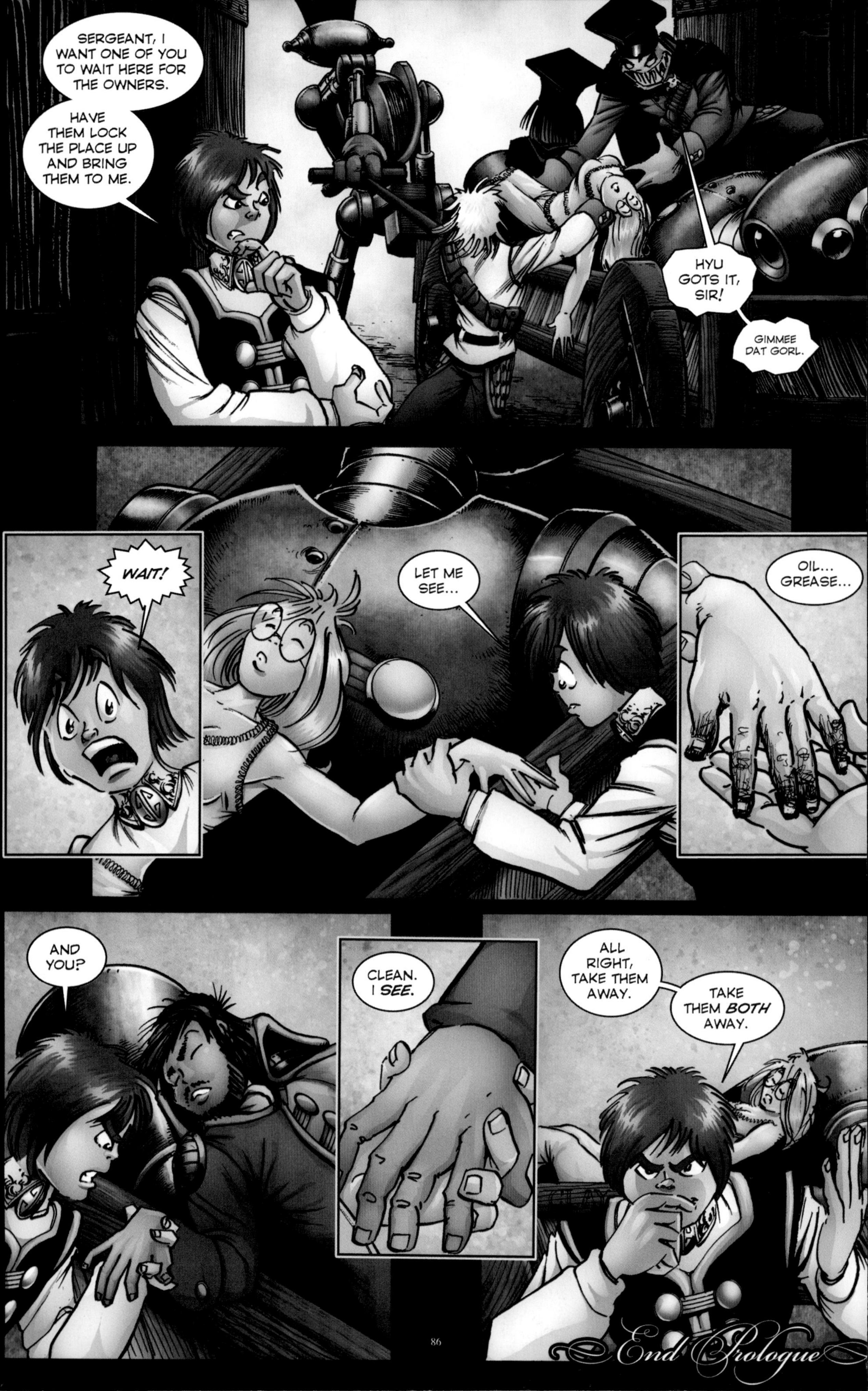
SERGEANT, I WANT ONE OF YOU TO WAIT HERE FOR THE OWNERS.
HAVE THEM LOCK THE PLACE UP AND BRING THEM TO ME.
HYU GOTS IT, SIR!
GIMMEE DAT GORL.
WAIT!
LET ME SEE...
OIL... GREASE...
AND YOU?
CLEAN. I SEE.
ALL RIGHT, TAKE THEM AWAY.
TAKE THEM BOTH AWAY.
End Prologue

TO BE CONTINUED IN:

GIRL GENIUS Book Two

AGATHA HETERODYNE & THE AIRSHIP CITY

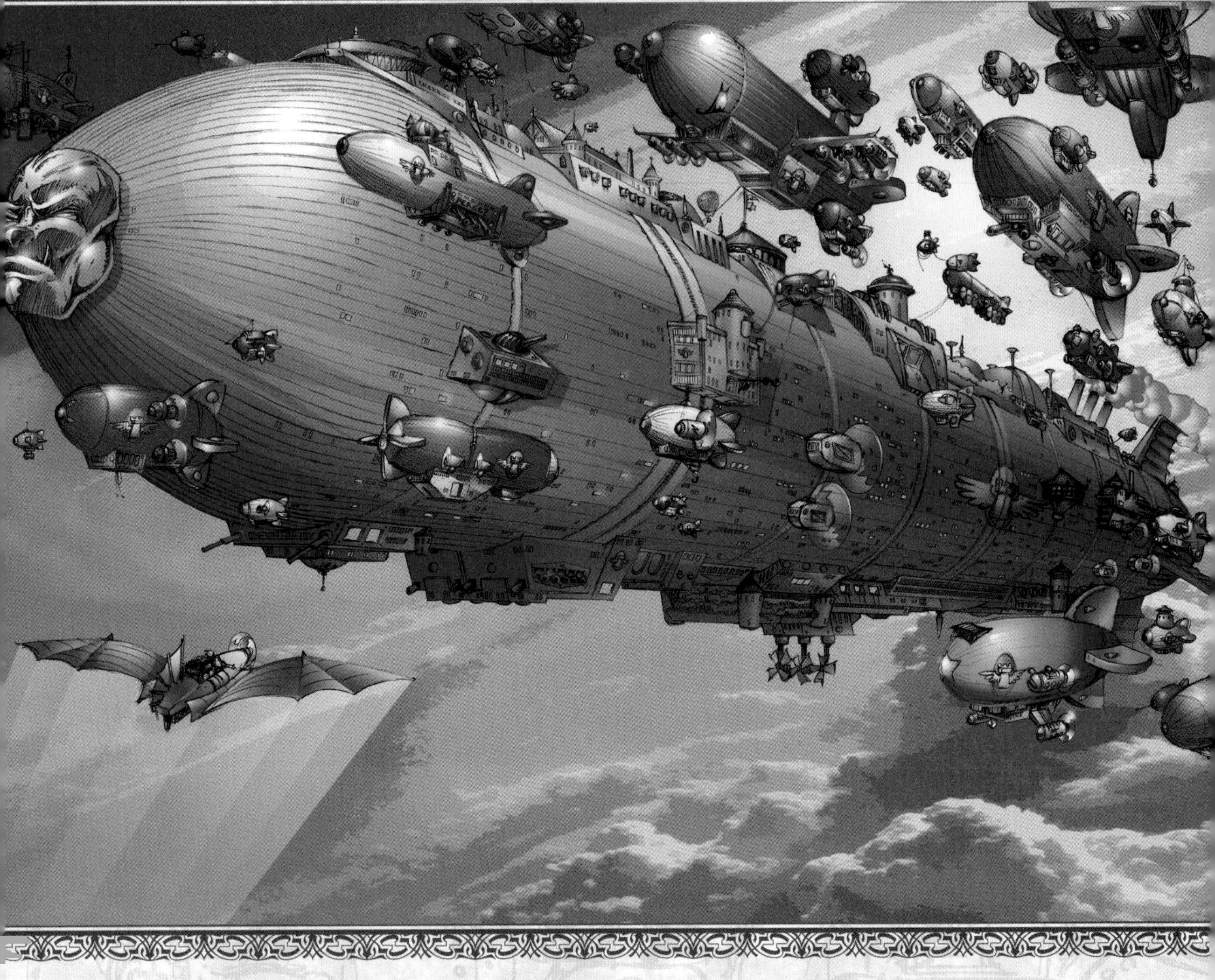

KEEP UP WITH THE STORY! READ NEW COMICS THREE TIMES A WEEK AT:

WWW.GIRLGENIUS.NET

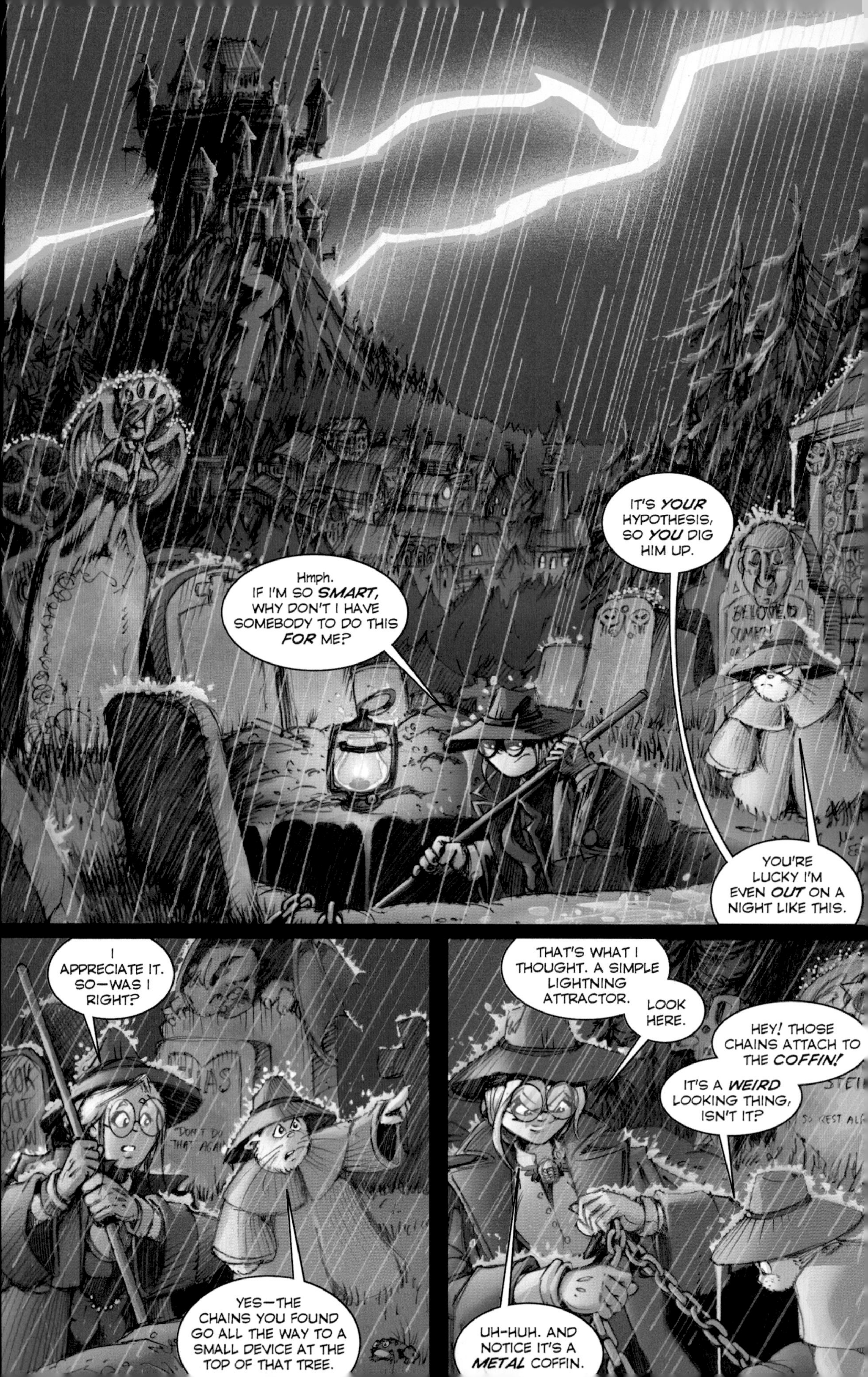

Hmph. IF I'M SO **SMART,** WHY DON'T I HAVE SOMEBODY TO DO THIS **FOR** ME?
IT'S **YOUR** HYPOTHESIS, SO **YOU** DIG HIM UP.
YOU'RE LUCKY I'M EVEN **OUT** ON A NIGHT LIKE THIS.
I APPRECIATE IT. SO—WAS I RIGHT?
YES—THE CHAINS YOU FOUND GO ALL THE WAY TO A SMALL DEVICE AT THE TOP OF THAT TREE.
THAT'S WHAT I THOUGHT. A SIMPLE LIGHTNING ATTRACTOR.
LOOK HERE.
HEY! THOSE CHAINS ATTACH TO THE **COFFIN!**
IT'S A **WEIRD** LOOKING THING, ISN'T IT?
UH-HUH. AND NOTICE IT'S A **METAL** COFFIN.

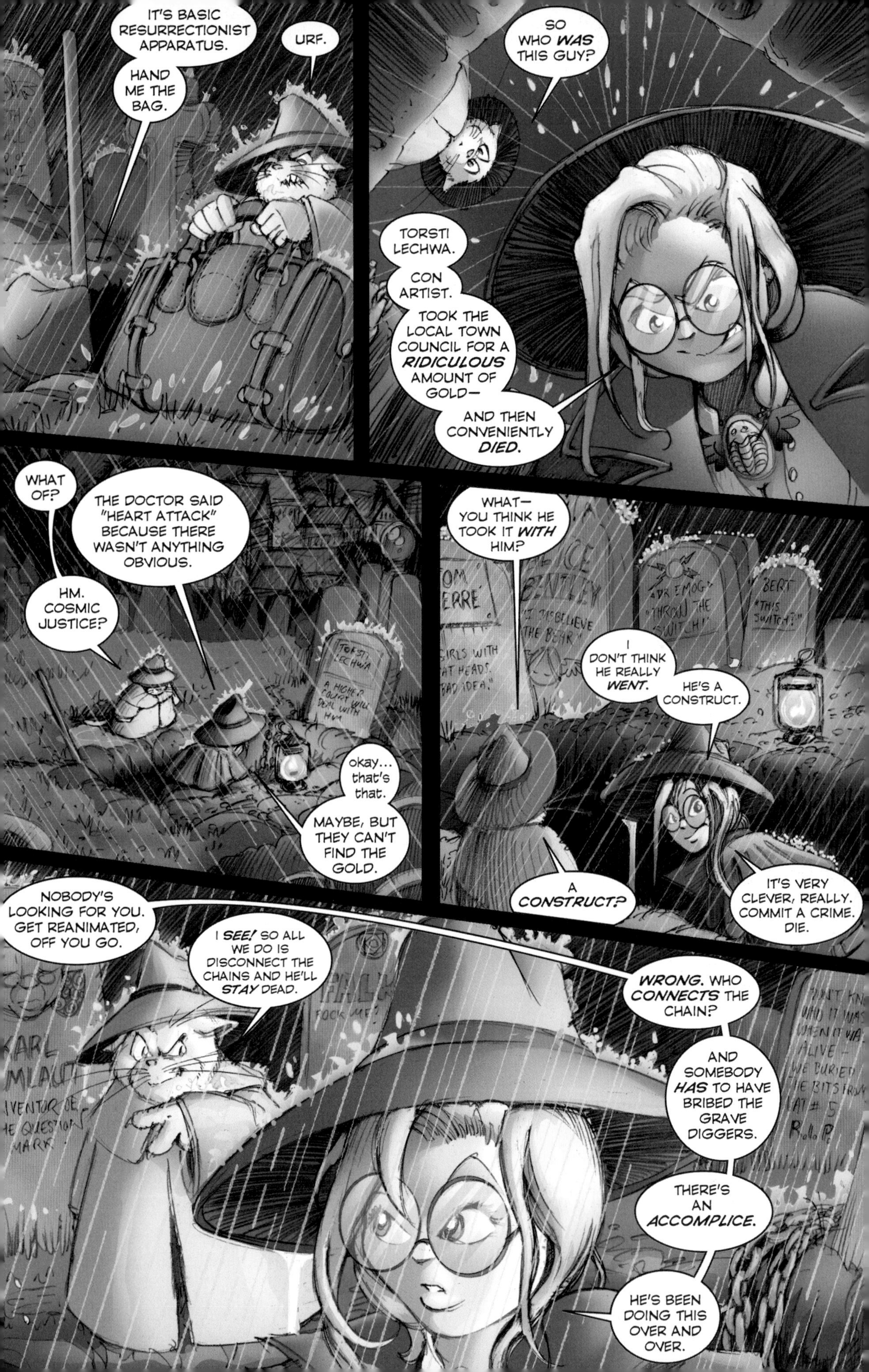
IT'S BASIC RESURRECTIONIST APPARATUS.
HAND ME THE BAG.
URF.
SO WHO *WAS* THIS GUY?
TORSTI LECHWA.
CON ARTIST.
TOOK THE LOCAL TOWN COUNCIL FOR A *RIDICULOUS* AMOUNT OF GOLD—
AND THEN CONVENIENTLY *DIED.*
WHAT OF?
THE DOCTOR SAID "HEART ATTACK" BECAUSE THERE WASN'T ANYTHING OBVIOUS.
HM. COSMIC JUSTICE?
okay... that's that.
MAYBE, BUT THEY CAN'T FIND THE GOLD.
WHAT— YOU THINK HE TOOK IT *WITH* HIM?
I DON'T THINK HE REALLY *WENT.*
HE'S A CONSTRUCT.
A *CONSTRUCT?*
IT'S VERY CLEVER, REALLY. COMMIT A CRIME. DIE.
NOBODY'S LOOKING FOR YOU. GET REANIMATED, OFF YOU GO.
I *SEE!* SO ALL WE DO IS DISCONNECT THE CHAINS AND HE'LL *STAY* DEAD.
WRONG. WHO *CONNECTS* THE CHAIN?
AND SOMEBODY *HAS* TO HAVE BRIBED THE GRAVE DIGGERS.
THERE'S AN *ACCOMPLICE.*
HE'S BEEN DOING THIS OVER AND OVER.

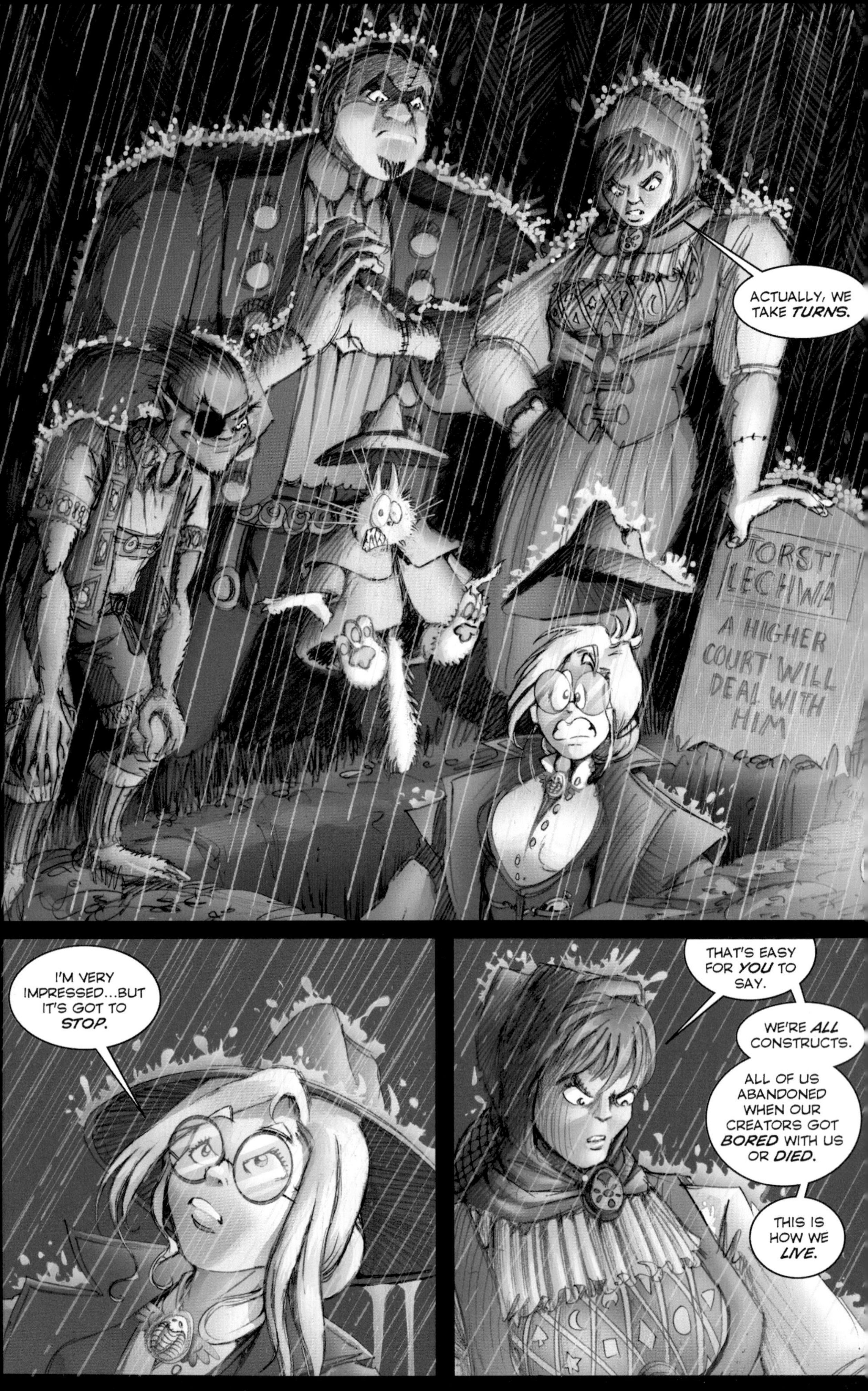
ACTUALLY, WE TAKE *TURNS.*
TORSTI LECHWA
A HIGHER COURT WILL DEAL WITH HIM
I'M VERY IMPRESSED...BUT IT'S GOT TO *STOP*.
THAT'S EASY FOR *YOU* TO SAY.
WE'RE *ALL* CONSTRUCTS.
ALL OF US ABANDONED WHEN OUR CREATORS GOT *BORED* WITH US OR *DIED*.
THIS IS HOW WE *LIVE*.

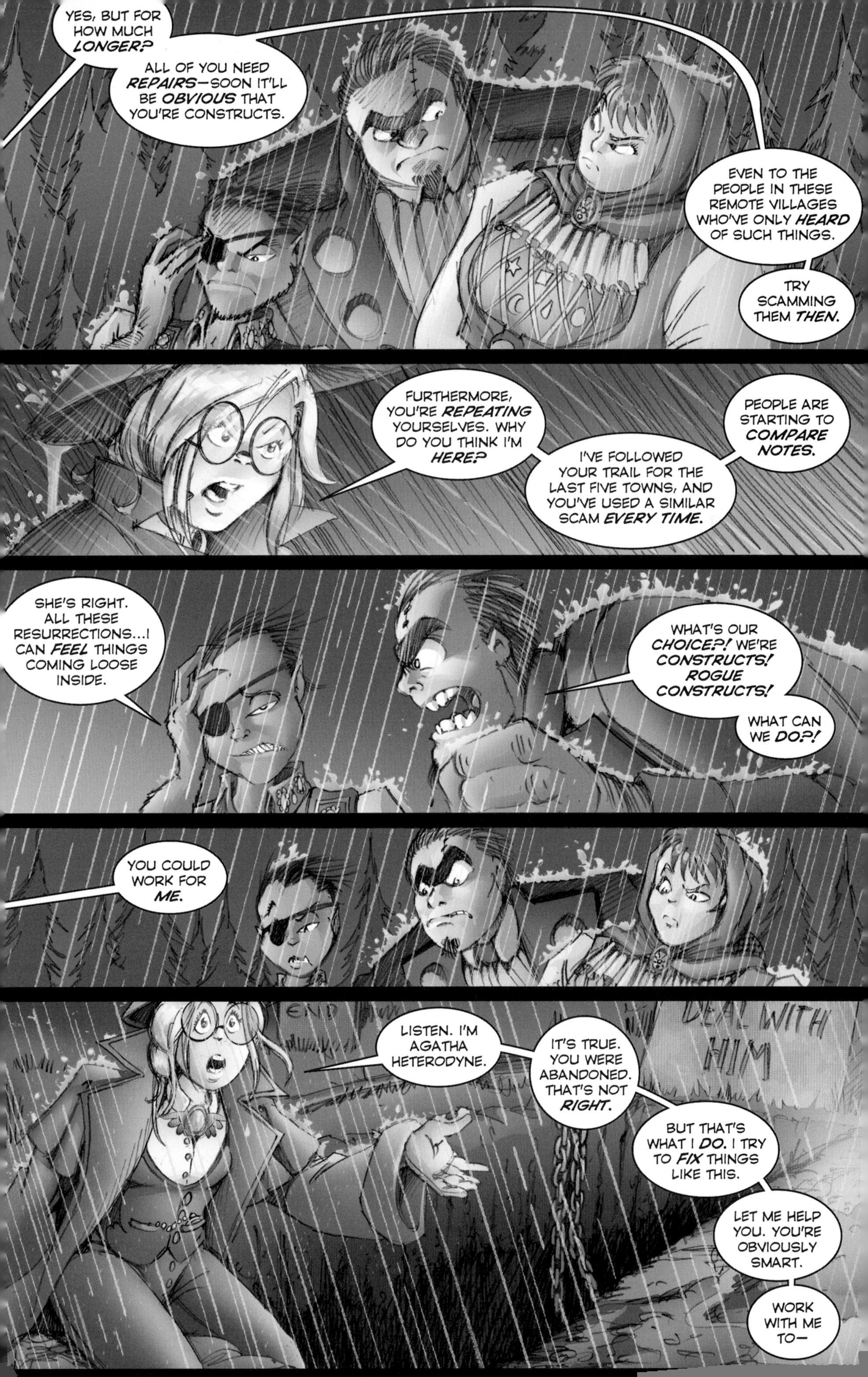
YES, BUT FOR HOW MUCH LONGER?
ALL OF YOU NEED REPAIRS—SOON IT'LL BE OBVIOUS THAT YOU'RE CONSTRUCTS.
EVEN TO THE PEOPLE IN THESE REMOTE VILLAGES WHO'VE ONLY HEARD OF SUCH THINGS.
TRY SCAMMING THEM THEN.
FURTHERMORE, YOU'RE REPEATING YOURSELVES. WHY DO YOU THINK I'M HERE?
I'VE FOLLOWED YOUR TRAIL FOR THE LAST FIVE TOWNS, AND YOU'VE USED A SIMILAR SCAM EVERY TIME.
PEOPLE ARE STARTING TO COMPARE NOTES.
SHE'S RIGHT. ALL THESE RESURRECTIONS...I CAN FEEL THINGS COMING LOOSE INSIDE.
WHAT'S OUR CHOICE?! WE'RE CONSTRUCTS! ROGUE CONSTRUCTS!
WHAT CAN WE DO?!
YOU COULD WORK FOR ME.
DEAL WITH HIM
LISTEN. I'M AGATHA HETERODYNE.
IT'S TRUE. YOU WERE ABANDONED. THAT'S NOT RIGHT.
BUT THAT'S WHAT I DO. I TRY TO FIX THINGS LIKE THIS.
LET ME HELP YOU. YOU'RE OBVIOUSLY SMART.
WORK WITH ME TO—

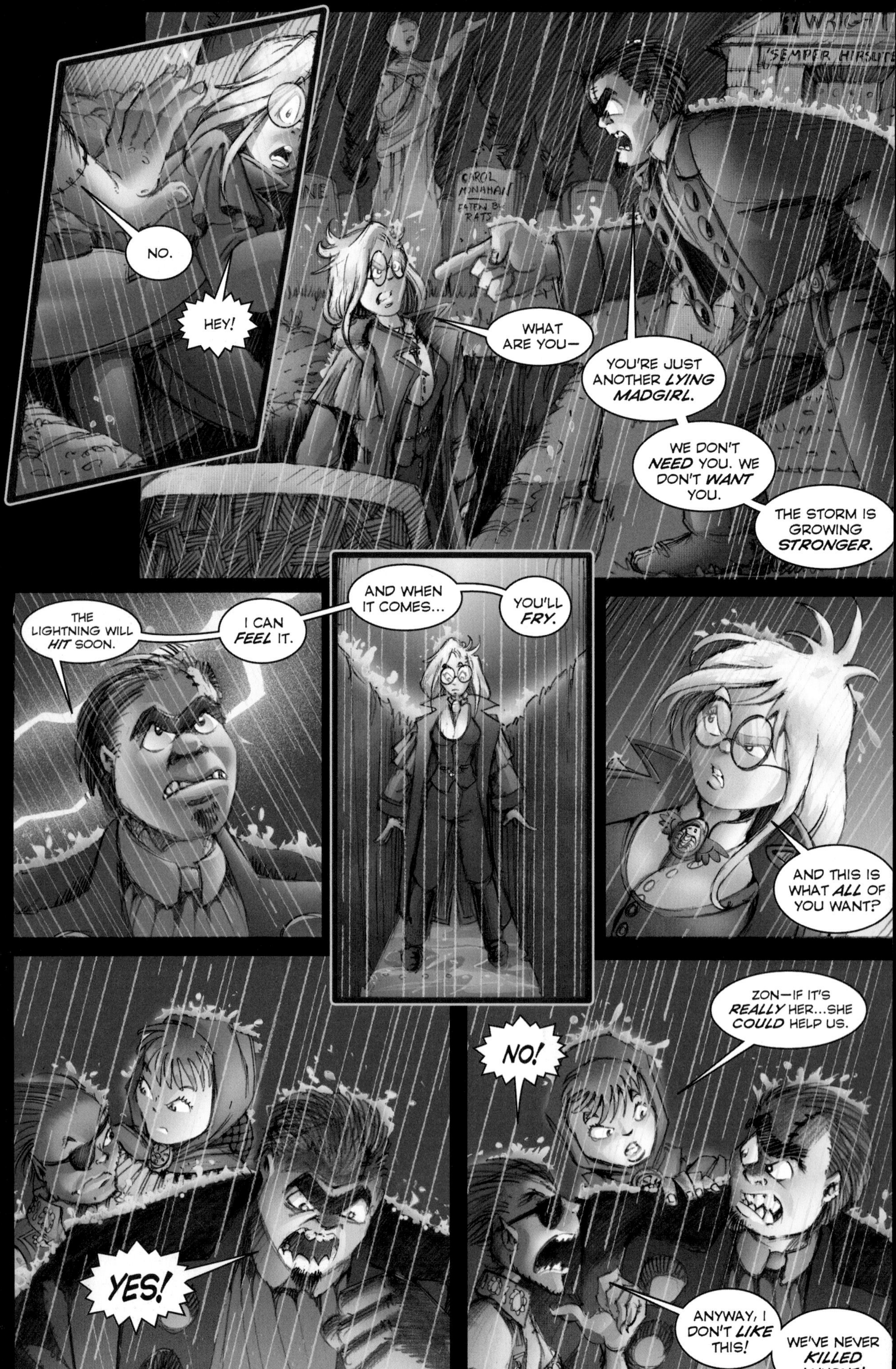
NO.
HEY!
CAROL MONAHAN EATEN BY RATS
WHAT ARE YOU—
YOU'RE JUST ANOTHER *LYING MADGIRL.*
WE DON'T *NEED* YOU. WE DON'T *WANT* YOU.
THE STORM IS GROWING *STRONGER.*
THE LIGHTNING WILL *HIT* SOON.
I CAN *FEEL* IT.
AND WHEN IT COMES...
YOU'LL *FRY.*
AND THIS IS WHAT *ALL* OF YOU WANT?
YES!
NO!
ZON—IF IT'S *REALLY* HER...SHE *COULD* HELP US.
ANYWAY, I DON'T *LIKE* THIS!
WE'VE NEVER *KILLED* ANYONE!

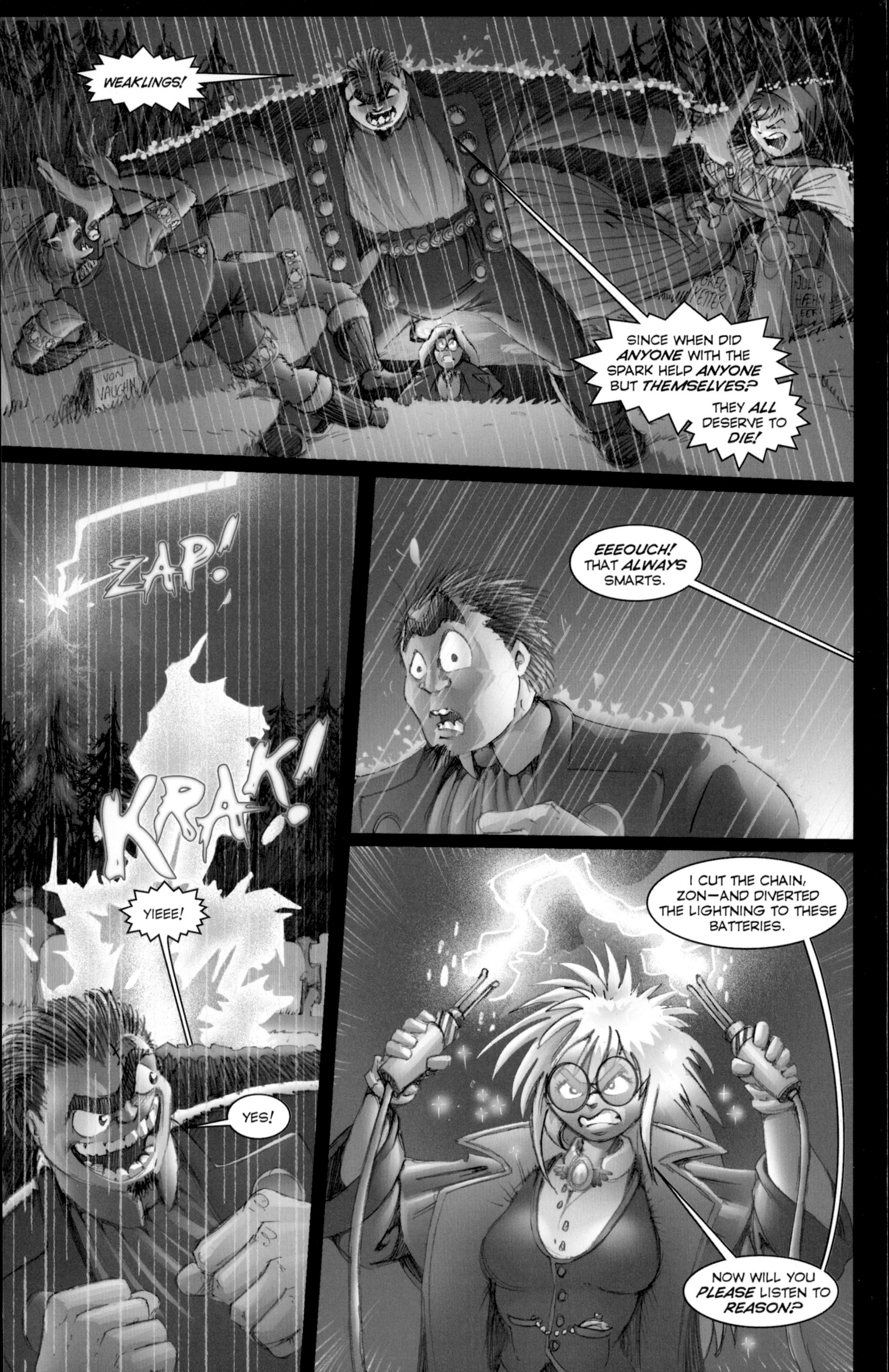
WEAKLINGS!
SINCE WHEN DID ANYONE WITH THE SPARK HELP ANYONE BUT THEMSELVES?
THEY ALL DESERVE TO DIE!
VON VAUGHN
ZAP!
KRAK!
YIEEE!
YES!
EEEOUCH! THAT ALWAYS SMARTS.
I CUT THE CHAIN, ZON—AND DIVERTED THE LIGHTNING TO THESE BATTERIES.
NOW WILL YOU PLEASE LISTEN TO REASON?

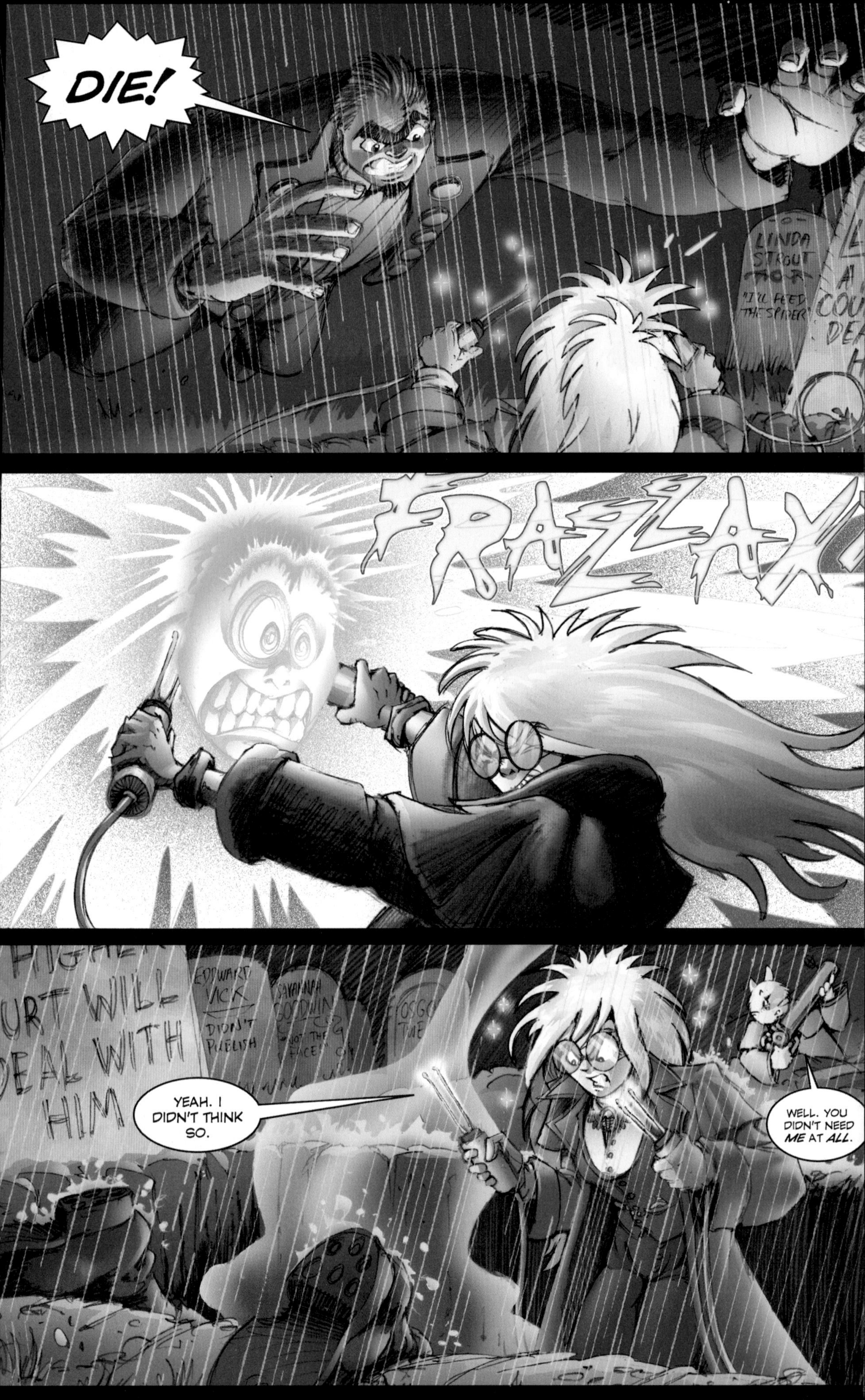
DIE!
LINDA STROUT
"I'LL FEED THE SPIDER"
FRAZZAX
EDDWARD VICK
DIDN'T PUBLISH
SAVANNAH GOODWIN
YEAH. I DIDN'T THINK SO.
WELL. YOU DIDN'T NEED *ME* AT *ALL*.

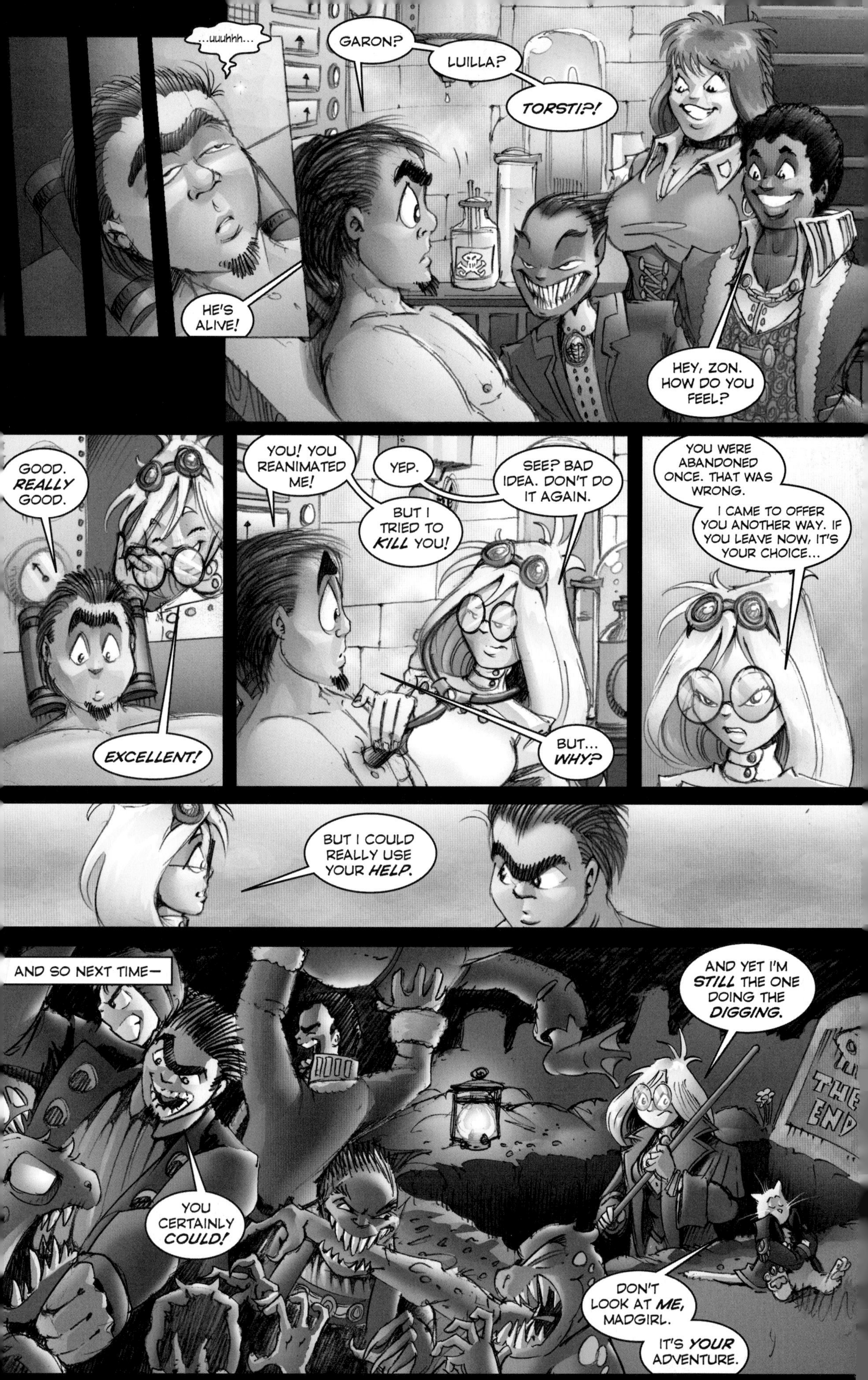
...uuuhhh...
GARON?
LUILLA?
TORSTI?!
HE'S ALIVE!
HEY, ZON. HOW DO YOU FEEL?
GOOD. REALLY GOOD.
EXCELLENT!
YOU! YOU REANIMATED ME!
YEP.
BUT I TRIED TO KILL YOU!
SEE? BAD IDEA. DON'T DO IT AGAIN.
BUT... WHY?
YOU WERE ABANDONED ONCE. THAT WAS WRONG.
I CAME TO OFFER YOU ANOTHER WAY. IF YOU LEAVE NOW, IT'S YOUR CHOICE...
BUT I COULD REALLY USE YOUR HELP.
AND SO NEXT TIME—
YOU CERTAINLY COULD!
AND YET I'M STILL THE ONE DOING THE DIGGING.
THE END
DON'T LOOK AT ME, MADGIRL.
IT'S YOUR ADVENTURE.

READ MORE COMICS ONLINE AT:

www.GirlGenius.net

MONDAY · WEDNESDAY · FRIDAY